W9-DEP-204

A WAY TO
PEACE, HEALTH, AND POWER

A WAY TO
PEACE, HEALTH, AND POWER

STUDIES FOR THE INNER LIFE

BY

BERTHA CONDÉ

AUTHOR OF "THE HUMAN ELEMENT IN THE MAKING OF A CHRISTIAN," ETC.

GEN. THEO. SEMINARY
LIBRARY
NEW YORK

NEW YORK
CHARLES SCRIBNER'S SONS
1925

109618
241.45
C751

COPYRIGHT, 1925, BY
CHARLES SCRIBNER'S SONS

Printed in the United States of America

The extracts from the Revised Version of the Bible contained in this volume are printed by permission of the Universities of Oxford and Cambridge, but all editorial responsibility rests with the author of the present volume.

TO

E. M. H.

WITH WHOM SIGHT IS INSIGHT

CONTENTS

FOREWORD

PSYCHOLOGY is the pet academic word today. People have waked up to the truth that the human mind has unsuspected powers for the conquest of limitations. Everybody has something he wants to escape; hence this eager rush to find some formula for omnipotence. Those who have the leisure and privilege of higher education are so engrossed in studying the possibilities of the mind; and are so enamoured of their technical vocabulary, that they are usually inaccessible to the average person who insists on having what he wants *now*. As a result, a legion of commercial enterprises has sprung up to supply the popular demand. They have seized upon the cravings of people for health, money, prosperity, and peace of mind and have promised all these things to those who would enroll in their classes and learn "the tricks of mental power."

Even more serious than this, are the religious problems which have been raised. People do not know how to fit these new thoughts to what they have been taught by the Church. They are wondering what relation psychology has to the teachings of Christianity. They need new reasons for confidence in the philosophy and the inevitable triumph of Jesus Christ.

This book is *not* a mental "patent medicine" for all the ills of humanity. If anyone is expecting to get the usually promised "instant relief" he desires, it will be useless to read these pages. The evil of a patent medicine lies in the fact that people buy it because of certain symptoms rather than causes. Symptoms are acute warnings of hidden causes. These must first be searched out before the symptoms will disappear. The writer claims no resources of wisdom beyond that of the ordinary Christian. She believes that the life of Jesus discloses certain laws and principles by which every one of us may sense a vital connection with God, and be able to draw on His infinite power for the task of living. When spirit, mind, and body are alike controlled by God, unusual experiences are likely to occur. Bodily weakness may disappear, mental disturbance may be removed, and spiritual longings may be satisfied. If we can hold ourselves in patience and steadiness long enough to get the point of what God has been trying to teach us, we shall discover the greatest secret of power we have ever known.

As far as possible these Studies have been kept free from technical terms. They do not pretend to make any contribution to psychological thinking, nor to theology. The Biblical material has not been used to prove any theories, but as a faithful and most reliable record of some of the experience through which people have discovered God, and His ways. If this book succeeds in steadying the thinking of anyone who is looking for a rational basis for faith in eternal realities, it will have accomplished its purpose. Jesus Christ is adequate for all human need.

Grateful acknowledgment is made to many books and friends consulted by the author; likewise to Lothrop, Lee & Shepard Company, Boston, Massachusetts, for permission to use two stanzas of "The Higher Catechism" from "Songs of the Average Man" by Sam Walter Foss; to the Oxford University Press, London, for permission to use the Revised Version of the Bible; to George H. Doran Company, New York City, for permission to use quotations from the Moffat translation of the New Testament; and to E. P. Dutton & Company, New York City, for permission to use certain prayers from "A Chain of Prayer Across the Ages."

May God help us all to discover the methods by which mind, body and spirit may disclose Him as a reality, and as the only power for transcendent living.

B. C.

New York City,
January 1, 1925.

A WAY INTO THE SECRETS OF THE INNER LIFE

WHICH WE DARE NOT OVERLOOK
LEST WE MISS THE LIVING SPIRIT
AND LOSE OURSELVES IN THE FOREST OF WORDS

Each morning of this new year, as we stand at our open window, or look off to the hills, or up to the heavenly blue limit, let us think of God and speak to Him in low clear tones:

> Every day and every hour,
> Father, I breathe in Thy life-giving power:
>> Power to love,
>> Power to be pure,
>> Power to be well,
>> Power to endure.

We have walked the road of daily life so long alone, that we need to say these words over and over until we begin to sense some connection between ourselves and our heavenly Father. The repetition of this act of faith will slowly but surely change our dull mind into the receptive spirit of a little child without which we may not enter into the kingdom of heaven. When the open heart of a little child becomes ours, we shall be ready to receive the teaching of God.

A WAY TO
PEACE, HEALTH, AND POWER

THE CONNECTING CURRENT OF LIFE
BETWEEN THE HUMAN SPIRIT AND GOD

HOW WE KNOW IT

In the life history of the human race, all peoples of every generation have been aware of a God; a creative spirit of life and energy. Individuals, through personal limitations, may be unaware of Him, but the people in general have an instinctive knowledge that there is Someone, however shrouded in mystery, with whom they inevitably must reckon; the Father of their spirits. The wisest philosophers have called man "a religious animal" because through all ages, men and women have had a hunger for God as real as their hunger for food. A little girl, born blind and deaf, whose spirit was imprisoned in utter darkness and silence, was told about God by touch signs on the palm of her hand. Her face lighted up with the joy of a new discovery as she signalled back: "God! Is that what you call Him? I have known Him a long time; but I never knew His name." Sooner or later, we too, discern that there is in the world "the true light, which lighteth every man."

One way in which we show this instinct for God is in our judgments of others. We estimate their moral worth or weakness by an inner God-like standard which we hold as our ideal. We say of another's deed: "That was an unchristian act"; or "He is not what I expected him to be." What we really mean is that this one has failed to measure up to our inner conception of God-like conduct. We may come short ourselves; but, instinctively, we apply the rule of perfection to the conduct of others.

Even though we are careless about our own standards, we train up little children to respect the highest law in their hearts, and count education in ideals a necessity. We toil and sacrifice ourselves in order that our children may reach a higher plane of living than that which we have attained. Long years — practically one fourth of the life span — is devoted to this training. Why should we do this, age after age, if there were no conscious connection with an unseen Spirit to whom we hold ourselves responsible?

1

In spite of our decisions to the contrary, we never actually consider the search for God a closed question, until we find Him answering to our human spirit. Our spirit compels us to continue the quest, with wistfulness or pessimism; with confidence, or restless uncertainty; but always with a resistless urge. As in ages ago, so now, we too, say in the silence of the night, or under the crushing experiences of life, "Oh that I knew *where* I might find Him."

> "Dark is the world to thee: thyself art the reason why;
> "For is He not all but thou, that has power to feel, 'I am I?' "

In a closer way we sense our connection with an infinite Power. Who of us has not experienced flashes of illumination at times when we were at our wit's end? Something happened, beyond our wisdom. We called it truly an inspiration. At that moment of our need, God breathed into the mind a thought; a guiding torch, and we found our way out of our trouble. Again, we were exhausted with our vigils and our tasks; we had not the physical strength to go on. Soon there came what we called our "second wind"; a vigor drawn from some hidden depth; and we did what before we could not do. The ancient seers understood the prime source of that power: "The Creator of the ends of the earth fainteth not, neither is weary. He giveth power to the faint: and to him that hath no might he increaseth strength . . . I will gird thee, though thou hast not known me."

If we have the wisdom to relate our experiences not to secondary causes only, but to the great first Cause, we shall begin to understand the limitless possibilities of our human life.

> "Thou hidden love of God, whose height,
> Whose depth unfathomed no man knows,
> I see from far thy beauteous light,
> Inly I sigh for Thy repose:
> My heart is pained, nor can it be
> At rest, till it find rest in Thee."   *1729 G. Terstegen.*

FOR STUDY AND THOUGHT

Ye worship that which ye know not: we worship that which we know: for salvation is from the Jews. But the hour cometh, and now is, when the true worshippers shall worship the Father in spirit and truth: for such doth the Father seek to be his worshippers. God is a Spirit: and they that worship him must worship in spirit and truth. The woman saith unto him, I know that Messiah cometh (which is called Christ): when he is come, he will declare unto us all things. Jesus saith unto her, I that speak unto thee am he.   *John 4:22-26.*

Then Job answered and said, Oh that I knew where I might find him, that I might come even to his seat! I would order my cause before him, and fill my mouth with arguments. I would know the words which he would answer me, and understand what he would say unto me. Would he contend with me in the greatness of his power? Nay; but he would give heed unto me. Behold, I go forward, but he is not there; and backward, but I cannot perceive him: On the left hand, when he doth work, but I cannot behold him: he hideth himself on the right hand, that I cannot see him. But he knoweth the way that I take; when he hath tried me, I shall come forth as gold. *Job 23 : 3–6; 8–10.*

An intellectual conception of the immanence of God did not keep the non-christian world from idolatry. It is not enough to admit theoretically the fact that we are the offspring of God and that our life and breath are dependent on Him. We must *"feel* after Him and find Him." Plotinus expressed the problem of life in his dying words: "I am striving to bring the God which is within into harmony with the God which is in the universe."

Jesus put His finger on the point where God and man meet, when He said to the woman of Samaria "God is a Spirit; and they that worship Him must worship in spirit and truth." She was like the multitude who are interested in religious questions and forms of worship as intellectual opinions, but whose inner life is at cross purposes with the moral law of God. The great discovery of the Hebrews was the God of righteousness and truth who required the same standards of character in His children. If God is the infinite Spirit of holiness, and we are His children, it is fitting that we should follow the instincts of our spirit toward spiritual values and away from the desires of the flesh. Sometimes we are upset in our thinking when we are told that science has never seen God in the heavens, nor discovered the human soul. "We recover ourselves" as Bishop Gore observes "as we recollect that, if God be what we believe Him to be, immaterial and spiritual, then He would cease to be Himself if He were visible through a telescope: and that if the spirit of man be what we believe it to be, that is the very reason why no surgeon's knife can ever arrive at it."

> "Thou Life within my life, than self more near,
> Thou Veiled Presence infinitely clear;
> From all illusive shows of sense I flee
> To find my center and my rest in Thee."

We do not have to grope after God: He is seeking us, waiting to reveal Himself to the spirit within. Job, long before Jesus unfolded the kingdom of the inner life, felt this truth instinctively. The God he discovered lifted him above the struggles and trials of earth. He *knew* God would attend to his need, if he could but find Him, and his spirit knew that God cared about the path his soul was taking and that in the end it would come forth free from its earthly struggles like the pure gold refined in the fire. Nothing can hold down a spirit — it gathers new power from every experience.

How do we know that we are one with God? Is our knowledge instinctive or reasoned? In what does our dominant interest in religion centre? What holds the centre of importance? — forms and human opinions or the task of sublimating our desires and instincts into the character and purposes of God? Are we as far along in our understanding of God as

Job was thousands of years ago? If not, why not? Does our spirit triumph as did his in spite of boils? What is the horizon of our soul?

Almighty God, we invoke Thee, the fountain of Everlasting Light, and entreat Thee to send forth Thy truth into our hearts, and to pour upon us the glory of Thy brightness, through Jesus Christ our Lord. *Amen.*

Sarum Breviary, A. D. 1085.

HOW WE STRENGTHEN IT

Our consciousness of anything becomes vivid as we give it our earnest attention. To us the world, teeming with infinite wonders, is no greater than our thought of it. The greatest facts fail to register unless we give heed to them. Many a time we have walked down a street, with our thought so fixed on some inner problem, that we failed to see the sunset, or the look of joy in the eyes of a child, or the beauty of line in a bit of sculpture, or the suffering on some old woman's face. All of these might have stirred our souls to new life; but we were dead to all that might touch us, save that one problem on which our mind was set. There is a precise ratio between the size of our world and our mental alertness. It is true also in the spiritual world. Our sense of God becomes keen only as we make room in our mind for the thought of Him, and turn steadily to Him, concentrating our attention on Him.

Attention is only perfect when it is linked with a sympathetic, open-minded spirit. When our mind is in the turmoil of an inner argument, when we are more intent on balancing our opinions than on receiving more light outside of ourselves, we make ourselves inaccessible to God.

Some silent place, where our inner spirit is alone, is necessary for concentration. It may be in the still depths of nature, or within four walls; in the uninterrupted quiet of a sanctuary, or in the loneliness of the crowd. For many of us, conditions of living make physical silences impossible; and a waking hour in the night is the only time when God can get our attention. We may find peace and relaxation then; but usually the mind is too fatigued after the day's work to think constructively. The business of strengthening our connection with infinite powers deserves a time in the morning and evening, when, in the full vigor of our spirit, we may be open-doored to God.

> "As, in life's best hours we hear
> By the spirit's finer ear
> His low voice within us, thus
> The All-Father heareth us;
> And His holy ear we pain
> With our noisy words and vain.
> Not for Him our violence
> Storming at the gates of sense,
> His the primal language, His
> The Eternal silences!" *The Prayer of Agassiz.*

We must also take it for granted that the God who made us and holds us in life, desires to come near us even more than we can possibly desire to come near to Him. When two spirits have the same longing, there is every possibility for self-revelation, which is the basis of all friendship. A friend reveals himself to his friend, and receives also the self-revelation of his comrade.

One of the joys of friendship is the discovery of ourselves in our life with our friends. Each friend sounds depths in us which we scarcely suspected. So, when our human spirit reaches out to God, the Infinite Spirit, we become conscious of hidden desires and dispositions, and are influenced by His desires and character until we see in ourselves a new personality which no human friend has ever called out. There is no better way to see ourselves in true perspective than to place ourselves consciously in relationship with the Divine Source of our life. We may not understand how God can be, but of one fact we may be sure: from some source we have derived our life and we must be a part of the great whole. Like begets like, and God who wills and understands must be able to impart power to us. The experience will humble us and exalt us. We shall grow into a larger consciousness of ourselves, and God; which naturally brings with it new strength and power.

> "I see Thee not, I hear Thee not,
>   Yet art Thou oft with me;
> And earth hath ne'er so dear a spot
>   As where I meet with Thee."   *Ray Palmer 1858.*

FOR STUDY AND THOUGHT

"Ye shall seek the Lord thy God, thou shalt find Him, if thou search after Him with all thy heart and with all thy soul." *Deut. 4 : 29.*

"Ask, and it shall be given you; seek, and ye shall find; knock, and it shall be opened unto you: for every one that asketh receiveth; and he that seeketh findeth; and to him that knocketh it shall be opened. Or what man is there of you, who, if his son shall ask him for a loaf, will give him a stone; or if he shall ask for a fish, will give him a serpent? If ye then, being evil, know how to give good gifts unto your children, how much more shall your Father which is in heaven give good things to them that ask him?" *Matt. 7 : 7–11.*

"Be still, and know that I am God." *Psa. 46 : 10.*

"My soul, wait thou only upon God;
    For my expectation is from him." *Psa. 62 : 5.*

We cannot be casual about our religious life and expect to gain real knowledge of God. Anything that is worth while deserves all the concentration we can command. We need to examine our mental habits and see whether our natural tendencies hinder our being able to discover God within us. Are we increasing or decreasing our ability to concentrate? What type of thought holds us when we voluntarily choose our own subject? Do we ever lose ourselves in thought over anything? Each day we are forging chains of habit, and we may find it growingly difficult to search for God with all our heart and soul, unless we begin at once to train our mind to become spiritually attentive.

The dominant desires of our heart are answered. Whatever we concentrate upon as our goal is likely to come. If our dominant desires are spiritual and in harmony with the great laws of God, nothing can prevent their fulfillment. Is God a thesis or an experience in our life? What proof of His reality do we seek most to have?

All the advance in knowledge in the world has come because earnest minds were persistently seeking, and knocking. They always get light for the next step toward their goal. God compares Himself with the parent who lives for his child and gives it every good thing he possesses. Surely the heavenly Father from whom we come is infinitely more loving and ambitious for His children than any earthly father can be. This marvelous conception of God is Jesus' special contribution to the world and is the most satisfying one we have known. Therefore if we do not strengthen our relation with God, it is because we are holding other things more important than our spiritual life.

Concentration of mind on a dominant desire always means a silencing of other thoughts. Two interests cannot occupy the attention at the same time. If God alone is sought then there will be utter quietness when His voice is heard. We can prepare the way for God if we enter each day into silence. "Let a man meet with men: but his life is not whole, Till he goes to waste places and talks with his soul." The time we spend there will depend upon the ability we have to shut the door on other voices. Most of us do not seek an inner silence because we are not on good terms with ourselves. If this is so what are the real reasons? "Today if ye shall hear His voice, harden not your hearts."

> Our Lord who seest that all hearts are empty except Thou fill them and all desires balked except they crave after Thee; give us light and grace to seek and find Thee, that we may be Thine and Thou mayest be ours forever. *Amen. C. Rosetti.*

HOW WE MAKE THE CONNECTION

It is awesome to know that every spoken word quivering out into the air, beyond our recall, exerts its influence through its vibrations far beyond our ken. It has always been so; and we are only now beginning to understand how to gather up the sounds and make them audible to our poor limited ears. A friend, living far out in the open country, told of the peculiar emotion which gripped her one summer midnight when she "tuned in" on her radio and heard in the silent farmhouse the words of greeting broadcasted from a ship nearing the North Pole. Trembling with excitement, she put down the receiver. "It's terrible," she said. "The whole world hears a whisper!"

We have a greater power. We can choose from among all the voices those which we will hear, and those which we will shut away from us. It is as we will. Some day we shall understand how true this is also in the realm of the mind. In its silent depths we can tune in with the strident voices of human opinion, or we can let the voice of God become vocal within us and harmonize ourselves with His thought. It is in the inner room of the mind and heart that the receiving station for God's voice is located.

It is difficult to describe the speaking of God within us. One ancient seer speaks of it as a "still, small voice." Many times it has been heard in a dream, or in those moments before waking, while under the spell of sub-conscious connection with God. Sometimes the voice is heard in the pressure of a thought which is so insistent that it must be heeded. A noted Christian teacher once pointed out that one could account for many replies to the desires we voice to God, if we believe that it is possible for God to put a thought into the heart of a man. This opens to us a whole realm of possible experience in our relationship with God.

Our mind is played upon often by thoughts from other minds. Two friends who have lived together often sense in each other unspoken thoughts. Their close association gives them perfect understanding. Perhaps some of us doubt the possibility of hearing God's thoughts. Have we any right to do so until we have made the test, after weeks and months of living in the atmosphere of the finest and holiest ideals? It is the pure in heart who not only see God, but hear His voice.

Sometimes sudden memories of the past and a new association of ideas become full of significance when our mind is at rest. Holy

8

suggestions may come to us to-day. We shall know that they are from God because they transcend our human wisdom. It is only the quiet pool which catches reflections. Some of us are so blown about by the distracting winds of men's affairs and opinions that we make it impossible for God to give us any wisdom.

The pressure of heavy responsibilities and baffling experiences beyond our control often create a sensitiveness to the voice of God. There is no stimulus like that of utter helplessness. When help comes, we are more likely to recognize its heavenly source. If a family is starving, a basket of food, sent by a friend unexpectedly, comes as a miraculous gift from heaven. When daily needs are met and hunger is not poignant all seems to come as a matter of course and God as the constant source of supply is forgotten. Those of us who see God related to the events of every day, see in His unremitting faithfulness, evidences of His Fatherhood. We are so shortsighted that we look only at the experience of the present moment, forgetful of the long chain of connected events which have worked out the purpose of God for our lives. Before we call, He answers:

> "Breathe through the pulses of desire
> Thy coolness and thy balm;
> Let sense be dumb, its heats expire;
> Speak through the earthquake, wind and fire,
> O still small voice of calm." *1872 J.G. Whittier.*

FOR STUDY AND THOUGHT

"And, behold, the Lord passed by, and a great and strong wind rent the mountains, and brake in pieces the rocks before the Lord; but the Lord was not in the wind: and after the wind an earthquake; but the Lord was not in the earthquake: and after the earthquake a fire; but the Lord was not in the fire: and after the fire a still small voice. And it was so, when Elijah heard it, that he wrapped his face in his mantle, and went out, and stood in the entering in of the cave. And, behold, there came a voice unto him, and said, What doest thou here, Elijah?"

I Kings 19 : 11–13.

And the child Samuel ministered unto the Lord before Eli. And the word of the Lord was precious in those days; there was no open vision. And it came to pass at that time, when Eli was laid down in his place, (now his eyes had begun to wax dim, that he could not see,) and the lamp of God was not yet gone out, and Samuel was laid down to sleep, in the temple of the Lord, where the ark of God was; that the Lord called Samuel: and he said, Here am I. And he ran unto Eli, and said, Here am I; for thou calledst me. And he said, I called not; lie down again. And he went and lay down. And the Lord called yet again, Samuel. And Samuel arose and went to Eli, and said, Here am I; for thou calledst me.

And he answered, I called not, my son; lie down again. Now Samuel did not yet know the Lord, neither was the word of the Lord yet revealed unto him. And the Lord called Samuel again the third time. And he arose and went to Eli, and said, Here am I; for thou calledst me. And Eli perceived that Jehovah had called the child. Therefore Eli said unto Samuel, Go, lie down: and it shall be, if he call thee, that thou shalt say, Speak, Lord; for thy servant heareth. So Samuel went and lay down in his place. And the Lord came, and stood, and called as at other times, Samuel, Samuel. Then Samuel said, Speak; for thy servant heareth.

I Samuel 3 : 1-10.

When the thunderings and fires of life have passed by and we are in expectant silence, we hear the still small voice of God. We are more sensitive to silence immediately after the roar of thunder or any loud voice has ceased. There is a moment or two when our spirit is in the atmosphere of utter quietness. Sometimes it takes a contrast like this to make us mindful of it. Two street urchins were taken away from the noise of the city to the country for the first time. A few minutes after they arrived one came close to the other and whispered, "Let us go back. The silence — it sounds awful!" How many of us have the same feeling? Are we frightened at being alone with ourselves — and a possible realization of God? Even Elijah wrapped his face in his mantle and stood there in hushed expectancy. He had run for his life away from the strife of the enemy and went to the mount of God for some help, he knew not what. That still small voice of God within him revealed him to himself and gave him that poise within which is always power.

When we seek for the wisdom of human opinion we are usually dismayed by the conflicting views of perfectly sincere folk. They can give us the light of their own experience and help us in assembling all the varied points of view, but in the end we shall not find peace and power until we focus our spirit expectantly on what may come to our mind out of the silence of eternity. The ancient prophet Habakkuk knew what to say for the guidance of the people because he waited for the word of God. He learned this lesson from his dealings with God, "The vision is yet for the appointed time, though it tarry, wait for it; because it will surely come, it will not delay."

Note the pathos of the old high priest Eli, who after years of living in the atmosphere of holy things could not hear the voice of God because he did not act on visions which he had had. He had become callous in his spirit and God could not reach him with his still small voice; so He turned to the heart of a little child who had not lost his sensitiveness. The alertness of the boy Samuel who was so willing to rise in the night at the least call, furnished the quality of heart which brought the vision of God. His desire to serve Eli, which drew him out of bed three times in his anxiety to do his full part, fitted him for a supreme revelation.

> "When the fires burn low and red
> And the watch is ticking loudly
> Beside the bed:
> Though you sleep, tired out, on your couch,
> Still your heart must wake and watch
> In the dark room,
> For it may be that at midnight
> I will come."

Is our habit of life making us more sensitive to the whisper of God's Spirit? It is possible to dwell so constantly in the realm of the commonplace and the mechanics of living that we become automatic in our reactions to life and lose the sense of God. No sacrifice is too great to rescue our spirit from the plight of Eli who had the office of revelation without anything to reveal.

> Our Father, God: Give us the courage to be still and know that thou art God: Thou didst speak to men of old in a still small voice. Speak thou also unto us this day. *Amen.*

HOW TO PUT IT TO USE

Our human spirit clothed with a material body, in the midst of a material world, needs continually to draw upon the limitless power of God, the Father of our spirit, that it may live in triumph. Therefore, each day, we need to lift the heart consciously to Him in a definite act of devotion, until it grows to be an irresistible habit.

As we concentrate on this, we begin to vibrate with the vital, inexhaustible energy of God. If we neglect this inner act, we merely exist — a prey to our moods and whims and to the uncertain domination of other personalities. Most people live in this slavery. The only way in which we can resist the combined influences of the crowd, is to ally ourselves with the strength of God, who is infinitely stronger than the united power of lesser spirits.

These acts of devotion, by which we increase our consciousness of God, are what is called prayer. Prayer avails at once in taking away that sense of loneliness and helplessness which haunts the heart and brings despair. No one can have peace, health, or power who is living in despair. Countless people are in sanatoriums and hospitals for the insane, who would not be there if simple, childlike prayer had been the daily habit of life.

> "We kneel how weak, we rise full of power,
> Why therefore should we do ourselves this wrong
> Or others — that we are not always strong,
> That we are ever overborne with care,
> That we should ever weak or heartless be,
> Anxious or troubled, when with us is prayer,
> And joy, and strength, and courage are with Thee?"
>
> *Archbishop Trench.*

The human spirit shares the power of God to the extent that it shares His nature and the qualities of His spirit. In the Christian scriptures, we have the highest revelation of what God our Father is like, as we see Him in the life and character of Jesus around whom these scriptures are centered. It has been the experience of those who honestly study the teachings of Jesus, that they know instinctively, that his words are true; and that they stand the tests of life. He is the great specialist in the knowledge of God. Therefore, at any cost, we dare not miss the secret of His power, nor fail to follow Him on the open road to peace, health, and victory.

Jesus is the only personality who never broke the vital connection with His Father, God. Every act and word of His thirty-three years of incarnation in human flesh, was dynamic with more than human power. He was human, and more than human; He was the perfect conductor for the infinite power of God. It would be foolish to think that we can learn how to live without constant study of the life of Jesus, in order to discover the true characteristics of the life that is inevitably immortal.

According to the teaching of Jesus, the basis of prayer is personal trust in the character of God, as a loving Father. This conception of God we know to be true because it satisfies all the desires and longings of the human heart. The spirit of prayer which is born of this ideal opens up vast possibilities for life. If God is Father, then we can be sure that he is vitally interested in what concerns his children — It also means that childhood is a training for the inheritance of power; that life does not begin and end in weakness, but rises continuously to new heights of wisdom and achievement. Prayer becomes the meeting place where Father and child talk together; the state of mutual understanding; the moment where the spark of living energy leaps from heart to heart.

All this would be impossible if God were merely an unknown sinister Being who must be placated by endless sacrifice and served in craven fear. The generations which have had such a conception have known only the pleadings of fear: not the prayer of faith which works wonders. Therefore it is of infinite importance that we make Jesus' conception of God our own, and begin to avail ourselves of the vast resources of power which can only be released through a faith that is a personal trust in a God of love. Any other idea of God except the one Jesus taught cripples the possibilities of prayer. All people have lighted their darkness with some kind of light, if it were but a flickering torch, but those of us with the highest ideal turn darkness into day by the power of electricity. Even so, all men everywhere have prayer, but not all men have known its full power. That has been experienced in proportion to our faithfulness in following in the steps of Christ. The Bible is full of this teaching, available for anyone, however weak and needy. If we struggle on in helplessness, it will not be because God is unwilling to answer prayer, but because of our unwillingness to know the secret of the power which is revealed by Jesus Christ.

"Prayer is the soul's sincere desire,
Uttered or unexpressed,
The motion of a hidden fire
That trembles in the breast.
Prayer is the burden of a sigh,
The falling of a tear,
The upward glancing of an eye
When none but God is near."

J. Montgomery.

FOR STUDY AND THOUGHT

And when ye pray, ye shall not be as the hypocrites: for they love to stand and pray in the synagogues and in the corners of the streets, that they may be seen of men. Verily I say unto you, They have received their reward. But thou, when thou prayest, enter into thine inner chamber, and having shut thy door, pray to thy Father which is in secret, and thy Father which seeth in secret shall recompense thee. And in praying use not vain repetitions, as the Gentiles do: for they think that they shall be heard for their much speaking. Be not therefore like unto them: for your Father knoweth what things ye have need of, before ye ask him. After this manner therefore pray ye: Our Father which art in heaven, Hallowed be thy name. Thy kingdom come. Thy will be done as in heaven, so on earth. Give us this day our daily bread. And forgive us our debts, as we also have forgiven our debtors. And bring us not into temptation, but deliver us from the evil one. For if ye forgive men their trespasses, your heavenly Father will also forgive you. ᴅ᎑. if ye forgive not men their trespasses, neither will your Father forgive your trespasses. *Matt. 6 : 5-15.*

Jesus never argued with people about the philosophy of prayer. He knew people could not help praying any more than they could help breathing. It is the instinct of the human heart to lift its thought to God. Therefore note that Jesus does not say, "If you pray," but "When you pray." How much time people waste in discussing the value of prayer when it is the spirit, and method, and range of prayer that is important. Prayer is not a religious performance in order that public proprieties may be observed, but a communion with the Father in secret where the spirit of man waits silently for God. It is at the dynamic centre of that world within where all our instincts and desires clamor for control. Whatever reigns there determines all the outward life.

In responding to the pressure of the Divine Spirit we have all we need for guidance, wisdom and power. Jesus assures us that the Father is far more willing to pervade our inner life with His spirit than we are to give our children bread. He is ever at the door pressing in upon us. When we relax and throw open every entrance of our being to His coming, our spirit becomes alive to the sense of higher realities. As Whittier wrote:

"So sometimes comes to soul and sense,
The feeling which is evidence
That very near about us lies
The realm of spiritual mysteries.
The sphere of the supernal powers
Impinges on this world of ours.
The low and dark horizon lifts,
To light the scenic terror shifts;
The breath of a diviner air
Blows down the answer of a prayer:
That all our sorrow, pain, and doubt
A great compassion clasps about,
And law and goodness, love and force
Are wedded fast beyond divorce."

The model prayer which we call the Lord's Prayer has at its heart the two-fold consciousness; our relation to our Father and our relation to all mankind. It is an acid test for all desires. Are they according to the "manner" of speech taught us by Jesus? In voicing the desires of our hearts which objective is used more: "us" or "me"? What possible explanation may there be in this for a limited experience with God? In naming what is most important to our life how much of it harmonizes with the prayers of others? Is competition or coöperation the mainspring of devotion?

The primitive needs of humanity are all of concern to the love of God. Eating, drinking, clothing, wisdom, work, these are the necessary outfitting for the soul when it is incarnate in human flesh — "Your Father knoweth that ye have need of these things," says Jesus, "Be not therefore anxious." Woe to him who tries to restrain God from answering these needs. "He that selleth the needy for a pair of shoes" will not find any inspiration in prayer. All the resources of God are against the selfish soul.

"Search me, O God, and know my heart:
Try me and know my thoughts:
And see if there be any way of wickedness in me,
And lead me in the way everlasting." *Amen.*

THE PERVADING PRESENCE OF A PERSONAL GOD

AN OUT-SHINING PRESENCE IN HIS WORLD

From earliest days, even the most primitive people have connected the material world with a spiritual presence. They pictured a spirit in the mountain, a spirit in the sunrise, a spirit in plants and trees, and a spirit within the stars. Later thinking viewed the world without, not as possessed by many different spirits, but pervaded by the presence of the Infinite Spirit of God, intimately near to all of us.

We know what a man is like, by the quality of his work; sooner or later the day declares it. We know God, also, by His workmanship in His World. Sometimes we look at another person and say: "One cannot judge by appearances; the man looks honest, but we have had no dealings with him, and cannot say what the dominant qualities of his character may be." With God we do not depend on His outward appearance, because no man hath seen God at any time. But far more important knowledge of Him is ours. He has conducted vast enterprises in the universe, and we can study His methods, and through them know unerringly His real character and heart.

We discover that God is the soul of *perfection*. His work is flawless. The most complex living creature is intricately fashioned, and marvelously adapted for every exigency. Each tiny cell functions in silent efficiency; the mark of perfect workmanship. Each flake of snow that falls from heaven is perfect in its beauty and design, though it be only one of millions, and melt away under the sun's first rays. We may drill down into the earth and bring up a bit of rock only to discover that it, too, is perfect in its geometrical crystals and formation. A hair on the body of the smallest insect and the eye of a man are both fashioned in utter completeness. There is no sham or untidy spot in God's world; hidden away or open, it defies all critical inspection. God is everywhere and in all things absolute perfection.

We discover also that God is *faithfulness*. We go to sleep in peace, each night, knowing that the sun will shine in the morning, the waters of the mighty deep will surely be held true to the tides, and the harvest

16

will come from the seed. We look up in quietness to the stars in the sky, knowing that they will swing in their orbits and that God's plan for the universe will not fail. We can rely on His faithfulness.

We know, too, that God has an extraordinary purpose for *mankind*. In all the world about us, human beings have supreme privileges. We are endowed with peculiar powers of mind by which we can make use of God's created works, and by new combinations carry on the God-like work of creation. We came into life as helpless infants and by the use of our creative powers may develop great personalities; capable of thinking God's thoughts and working with Him. Evidently God's great heart purposes a mighty destiny for man, because He has arranged such a complex world of infinite possibilities for His training in greatness.

> "The earth with its stores of wonder untold,
> Almighty, Thy power hath founded of old,
> Hath stablished it fast by a changeless decree,
> And round it hath cast, like a mantle, the sea.
> Thy bountiful care, what tongue can recite?
> It breathes in the air, it shines in the light;
> It streams from the hills; it descends to the plain,
> And sweetly distills in the dew and the rain."
>
> *R. Grant 1839.*

FOR STUDY AND THOUGHT

For the wrath of God is revealed from heaven against all ungodliness and unrighteousness of men, who hold down the truth in unrighteousness; because that which may be known of God is manifest in them; for God manifested it unto them. For the invisible things of him since the creation of the world are clearly seen, being perceived through the things that are made, even his everlasting power and divinity; that they may be without excuse. *Rom. 1 : 18–20.*

To whom then will ye liken me, that I should be equal to him? saith the Holy One. Lift up your eyes on high, and see who hath created these, that bringeth out their host by number: he calleth them all by name; by the greatness of his might, and for that he is strong in power, not one is lacking. Why sayest thou, O Jacob, and speakest, O Israel, My way is hid from the Lord, and my judgment is passed away from my God? Hast thou not known? hast thou not heard? the everlasting God, the Lord, the Creator of the ends of the earth, fainteth not, neither is weary; there is no searching of his understanding. He giveth power to the faint; and to him that hath no might he increaseth strength. *Isa. 40 : 25–29.*

Therefore I say unto you, be not anxious for your life, what ye shall eat, or what ye shall drink; nor yet for your body, what ye shall put on. Is not the life more than the food, and the body than the raiment? Behold the birds of the heaven, that they sow not, neither do they reap, nor gather into barns; and your heavenly Father feedeth them. **Are not ye of much more value than they?** *Matt. 6 : 25–26.*

There are three great characteristics of nature which reveal a God who is adequate for all our need. One of them is the manifestation of power; so mighty that we can rest all our weakness upon it, and so humbling that there is no room for pride. If anything should keep a child-like heart within the majority of us, God's presence in His world ought to do it.

> "God moves in a mysterious way
>   His wonders to perform;
> He plants His footsteps in the sea
> And rides upon the storm."
>
> *William Cowper 1774.*

There is no room for vainglory if we view ourselves in the perspective of God's universe. David, the King, had a truer sense of values than most of us to-day. He looked up at the moon and stars, and the blue heavens, and in his sense of his insignificance exclaimed: "What is man that Thou art mindful of him?" Many of us stop there and do not get the other side of the truth that he discerned in the next breath, "Thou hast made him but little lower than God, Thou hast put all *things* under his feet." Many a student, delving into astronomy has reeled with the immensity of the heavenly spaces and inferred that man is after all only a handful of animated atoms. But the miracle of all nature is that man, a mere speck on the horizon, has the capacity to sweep the heavens, and pilot his way over the trackless seas by stars that are millions of miles away.

We stand in awe also before the omniscience of God. Stumblingly we grope our way to knowledge which is locked up in the libraries of nature. We try to reproduce awkwardly what nature creates silently and without effort. We never plumb the depths of the wisdom of nature. The wisest of men of all ages have scarcely gone beyond the alphabet. How can any of us regard his small problems as unsolvable when there is no searching of God's understanding!

We see also a benevolent nature. Nothing is forgotten. Every provision is made for the care of her children. The feeding of the birds is the Creator's concern, and the color of the lily. Wounds are healed by the marvelous recuperative powers. Nothing has been left undone to help us to grow up and fulfill all the possibilities of our being. When obstructions come they are of our own creation; for man, and not God, is the enemy of man.

We are indeed without excuse if we ignore these lessons from the world about us. If we throw aside our God-given powers and lead a parasitic life we shall lose our capacities of soul. The earth is one mighty workshop for the development of man. God trusts us with His unharnessed forces and promises strength and wisdom for all our needs. Why then are we so foolish in doing only what our frail strength can bring to pass and neglecting the coöperation with God for miraculous works? How do we measure our resources — by our ability or by our willingness, to let God work through us? Where do we set our limits and say, "Beyond this lies impossibility?" "The things that are impossible with *man, are possible with God.*"

"Lord I believe! Help Thou my unbelief." Amen.

AN OUT–SHINING PRESENCE IN JESUS

To see God in the world, in all His creative power, is sublime and humbling. In the perspective of the universe, man seems the merest atom. May he hope to have real companionship with the Infinite? Can it be possible that frail humanity may push through to the higher plane, where the destiny it hungers for becomes a reality?

This hunger for relationship with God is a mark of our supremacy in the created world and indicates qualities which tend to fit us for a higher realm of life. These qualities make us individuals with boundless personality. This separates us from the world of things. Every little child knows this. No amount of material things can satisfy its heart, if the mother, the great personality in its tiny world, is beyond reach. All of us, children of larger growth, need the presence of a personality wiser than our own, to guide us in our search for God.

In the pages of history, certain personalities tower above all others in their understanding of God. Among them all, Jesus, in the simplicity of His teaching transcends the highest in mankind.

The most discerning men of wisdom echo Sidney Lanier's words:

> "What least defect or shadow of defect,
> What rumor, tattled by an enemy
> Of inference loose, what lack of grace,
> Even in torture's grasp, or sleep's or death's —
> O what amiss may I forgive in Thee,
> Jesus, good Paragon, thou crystal Christ."

He alone qualifies as the guiding expert in our search for peace, health, and power. If we are mentally honest and sincere, we shall be willing, in a spirit of scientific inquiry, to follow Jesus as the best working hypothesis for discovering as much of God as mortals may know.

We should still be living in incoherent uncertainty were it not that God has come near to us in the person of Jesus. In His life untold millions, through the centuries, have seen God. History concedes that He is as much of God as has ever been compassed within the limits of human personality; a perfect medium for the revelation of the heart and mind of God. As we study Jesus, it begins to dawn on us that every quality we long for in God is radiant in Him. The perfection of His relationship with God gives us hope that we too may inherit the same friendship: one like unto the perfect relation of father and child with all the loving expectancy, the tender protection and the reverence that it involves.

We may well heed the ways in which Jesus conquered the world by His spirit. He naturally and instinctively used the laws which the wisest philosophers have groped after uncertainly. He lived on a plane where the laws of the spirit are dominant and overcome the desires of the flesh. Those who discerned His heart, knew He was unlike any personality the world had seen, in spite of the limitations of His human incarnation. We who see Him in the perspective of history, know that even yet He towers high above the poor best that mankind has been able to achieve, after two thousand years of testing His methods.

The records of the life of Jesus in the New Testament will yield all that the world now hails as new truth in the realm of the spirit. His character bears any scrutiny. Even the critical Renan writes, "Whatever the surprises of history, Jesus will never be surpassed." More than nineteen hundred years have passed and today when our discoveries in science are pushing up into the unseen powers of the natural world we are beginning to see that Jesus is the only One who is perfectly at home in these higher planes that the eyes of the mind are only beginning to discern. He still leads the way up and out from all limitations. Those of us who have demonstrated in some small degree the reality of His teaching know within our hearts the truth of His power. Even from unexpected sources we find a discerning witness to the power of Jesus. The words of Napoleon bear this out.

"Alexander, Cæsar, Charlemagne, and I have founded great empires, but upon what did these creations of our genius depend? Upon force! Jesus alone founded His empire on Love, and to this very day millions would die for Him, I think I understand something of human nature, and I tell you that all these were men, and I am a man. None else is like Him. Jesus Christ was more than a man."

> "Jesus thou joy of loving hearts,
> Thou fount of life, thou light of men;
> From the best bliss that earth imparts,
> We turn unfilled to thee again."
> *Bernard of Clairvoix 1150 A. D.*

FOR STUDY AND THOUGHT

And there were shepherds in the same country abiding in the field, and keeping watch by night over their flock. And an angel of the Lord stood by them, and the glory of the Lord shone around about them: and they were sore afraid. And the angel said unto them, Be not afraid;

for behold, I bring you good tidings of great joy which shall be to all the people: for there is born to you this day in the city of David a Saviour, which is Christ the Lord. And this is a sign unto you; Ye shall find a babe wrapped in swaddling clothes, and lying in a manger. And suddenly there was with the angel a multitude of the heavenly host praising God, and saying, Glory to God in the highest, And on earth peace among men in whom he is well pleased. *Luke 2 : 8–14.*

I am the door: By me if any man enter in, he shall be saved, and shall go in and go out, and shall find pasture. The thief cometh not, but that he may steal, and kill, and destroy: I came that they may have life, and may have it abundantly. I am the Good Shepherd; the good shepherd layeth down his life for the sheep. *John 10 : 9–11.*

Again therefore Jesus spake unto them, saying, I am the light of the world: He that followeth me shall not walk in the darkness, but shall have the light of life. *John 8 : 12.*

All things have been delivered unto me of my Father: and no one knoweth the Son, save the Father; neither doth any know the Father, save the Son, and he to whomsoever the Son willeth to reveal him. Come unto me, all ye that labour and are heavy laden, and I will give you rest. Take my yoke upon you, and learn of me; for I am meek and lowly of heart: and ye shall find rest unto your souls. For my yoke is easy and my burden is light. *Matt. 11 : 27–30.*

The heart of Christianity is the personality of Jesus. He is the centre of its power and the One who gives meaning to the whole of life. He is the spirit of triumphant victory and joy. Of all the religions in the world Christianity is the most joyous. Songs and praises began at His birth and have never ceased through the centuries. When we face our sins and the sorrows that surrounded the death of Christ we forget the joy and triumph of His life. He came to burst the bonds of death and sorrow and to bring the joy of deliverance. Naturally the Christmas bells ring when the triumphant song is heard: "Glory to God in the highest and on earth peace among men in whom He is well pleased."

Jesus is everything that men long for: light in darkness; protection in danger, freedom from sin, rest for weariness, strength for weakness, faith for fear, life for death. No other religion has ever promised such perfect freedom. Even in the face of the crucifixion Jesus says to His intimate friends during their last supper together: "These things have I spoken to you that my joy may be in you, and that your joy may be full." (John 15 : 11) Why then, are we so slow to possess our spiritual inheritance. We do not have to go about bearing depressing burdens. Jesus has conquered death and all those things that make life hard for us.

In the light of these triumphs of Christian thinking it is well for us to face our motives for ignoring an out and out allegiance to Christ. Why do we not believe in the power of Jesus? Is He too great to be true? Dare we cling to any other ideal of God than that of Jesus? We are constantly yearning for the very experiences which He said we might have. Why do we not rise up in faith and prove the truth of His words? What most of us need is *hope* to lift us out of the rut of our thinking and the inhibitions of our fears. We do not get it from outer circumstances: we find it only by taking the words of Jesus at their full face value. He challenges the moral honesty of all of us to come and see for ourselves whether His point of view about life and death and sickness and sin will not bring us the freedom for which we long.

There is no other way of finding God save through Jesus. He has blazed the trail by which the human spirit can become one with the Father, God. We would still be groping in our intricate philosophical speculations, going round in circles, victims of an impersonal scheme of things and impotent to attain to spiritual life. The way of Jesus is *the* way , *the* truth, *the* life. The fact that some have been half-heartedly interested in it, or have stumbled in following their Lord, is not a reflection on Him, but rather a witness to the universal desire to be related to Him in some way as a goal, even though it be far ahead of our present realization. It proves, too, how far above human effort the transcendent Christ lives, making us feel after twenty centuries that He is as far above us as the heavens are higher than the earth. Millions more people now look to Him as their Ideal than during all the years He lived on earth. His spiritual dominance is greater with each passing century.

> O blessed Saviour, draw us; draw us by the cords of Thy love; draw us by the sense of Thy goodness, draw us by the unspotted purity and beauty of Thy example; Draw us by the merit of Thy precious death and by the power of Thy Holy Spirit; Draw us good Lord, and we shall run after Thee; for Thy Name's sake. *Amen.*   *Isaac Barrow A. D. 1630.*

AN OUT-SHINING PRESENCE WITHIN US

We have already seen that it is our inner spirit which lifts us above the material world and connects us with God. It is the thinking, feeling, willing part of us which has the power to hear the "still, small voice" of God.

Spirit is all-living, all-pervasive, all-powerful, ever reaching out, and up, and irresistible. The gift of spirit to man makes him the offspring of God. It is the I, the conscious I am, by which I am aware that I am a living person. We may enslave ourselves voluntarily in a dark prison of material things and in the shadowy life of the senses, but try as hard as we may to forget, the inner spirit restlessly yearns to be free once more.

Jesus came, all glorious, because His spirit and God were one. God shone out in living presence in Him so much that some of those who were with Him, cried out : "My Lord and my God!"

An amazing secret Jesus has shared with us. He said to those earnest folk who wanted to understand spiritual mysteries, "The kingdom of God is within you." He voiced it also in a prayer which, He said, was not only for His disciples, but "for them also that believe on me through their word." Thus He includes each one of us who longs to be like Him. His words seem almost incredible. "The glory which thou hast given me I have given unto them; that they may be one even as we are one."

When we think of the character of Christ, — the glory which lifted Him above all men who have ever walked the earth; a glory which made Him triumphant over sin, and death, and hatred; a glory which bestowed upon Him such powers of love and wisdom that no one could find a flaw in Him, we can scarcely understand how that glory could be given to us. What inexhaustible riches are within our grasp because Jesus has invited us into His kingdom of love!

God, then, is within us, bringing us if we will it to be so, into oneness with Him and into oneness with all other spirits who are one with Him!

If, each day, we turn away from all outer life for a while and concentrate our thought upon our inner life, silently and expectantly, we shall find that God is within us illumining our mind, and diffusing the love of Himself in our secret heart. It is vain to try to penetrate the distant heaven to find God. He is within us: how then can God be far away.

"Speak to Him, thou, for He hears, and Spirit with Spirit can meet —
Closer is He than breathing, and nearer than hands and feet!"

Browning.

In spite of this possibility we feel also the tug of another influence: a pressure toward the things of sense; a rebel impulse which fights against the God-spirit within us. So long as we yield to it, we live without spiritual hope and without God. It is we who shut ourselves out from His presence. He is there, within us, ready to meet us when we enter our inner room and shut the door upon the world without.

There are other ways in which we are conscious that God is within us. In that moment of hesitation before we make a moral choice for or against our highest self, we instinctively think of God. Like Wordsworth, we too "feel a Presence that disturbs" us, and that sense of God becomes the sensitive guide for conduct.

"Therefore I walk as one who sees the joy shine through
Of the other life behind our life, as the stars behind the blue."

Jesus told his disciples to pray until the Holy Spirit of God should come into their inner lives. He fully expected that the life of the body should be controlled by spiritual laws and that we should be living temples, the home of His Spirit. In this way He means to dwell among men, so that people may come to know Him through our walk, and conversation, and contacts with life. Bishop Gore points out that because the special quality of the Holy Spirit is holiness, "it is in *rational* natures, which alone are capable of holiness, that He exerts His special influence."

There is no way of gaining power from the indwelling spirit of God unless we are willing to have the *character* of God wrought out in us. "He giveth His Spirit to them that *obey* Him" said St. Paul. It is only as representatives of God on earth that we can be entrusted with the outshining Presence. It is not for a selfish luxury of emotion nor for the degrading of power for selfish ends. It is that we may be able to work the works of God and bring nearer the day when His will may be done on earth as it is done in heaven.

"For Thou within no walls confined,
Inhabitest the humble mind.
Such ever bring Thee when they come,
And going take Thee to their home.".

W. Cowper 1769.

FOR STUDY AND THOUGHT

And being asked by the Pharisees, when the kingdom of God cometh, he (Jesus) answered them and said, The kingdom of God cometh not with observation: neither shall they say, Lo, here! or, There! for lo, the kingdom of God is within you.   *Luke 17 : 20–21.*

If ye love me, ye will keep my commandments. And I will pray the Father, and He shall give you another Comforter, that he may be with you forever, even the Spirit of truth: whom the world cannot receive; for it beholdeth him not, neither knoweth him: ye know him; for he abideth with you, and shall be in you.   *John 14 : 15–17.*

How be it when he, the Spirit of truth, is come, he shall guide you into all the truth: for he shall not speak from himself; but what things soever he shall hear, these shall he speak: and he shall declare unto you the things that are to come. He shall glorify me: for he shall take of mine, and shall declare it unto you.   *John 16 : 13–14.*

Then shall the righteous shine forth as the sun in the kingdom of their Father. He that hath ears, let him hear.   *Matt. 13 : 43.*

The story goes that in pioneer days a community of people suffered from the cold during a bitter winter. There was a scarcity of fuel and they met in their churches to pray for milder weather. Later on, when they were digging in the earth, they discovered large quantities of soft coal; — enough to keep multitudes in comfort. While they had been looking for help from God without, He had provided resources within their reach. Even so we look up to God in heaven and try to find Him, when lo! He is within us, waiting for us to release Him in all His power. As St. Paul says:

"Work out your own salvation with fear and trembling; for it is God who *worketh in* you both to will and to work for His good pleasure."
Phil. 2 : 12–13.

Note how the presence of the Spirit within us is conditioned by our love of Christ and our willingness to keep His commandments. It could not be otherwise when the purpose of God's Presence in us is to transform us into the likeness of Christ. It means a more intense life made richer in personality because the life of Christ is added to our life, bringing to it a new completeness. Thus every natural gift we have becomes luminous with the beauty of God. This is what some call inspiration. It is the experience which comes to us when we step out from a close stuffy room into the fresh air. We begin to glow with new life. Our thoughts become clearer, we breathe more easily and we have a new vitality and freedom. The breezes of heaven have entered our being and we are more fit to use our powers. This is not an original simile. Jesus used the thought when he said to Nicodemus who sought a scientific explanation of the phenomenon of the Spirit's coming into a man, "The wind bloweth where it listeth, and thou hearest the voice thereof, but knowest not whence it cometh, and whither it goeth: so is everyone that is born of the Spirit." (John 3 : 8.) We know that God dwells in us by the new illumination which comes to us,

> "I ask no dream, no prophet-ecstasies;
> No sudden rending of the veil of clay;
> No angel visitant, no opening skies;
> But take the dimness of my soul away." *George Croly.*

The most important change within us will be in our desires. They will be fused together into a love for God and for others. Jesus says: "By this shall all men know that ye are my disciples, if ye have love one to another" (John 13 : 35).

We shall not be conscious of the Presence within. The more completely God and our spirit become one the less shall we be able to distinguish between them. God and our conscience become one voice. We shall not know that our face shines with the light of our secret life with Him, but others will know that the inner springs of our life are unfailing and that everything absorbs new vitality from association with us. "And thou shalt be like a watered garden and like a spring of water, whose waters fail not" (Isa. 58 : 11).

> Oh God, deliver us from blindness of heart, that we may not miss the destiny which Thou hast purposed that we should inherit. Turn Thou our hearts that we shut not ourselves away from Thy indwelling Presence. *Amen.*

AN OUT-SHINING PRESENCE IN OTHERS

Someone once said that prejudices are our dearest possessions relinquished only at death. It is probably true. We accumulate so many fixed ideas and unyielding habits of thought along the road of life. Most of them come from hasty judgments and inherited traditions. Reverence for the experience of the past is a virtue so long as we can view it open-mindedly; but it becomes a fault if it prevents our mental growth or makes us wise in our own conceit.

One of the danger symptoms of prejudice is an easy contentment with our own point of view which leads us to look down on others who see life from a different angle. Few of us question our opinions or our sense of values. We seek friends who think as we think, read books which repeat our thoughts, and tend to become more and more what we already are. This habit of mind colors our thought of God. We picture Him to be what we think Him to be from our background and ideas, and our religion harmonises with our particular conception of Him.

When we stop to think that the same God who is within us is also within others, we have a new consciousness of His infinite revelation to the world. He has incarnated living spirits in varied races and nationalities both of men and women, with all their differences in characteristics, temperament and experience, in order that there might be an infinite manifestation of His indwelling Presence. Each is meant to add his own expression of the Divine life to the glory of the whole. Every color of thought may enrich all others. There is only one condition to be fulfilled: each human being must be open-doored to God, relating himself to the Infinite Spirit. Each must be a willing medium for the abundant life.

In an old cathedral there is a famous rose window of exquisite design and artistic craftsmanship. Hundreds of tiny bits of glass of all colors and shades are fitted into the pattern. Behind it the sun shines, revealing the beauty of each color and the greater beauty of the whole design. The sun becomes more radiant and intimate because of the colors, and the colors are transfigured by the sun. Without the sun the colors could not reveal themselves. The whole window is fittingly symbolic of the Presence of God in people. One soul cannot give the full vision of the heart of God; all others are needed; fitting together in intimate unity. If we could believe this with all that there

28

is in us, most of our troubles would be over, and we would learn so much from one another that the whole world would bound forward into light.

We love others in proportion to the degree in which their quality of spirit transcends our own and calls forth our adoration. The experiences in life bring out in each of us some dominant quality of character. The aviator shows courage, the friend is faithful. Everyone is radiant in *something* that is God-like. If these marks of character are possible in others they can be grown also in us. The lives of others are a challenge to our own. The total of all these transcendent qualities in all human beings makes a composite spirit which shows us in part what God must be like. In the Christ we see all these qualities embodied and functioning in one personality. He thus becomes the standard for us, revealing in us whatever is like Him, and pointing to all that stretches ahead.

It is good for us to see ourselves as only one variety of flower in God's garden. We lose our egotism, and sense of importance and get closer to the common life of all humanity. This makes us tender toward all the children of men, so that we say *"Our* Father" with new humility. It is also easier to believe that God is adequate for the whole world, as well as for our simple needs.

> "Old friends, old scenes will lovelier be,
> As more of heaven in each we see:
> Some softening gleam of love and prayer
> Shall dawn on every cross and care."
>
> *J. Keble.*

FOR STUDY AND THOUGHT

And Stephen, full of grace and power, wrought great wonders and signs among the people. And they were not able to withstand the wisdom and the Spirit by which he spake. Then they suborned men, which said, We have heard him speak blasphemous words against Moses and against God. And they stirred up the people, and the elders, and the scribes, and came upon him, and seized him, and brought him into the council, and set up false witnesses, which said, This man ceaseth not to speak words against this holy place, and the law: for we have heard him say, that this Jesus of Nazareth shall destroy this place, and shall change the customs which Moses delivered unto us. And all that sat in the council, fastening their eyes on him, saw his face as it had been the face of an angel.

Acts 6 : 8, 10–15.

But if the ministration of death, written, and engraven on stones, came with glory, so that the children of Israel could not look stedfastly upon the face of Moses for the glory of his face; which glory was passing away: how shall not rather the ministration of the spirit be with glory?

II Cor. 3 : 7–8.

Unto each one of us was the grace given according to the measure of the gift of Christ. And he gave some to be apostles; and some, prophets; and some, evangelists; and some, pastors and teachers; for the perfecting of the saints, unto the work of ministering, unto the building up of the body of Christ: till we all attain unto the unity of the faith, and of the knowledge of the Son of God, unto a full-grown man, unto the measure of the stature of the fulness of Christ.   *Eph. 4 : 7, 11–13.*

Character speaks more loudly than words. People do not have to explain themselves. Their presence creates a personal atmosphere which reveals the inner soul. Some people depress us without saying a word, others lift us into buoyant life. If selfishness is the center of the heart all the world knows it in spite of our denials. If the Spirit of Christ rules us people will know it instinctively.

The Spirit of Christ does not always meet with the approval of men. As Jesus once said, there are men who love darkness rather than light because the light reproves their deeds. The life of a true spiritual leader is never smooth. Stephen was an example of this. He was chosen by the multitude to supervise the social service of the early Christian Church because they trusted his spirit and wisdom. It is said of him that he was "full of grace and power" and "wrought great wonders" and that people were not able to withstand the wisdom and spirit by which he spake. Yet they stoned him and cast him out as they had rejected Jesus. He was persecuted because of His right-eousness. There is also a persecution which we bring on ourselves because of unrighteousness. Which kind has been true in our exper-ience? Note the effect of this persecution on Stephen's spirit. He died praying forgiveness for his enemies and with a face radiant as an angel with the love of Christ. What is our reaction to opposition? Is it wounded vanity or pride of opinion or forgiving love? Are we tempted to avoid moral issues when they come naturally in the exper-ience of a day? We say we seek the way of peace and power. Does it rest on the approval of men or the inner voice of God? Moses and Stephen found themselves separated from people because of their inner radiance, but it gave Moses the power to transform a multitude of slaves into a nation which brought the Christ into the world. The face of the dying Stephen won for the cause of Christ, St. Paul, the mightiest apostle of the ages. What would the world have missed had these men not paid the price of utter devotion to the Presence of God!

Our growth in the knowledge of God is dependent upon our appre-ciation of His Presence in others. No one soul or kindred group can fully manifest Christ. It requires all the varied experiences of His character to present an adequate picture. The reason why the world is not moved by the Christ it sees, is because we present only the one feature that appeals to us and do not add to our conception the features which shine out through the experience of others. Nothing is more dangerous than a half truth. Generations have stumbled on in error because men in their pride thought they had the whole truth. The radiance of Christ *is* greater in every age. Can we do better than to follow the example of St. Paul in his attitude of mind, "Unto me who am less than the least of all saints was this grace given to preach unto the Gentiles the unsearchable riches of Christ" (Eph. 3 : 8)

> Our Father, unto Thee, in the light of our Saviour's blessed life, we would lift our souls. We thank Thee for that true light shining in our world with still increasing brightness. We thank thee for all who have walked therein, and especially to those near and dear, in whose lives we have seen his excellent glory and beauty. May we know that in the body and out of the body they are with Thee, and that when these earthly days come to an end, it is not that our service of Thee, and of one another may cease, but that it may begin anew. Make us glad in all who have faithfully lived; make us glad in all who have peacefully died. Lift us into light and love, and purity and blessedness, and give us at last our portion with those who have trusted in Thee and sought, in small things as in great, in things temporal and things eternal, to do so Thy Holy Will.   *Amen.*
>
> *Rufus Ellis 1819.*

THE WORLD WITHIN US

THE CREATIVE POWER OF THOUGHT

"As a man thinketh in his heart, so is he," wrote the Hebrew seer thousands of years ago. He knew then instinctively what the psychologist now heralds as a scientific discovery. Everyone knows this truth theoretically, but does not use the mighty weapon of thought practically. Most people still allow their minds to be an unfenced space where every kind of thought may come and go as it chooses. We allow ourselves to be played upon by all sorts of mental influences and because we do not always know whence they come, we assume a helpless attitude toward them. Archbishop Trench describes the common experience in his sonnet: —

> "A wretched thing it were, to have our heart
> Like a thronged highway or a populous street
> Where every idle thought has leave to meet,
> Pause, or pass on as in an open mart;
> Or like some roadside pool, which no nice art
> Has guarded that the cattle may not beat
> And foul it with a multitude of feet,
> Till of the heavens it can give back no part."

In the interests of that efficiency which we all seek, we are compelled to think more about this strange power of thought which can make or unmake our health, our mental ability, our business success, and our peace of mind. We have no right to disregard the importance of our power house merely because it seems so intangible, and silent in its working.

Every one of us should have a sentry at the door of our mind to challenge all uninvited, passing thoughts and see whether they be worthy to enter and to influence us. Once they are inside and allowed to linger, they begin to create situations and effects in which we may become deeply involved.

Thoughts create bodily conditions. We all know how our circulatory system is immediately affected by our thinking. It may bring a blush to our cheeks — so instant is the connection between our mind and the capillary blood vessels under the skin. A disturbing thought may so inhibit our nerve centres that we cannot eat, or sleep. A thought of fear may paralyze us so that we cannot move and, in the same way, a thought of happiness will create a new elasticity in our step and a glow of health in every organ of our body. When our thinking is morbid or depressed, every function of the body becomes so sluggish that it may create a condition of disease. Even thoughts that have shocked the mind unpleasantly in the past, by connecting certain emotions with certain experiences, may go on working powerfully for years in what is called a "repressed complex" although we have forgotten that we ever had such thoughts. No wonder the ancient prophet warned, "Guard thy heart with all diligence for out of it are the issues of life." We cannot change bodily conditions in a moment much as we long to do so; but we can put away the thought that caused the condition by fixing our mind on a more powerful, health-giving thought until the trouble-making one dies of inanition: — starved from lack of attention.

Our thoughts create mental powers or mental weakness. A man may go to sleep with a burden of mental anxiety saying over and over, "How shall I ever meet to-morrow's problems?" until he is nervously overwrought and mentally unfit to solve them. The same man may go to sleep thinking, "what a privilege and honor it is to be trusted with this difficult task; it is a compliment to my ability!" and lo! in the morning he rises with a new vigor and power which solves the problems easily. The difference lies in the aspect of the situation he chooses to think about. There is never an experience, however difficult, in which there is not at least one possible cheerful reflection which is the way of escape for us. We can begin now to demonstrate this for ourselves, and perhaps our faith in the power of a thought may become strong enough to move some age-long mountain of difficulty from our vision.

Thoughts pull the trigger for ends. The easiest way to keep from doing something is to think of something else equally absorbing. No temptation to an evil act engulfed us without much preliminary morbid thinking. A temptation which comes upon us swiftly "before we thought" as we say, in reality is the natural situation created by thoughts that have lingered in our minds so long that they have become subconscious and flash out into consciousness in response to pent-up emotions. We store up thought ammunition for months and then are surprised at the mighty effect of a small word-spark which touches it off.

It would be well for us if we had at least five minutes of serious self-examination at the close of each day, recalling the kind of thoughts we have been harboring, and casting away every destructive one that spells fear, worry, depression, jealousy, hatred, or selfishness. Then let us deliberately replace each of them with its opposite creative suggestion. We should hold them all in concentrated thought, and in a prayer of gratitude to God who makes these life-giving realities, and escape from spiritual death possible. We can never get rid of destructive thoughts by repressing them or burying them. They must be dragged out into the open, judged and cast out as real, but undesirable, enemies. Then, with a mind clear and empty, we can bring into a thankful heart those thoughts which bring peace, health and power.

> Our blest-Redeemer, 'ere he breathed
> His tender last farewell,
> A Guide, a Comforter, bequeathed
> With us to dwell.
>
> And His that gentle voice we hear
> Soft as the breath of even,
> That checks each thought and calms each fear,
> And speaks of heaven.
>
> And every virtue we possess,
> And every victory won,
> And every thought of holiness,
> Are His alone.
>
> *Harriet Auber.*

FOR STUDY AND THOUGHT

Seek ye the Lord while he may be found, call ye upon him while he is near: let the wicked forsake his way, and the unrighteous man his thoughts: and let him return unto the Lord, and he will have mercy upon him; and to our God, for he will abundantly pardon. For my thoughts are not your thoughts, neither are your ways my ways, saith the Lord. For as the heavens are higher than the earth, so are my ways higher than your ways, and my thoughts than your thoughts. *Isa. 55 : 6–9.*

Commit thy works unto the Lord, and thy thoughts shall be established.
Prov. 16 : 3.

The good man out of the good treasure of his heart bringeth forth that which is good; and the evil man out of the evil treasure bringeth that which is evil: for out of the abundance of the heart his mouth speaketh.
Luke 6 : 45.

And he called to him the multitude again, and said unto them, Hear me all of you, and understand; there is nothing from without the man, that going into him can defile him: but the things which proceed out of the man are those that defile the man. For from within, out of the heart of men, evil thoughts proceed, fornications, theft, murders, adulteries,

covetings, wickednesses, deceit, lasciviousness, an evil eye, railing, pride, foolishness: All these evil things proceed from within, and defile the man.
Mark 7 : 14–15, 21–23.

Finally, brethren, whatsoever things are true, whatsoever things are honourable, whatsoever things are just, whatsoever things are pure, whatsoever things are lovely, whatsoever things are of good report; if there be any virtue, and if there be any praise, think on these things.
Phil. 4 : 8.

We cannot always control outer circumstances but we can control our thoughts which create many circumstances. God made us supreme in the kingdom of our thoughts and therein lies our share of moral responsibility. Thoughts may be non-creative and center around ourselves, our pleasure, our likes and dislikes until like a boy with a nickel close to his eye, we see no horizon. Many diseases and forms of insanity, and a breakdown of physical vitality start in a thought life which begins and ends in oneself. What a change would come over us if our thoughts mounted to the stars and heavenly places where we come into the clear spaces of God. Many of us are ill because of the friction that results from trying to crowd down our immortal spirits into the confines of small bodies. The strain of keeping them there is too great for endurance and we break down under it. What is the way out? Give the mind a chance to mount up in thought like an eagle and stretch its wings in the heights. Any subject that is uplifting will take us out of ourselves; the thoughts of God as we catch them in the study of the stars, the wonders of physical science, and the glory of flowers, are some of the ways in which God meant us to stretch and grow. It is sin to center thought in ourselves. Christ died to set us free.

"We are here and all born little, just because
    We're here to grow.
What is sin? why sin's not growing; all that stops the growth within,
Plagues the eternal upward impulse, stunts the spirit — that is sin."
Sam Walter Foss.*

There is a connection between "works" and the control of our thoughts, concentration on some constructive program keeps the mind from being a prey to unwholesome thinking. Many invalids are made worse because they have no work to occupy their thoughts, therefore they react on themselves. Their symptoms get too much of their attention. With others there is another need. Their work becomes a burden of thought, which can only be relieved by entrusting the issues to God. They then find freedom from gnawing anxiety and gain steadiness of thought.

*From "The Higher Catechism in Songs of the Average Man," with permission of Lothrop, Lee & Shepard Co., Publishers, Boston.

Jesus puts great emphasis on the relation between thought and character. When He says that defilement comes not from without but from within, He is stating a truth now admitted by psychologists. Even thoughts which come into the mind from without cannot do harm until they are accepted by the will. If they are looked at in their true character and rejected, they fall powerless. Many people make the mistake of trying to suppress evil thoughts which clamor for entrance. Sooner or later they will gather enough strength to take possession. If they are allowed to show themselves so that they may be judged by the mind, they lose their appeal and the temptation is conquered. Unless they are so judged they come forth to create endless offspring like unto themselves. Some time in the future we shall see scientifically how an evil thought interferes with the harmony of life like a discord in a symphony. We know it now as a spiritual experience and find ample proof within ourselves.

St. Paul suggests that the positive thinking about all things which are true, and pure, and lovely as an education of the spirit, in time, will so refine our tastes that we shall unconsciously turn from all unworthy thinking. Some thoughts build strong foundations for life. They always create and never tear down. We undermine the wall of protection when we accustom our spirits to the presence of thoughts that are false and destructive. Sophistication may bring stagnation.

"Let the words of my mouth and the meditation of my heart be acceptable in thy sight, O Jehovah, my rock and my Redeemer." *Amen.*

THE SPIRITUAL USES OF THE IMAGINATION

The most fascinating gift of the human mind is its power of imagination. It is a proof of our spiritual citizenship that we can shut our eyes to all the material phenomena about us and live, move and have our being in a world which we create within ourselves. In it we fight noiseless battles, paint mental pictures, enter upon every possible experience, choose what we please to think about, and create characters and personalities, actors in powerful dramas. Imagination creates our destiny of triumph or defeat. It is the most compelling and the least understood of all our powers.

The materials out of which our imagination is woven come from that great storehouse of memories into which have been collected all our conscious and unconscious experiences, everything we have learned, our emotions, instincts, thoughts and repressed desires. We call this storehouse our subconscious mind and it is like Aladdin's cave; a veritable wonderland of vast possibilities.

Every one has an "organized self" which is strong or feeble according to the sentiments and dispositions which compose it. In his book on "Psychology and Morals," Professor Hadfield says "when the organized self moves toward its own completeness we call it the *Will*. The Will is the organized self in function, the self in movement." Ordinarily this will is powerful, but it has its limitations because often it is unable to control our emotions and desires.

It is our will, that function of our sentiments and dispositions, which chooses the plot of our mental drama and calls out from the storehouse of memory all those associated ideas which make up the imaginary picture. If our sentiments and dispositions are born of the Spirit of God, then quite naturally our "organized self" wills to create mental pictures which are pleasing to the God-controlled self. If our sentiments are unworthy, then our mental images will be unclean and demoralizing.

Imagination makes a powerful emotional appeal which is able to sweep our will before it. Therefore the wisdom of the scriptures bids us, "Keep thy heart (the secret place of spiritual desire) with all diligence; for out of it are the issues of life." And the prophet Isaiah put his finger instinctively on the secret of peace when he said of God, "Thou wilt keep him in perfect peace whose mind (or imagination) is stayed on Thee; because he trusteth in Thee."

37

It will help us to make our imagination an ally with God for peace instead of an enemy, if we understand how to use this power for spiritual ends. It can make God's presence real to us if we use it rightly and intelligently.

A negative habit of imagination is the direct cause of much ill-health; especially "nerves" and functional disorders. If our "organized self" moves toward selfishness and absorbing self-concern, so that we and our experiences are our chief interest, we will be tempted to picture things not as they are, but as a drama in which we are the pitiful heroines, appealing to the sympathies of the world. Many times we weep real tears over our imaginary woes, unaware of the undoing of our moral powers of self-control. Day dreams, also, may be our undoing. In them we create an imaginary world as we should like it to be, but unrelated to the actual circumstances in which God has placed us. We dream not in order to do, but to detach ourselves from our world and its challenges. Later on we realize in bitter sorrow that it is too late to do the work God entrusted to us, because we have idled the time away.

All the demoralizing emotions which rob us of peace, health, and power may be replaced by other emotions which build up the spirit, mind and body. There are times when the circumstances of life are overwhelming. We face them as they are in fearsome reality. Then we withdraw into our inner world and fix our imagination on God and His assurance of strength and wisdom and courage and companionship. We visualize ourselves as adequate for everything we have to face on the morrow because we picture ourselves hidden in God, and we say, "I can do all things in Him that strengtheneth me" and lo! our brain becomes clear and we *see* the way of escape. Our courage gives us a strength which brings us through in triumph.

When we forget ourselves we are free to think of others. One cannot see those who labor on without hope, neglecting children, the poor, and afflicted without picturing a new world of justice and mercy. God has need of some imaginations which being free from selfishness can visualize new social conditions and work to bring them about. This is what is implied in the prayer our Lord taught us when we say, "Thy kingdom come." The Bible is full of prophetic visions of days to come when deserts will blossom like a rose and men will beat their swords into plowshares. Well did Matthew Arnold sing:

> "Tasks in hours of insight willed
> May be in hours of gloom fulfilled."

There are big tasks awaiting the imagination of those who will use it to develop plans to hasten the time when the will of God will be done on earth as it is done in heaven. We lament that there are no prophets nowadays. We have the power to create visions, but most of it has been diverted from the Divine purpose.

As our minds remain steadfast in picturing visions of truth, and beauty, and mercy, and love, we shall discover that powerful emotions are reacting upon us, building up health, bringing in peace and drawing us into the atmosphere of the presence of God. Others will feel the effect of these purifying emotions and respond to them. Our strength will be reinforced by the strength we have kindled in them and possibilities for spiritual friendship beyond what we have ever experienced, will be realized.

> My thoughts before they are my own
> Are to my God distinctly known;
> He knows the words I mean to speak,
> 'Ere from my opening lips they break.   *I. Watts 1715.*

FOR STUDY AND THOUGHT

O Lord our God, all this store that we have prepared to build thee an house for thine holy name cometh of thine hand, and is all thine own. I know also, my God, that thou triest the heart, and hast pleasure in uprightness. As for me, in the uprightness of mine heart I have willingly offered all these things: and now have I seen with joy thy people, which are present here, to offer willingly unto thee. O Lord, the God of Abraham, of Isaac, and of Israel, our fathers, keep this forever in the imagination of the thoughts of the heart of thy people, and prepare their heart unto thee.   *I Chronicles, 29 : 16–18.*

And thou, Solomon my son, know thou the God of thy father, and serve him with a perfect heart and with a willing mind: for the Lord searcheth all hearts, and understandeth all the imaginations of the thoughts: if thou seek him, he will be found of thee; but if thou forsake him, he will cast thee off forever.   *I Chron. 28 : 9.*

Thou wilt keep him in perfect peace, whose mind is stayed on thee.
Isa. 26 : 3.

For though we walk in flesh, we do not war according to the flesh, (for the weapons of our warfare are not of the flesh, but mighty before God to the casting down of strongholds); casting down imaginations, and every high thing that is exalted against the knowledge of God, and bringing every thought into captivity to the obedience of Christ.
II Cor. 10 : 3–5.

A memory which is full of inspiring mental pictures is a priceless treasure. All of us are influenced by the memory of certain events which the mind paints for us. They are more real than what is actually before us. In this prayer of King David he asks God to keep a certain spiritual vision vividly in the imagination of the people. All of them have had a vivid picture of a temple, which was to be built to God.

They have created it with the eye of the mind and have given gold, silver and precious stones to make their dream come true. David knows that the people will build no greater temple than they have visualized, therefore he prays that their vision may not be dimmed. No great thing is achieved unless someone dreams it first. Every building is first built in the imagination of the architect before it is visible in brick and stone. "Where there is no vision," we are told, "the people perish." We have inspired moments when we see clearly, but the vision fades because we do not believe in it enough to part with our treasures to make it come true.

An imagination which begins and ends in the mind is weakening to character. An artist who does not paint the picture of which he dreams, or a Christian who does not do the good deed his mind moved him to do, weakens his creative power. We lose our capacity to have visions when we do not take steps to realize them. We also become sentimentalists because our emotions, which are stirred by our mental pictures, have no outlet in action.

Unless we control the use of our imagination it will enslave us. Self-pity, suspicion, fear, anxiety, sap our strength when they grip our thought. People become nervous wrecks from living under the spell of imaginary situations. As soon as they begin to hold the thought of Christ vividly before them, the sense of His understanding love relaxes the mind and peace comes. Marvellous cures often result naturally and the Psalmist's experience is reproduced: "I sought Jehovah and He answered me and delivered me from all my fears"

Holding every thought obedient to Christ is a habit of life that can be cultivated. A well-bred woman does not find it difficult to conform to the standard of good society, nor should a Christian find it hard to conform his thinking to the character and standard of the Christ. If it is hard it is probably due to the fact that there has been no personal acceptance of Christ as the authority of life. One cannot let all kinds of mental images dwell in the mind without seeing them reproduced in character. When we give a guest the freedom of our home we do not expect that freedom to express itself in damaging walls and breaking furniture. It means freedom to use the house according to the standards of good usage. Freedom of thought likewise implies standards. An evil imagination is not free; it shuts itself out from growth and creative power, and lives in a prison house of its own making.

"Create in me a clean heart, O God;
And renew a right spirit within me." *Amen.*

RECOLLECTED STRENGTH

A wise Christian teacher once gave this counsel to some students who were troubled because they could not realize the presence of God. "Form a daily habit of *recollecting* God and you will soon begin to realize His nearness." In this brief reply he showed them the possibilities of memory as a source of strength.

Memory is a wonderful provision for the accumulation of all the experiences of the past so that all its stored-up suggestions may be usable for the needs of to-day. It is also a fearful handicap to those who have amassed the wrong kind of experiences which come back later as painful reminders of folly. A continual vivid remembrance of all our sins and stumblings is all the punishment most people would ever need.

The Bible is full of appeals to memory, and we are urged to strengthen every link with the past which has been good and true so that we may build up reserves of strength and comfort. Every day experiences are being turned into mere memories. The actual situation is temporary, but the memory of it abides; therefore for the sake of our future peace we do well to order our daily conduct so that there shall be no life-long regrets. We can strengthen our inspiring memories by recalling them again and again until they come back habitually when the mind is at rest. We can also starve out regretful and unhappy memories until they die of inanition.

When our bodily powers are weakened and our minds are fatigued, we become a prey to memories that depress and unnerve us. Therefore it is good strategy to fix our mind on those things in life which bring strength and courage, in the hope that they will form the habit of returning to us when we need them most.

There are certain recollections which always bring strength. Chief among these are the memories of joy. The wisdom of the Proverbs says, "A merry heart is a good medicine: but a broken spirit drieth up the bones." We are too prone to forget our past joys. One has only to look at the crowds on city streets to see how few there are who are remembering happiness. Even if we have to work hard to resurrect our memory of a past joy it is worth the effort, because it replaces leaden boots with wings and lifts us nearer to the gate of

41

heaven. No child of God can afford to grovel in the depths of woe when his sins are forgiven and his strength as is dependent on joy as his blood is on oxygen.

Love also is strength. The memory of loved ones at home has brought buoyant energy to many a man. The letters of friends, the memory of loving words, the recollection of a warm handshake have infinite possibilities as a tonic for our strength if we bring them back again and again to our mind. Love can transform the expression of the face and bring back appetite and the zest of living. We all have enough memories of love to carry us through our present ills, even though at the moment we are denied it. "He that abideth in love abideth in God, and God abideth in him." Therefore let us recollect love until it becomes the atmosphere of our life.

To the spirit that is in harmony with God, the recollection of Him is the greatest strength. This may come through conscious prayer or the remembrance of some teaching of Christ which lifts us above the turmoil of life. If He is the undercurrent of all our thought there is no need to renew our strength by other suggestions. The other thoughts which bring vigor to the spirit will inevitably make God more real, for they are part of the expression of His Spirit. Too much importance cannot be laid on the daily reading of the Bible, for it is the soil out of which the sense of God's presence grows. Many of us find Him dim and far away, largely because we have stored up no treasure of sacred truth through which He can manifest Himself.

Nothing so squares our shoulders for courageous effort as the memory of another who needs our strength; a mother will go through anything for the sake of her child. The thought of one's country nerves thousands for battle. The cause of the poor and helpless is all some folk need to bring forth self-sacrifice. No normal human being can live only for himself without losing health and strength. What everyone needs is a purpose which commands devotion. Then the circulation will quicken and the whole nervous system will become electric with new energy. Find something worthwhile to do; some cause which needs you, and let it fill your mind with its concerns. You will then discover a new spring in your step.

The strong men of ancient days found help in the remembrance of the hills and far horizons. There should be some time each year when every human being climbs to the top of some mount of vision and places his soul in the perspective of far spaces. We need the sense of dignity and humility which comes from such experiences. The wideness of the sea, the height of the mountain, the length of the plain, the limitless heavens stretch the spirit to its full height. We cannot afford to miss the God of the open air.

For some temperaments, beauty, color and line are like the wine of life. We cannot fill our life too full of these emotional experiences, for they create a standard with which to measure real values.

What are your resources of recollected strength? According to the easy habit of your thought will the future be dark or full of light?

> Let holy thoughts be ours when sleep o'ertakes us;
> Our earliest thoughts be Thine when morning wakes us;
> All day serve Thee, in all that we are doing
> Thy praise pursuing.
>
> *Petrus Herbert 1566.*

FOR STUDY AND THOUGHT

Lord, thou wilt ordain peace for us: for thou hast also wrought all our works for us. O Lord our God, other lords beside thee have had dominion over us: but by thee only will we make mention of thy name. They are dead, they shall not live; they are deceased, they shall not rise: therefore hast thou visited and destroyed them, and made all their memory to perish. *Isa. 26: 12–14.*

I will put my law in their inward parts, and in their heart will I write it; and I will be their God, and they shall be my people: and they shall teach no more every man his neighbour, and every man his brother, saying, Know the Lord: for they shall all know Me, from the least of them unto the greatest of them, saith the Lord: for I will forgive their iniquity, and their sin will I remember no more. *Jer. 31 : 33–34.*

> My soul shall be satisfied as with marrow and fatness;
> and my mouth shall praise thee with joyful lips;
> When I remember thee upon my bed,
> and meditate on thee in the night watches. *Psa. 63: 5–6.*

I put thee in remembrance that thou stir up the gift of God, which is in thee through the laying on of my hands. For God gave us not a spirit of fearfulness; but of power and love and discipline. *II Tim. 1 : 6–7.*

A sin forgiven is a sin forgotten. Peace of mind is impossible unless religious faith meets the problem of past memories. The saddest of these are connected with those times in our experience when other dispositions contrary to the spirit of Christ dominated us. These "other gods" led us captive. There is much talk of "irresponsibility" these days when people are in the grip of some anti-social, or evil spirit and are impelled to deeds which their true self abhors after the spell is broken. Unless a spirit is controlled by the Spirit of God these "other lords" will take the reins. Every human spirit is under some kind of control: either evil or good. That control is gained at first by the consent of the spirit. Later he is helpless. Hence the vast importance of training children early to yield to the gracious Spirit of God until yielding to it becomes habitual. Fortunate are those children who do not have to carry with them the memories of immoral outbreaks to haunt them in later years.

Out of the fearful moral chaos of the prophet's days he sees a time coming when life on earth will be what it ought to be. It will be a time when *everyone* shall know the Lord from the little child to the greatest man and the memory of sin shall be no more. Lawlessness is beginning to be a vital question in our generation. How can we hasten the time when humanity shall be controlled by the Spirit of God? If we begin at the center of our influence, (our family, our social group, our business associates) each of us could shape the future of a considerable group. Have we a living experience with God to communicate? There are no painless methods of bringing in the golden age of peace. Mere intellectual discussion will not fire the spirit any more than an understanding of how matches are made will start a bonfire. The match itself must be struck and give up its life to start the fire. What memories need to be burned up by the fire of God's forgiveness before we can even begin to bring in that day when God's law shall be paramount in the heart? Tagore, in one of his stories, makes two of his characters say:

> " 'I only seek the result,' said I, 'which belongs to-day;
> 'The result I seek,' answered Nikhil, 'belongs to all time.' "

If we would make our personal decisions in the light of even one hundred years instead of merely vacillating in the midst of the present situation, we, too, might discover within ourselves the soul of a prophet and prepare the way for God.

The hours between two and four in the morning are the acid test for peace of mind. The life of the spirit is renewed or undermined in the midnight watches. It is the easiest time for us to relax in the enfolding strength of God. Dr. Sadler, the therapeutic specialist in an important medical college, writes: "The sincere acceptance of the principles and teaching of Christ with respect to mental peace and joy, the life of unselfish thought and clean living, would at once remove more than one-half the difficulties, diseases, and sorrows of the human race. The simple habit of keeping in mind some one teaching of Christ for use in wakeful hours will bring peace when memories sweep over our spirit and the world is "sicklied o'er with the pale cast" that Hamlet experienced. We can start forces of health working within us if we redeem our wakeful hours from despair.

Paul reminds Timothy that there are stores of wonderful memories in his life which can burst into flame and become the driving power for his life. It is not enough to have our evil memories blotted out by the Spirit of God. We must provide materials for inner resources. A man may rejoice that he has no debts to pay, but his position is more secure if he has resources in the bank for the times of future strain. Everything that will store the memory with wisdom and truth and goodness can become riches for the rainy day used for days to come. How are we building up our spiritual resources? Save something out of each day which has a permanent value. It will all be used before long for an occasion of need when we shall have no time to gather thoughts. Power, love and discipline are the gifts of a wholesome, clean memory.

> O Heavenly Father, in Whom we live and move and have our being, we humbly pray Thee so to guide and govern us by Thy Holy Spirit that in all the cares and occupations of our daily life we may never forget Thee, but remember that we are ever walking in Thy sight; through Jesus Christ our Lord. *Amen.*
>
> *Ancient Collect A. D. 440.*

THE EDUCATION OF A CONSCIENCE

We are living spirits clothed with material bodies, in the midst of a material world; therefore we face a perpetual struggle between higher and lower desires. When we bow to low desires we are yielding to temptation; when we turn toward high desires we are following the dictates of conscience. Hadfield, the psychologist, defines these opposing desires in these words: "Temptation is the voice of suppressed evil when good is dominant; conscience is the voice of the suppressed good when evil is dominant." Back of our conscious thought, lies what we call the sub-conscious mind. Into that region all impulses and desires retire when we are not giving them our attention. Out of that comes reinforcement or hindrance to our higher life.

There is a knowledge of right and wrong which is born within us. We do not have to argue it with ourselves; we know it by our very instincts. Therefore we all have some sort of rudimentary conscience which is the sum of all our highest desires. It pulls us up all the time when low desires beg to be satisfied. No one is wholly bad or wholly good. We are a mixture of impulses.

> "Within my inner temple there's a crowd
> There's one of us that's humble, one that's proud;
> There's one that loves his neighbor as himself
> And one who cares for naught but fame and pelf.
> There's one who sits and sorrows o'er his sins
> And one who, unrepentant, merely grins,
> From such corroding care, how soon I'd fly,
> Could I but once determine which is I."

Everyone classifies his desires as good or bad according to his ideals, and ideals differ according to education, and the life of the spirit. A South Sea islander may have no conscience about killing and eating a man, because his ideals are low. A man educated in high ideals has a conscience against such deeds. All our sense of right and wrong is relative to our ideals. What is right for an ordinary man may be entirely wrong for a man who measures his life by the standards of Jesus Christ. All men have not the same conscience because they are not controlled by the same standards of right and wrong. Even among Christians there are many varieties of conscience. Each holds the teachings of Christ as his standard, but differ from one another in what they consider the most important teachings; therefore their

46

consciences differ. Many of us rely on what we call the "public conscience" to keep us free from national perils, but there is no such thing unless the standard of education in national ideals is everywhere the same.

A strong moral conscience does not exist apart from training. Sometimes in a family, the moral ideals of the parents are so high that children and relatives are lifted up to the same plane for generations. Some ancestor who has been renowned for his moral ideals, and has influenced the thinking of his time, may hand down his standards to his children's children. Tradition and family pride become an inherited conscience. Thus it is possible for the conscience of one enlightened soul to influence thousands for good. The original leader made the choices and did the thinking and the multitudes accept his judgment and acknowledge his influence.

This inherited conscience may lift people to a high plane of living or may blind them with prejudice. It is of the utmost importance that we examine our standards and encourage an intelligent conscience in our thinking and living. Paul with a good conscience persecuted the Christians, thinking he did God service because he had inherited his standards from a religious system rather than from the character of God. Later he was startled to discover that he was fighting God and goodness and that conformity to tradition could no longer be his conscience. "For me to live is Christ" became his ideal and because of this he yet towers above other men down the centuries.

There is no education in conscience which compares with the study of the life of the Christ. He is the perfect ideal for the human life and for the revelation of God. If His followers really grasped the standards of His life, the whole world could be lifted, easily, up to a way of life which would bring in a golden age of peace. Sometimes national ideals are demoralizing in their effects. A "prosperity" slogan may lead countless people to adopt "wealth" as their ideal. If this becomes the dominant standard, a man will take every chance for wealth even though honesty and square dealing are sacrificed. Graft and exploitation may replace service and the Golden Rule and the whole moral tone of a country be lowered. Why then do we make this possible?

Conscience is also strengthened by good habits. A succession of the same choices forms a habit. Every day we accustom ourselves to right action we store up added power to overcome evil desires. An habitual desire to read good literature will safeguard us from many an attack of evil by a compensating interest in other things. A habit of taking exercise may so tone up the system that healthful desires will control our attention. It is almost impossible to resist an evil habit plus an evil desire: and the opposite is equally true. It is a good thing to change as many of our finest ideals into habits of life as soon as possible. In this way we form character; and we become what we desire to be.

A good character is a protection without and within. From without, people hold us to our best because they expect us to live up to our character. From within, it is a shield against evil because sincerity is usually one of our commonest ideals and we do not like to pretend to be what we are not. Such a moral contradiction is sure to betray us sooner or later. There must be oneness in desire, habits and character or health is wrecked, reputation is ruined, and we lose all we have gained. If we nullify a good character by following evil desires, the sham is soon detected and we suffer for it in mind and body.

A conscience which holds us to the ideals of Christ and is reinforced by habits which correspond to those ideals is the strongest basis for an enduring character and perfect health. Let us do our full part in preparing the way for the life-giving power of Christ to give us perfect victory.

> "Groping dim and bending lowly,
> Mortal vision catcheth slowly,
> Glimpses of the pure and holy;
> Now, Lord,
> Open Thou mine eyes, O Lord."   *J. S. Blackie 1876.*

FOR STUDY AND THOUGHT

Not the hearers of a law are just before God, but the doers of a law shall be justified: for when Gentiles which have no law do by nature the things of the law, these not having the law, are a law unto themselves.
Rom. 2 : 13–15.

Let us draw near with a true heart in fulness of faith, having our hearts sprinkled from an evil conscience, and having our bodies washed with pure water. *Heb. 10 : 22.*

Herein do I also exercise myself to have a conscience void of offence toward God and men alway. *Acts. 24 : 16.*

For our glorying is this, the testimony of our conscience, that in holiness and sincerity of God, not in fleshly wisdom but in the grace of God, we behaved ourselves in the world, and more abundantly to you-ward.
II Cor. 1 : 12.

Forbes Robinson wrote once to a friend, "You are born to be a saint, and you will be wretched until you are one. You are not the kind of man who can do things by halves." This is true of most of us, but we stand a deal of wretchedness before we can organize the self for right living. Some people think that inherited consciences are what rob the spirit of peace and there is a modern tendency to consider conscience as an early-Victorian prudery which should be ignored. Paul is right, however, when writing to the pagan Romans in describing the actual situation within the heart of every human being. Even the lowest of them have some elemental standard which has dawned upon them from experience. They have proved that certain things lead to life and other things lead to death. As soon as they begin to appraise values in life they develop a conscience; a reminder of their past wisdom concerning right and wrong.

As soon as one knows the best and does the worst, be it a high or low standard of life, his conscience strives to hold him to the best.

However, the best a man knows may be evil in the light of higher wisdom. A garment may look white by gas light, and yet be yellow in the light of the midday sun. What was lawful in the Middle Ages may be intolerable to-day. The standards of Jesus Christ reveal all the grades of inferiority. An easy contentment with low standards in the light of perfection is morally stultifying. Why then are so many content with inferiority in moral standards when they demand the highest in education, and material living?

Our relation to God, and to our fellows, is determined by the same conscience. If we try to separate the two we live in spiritual darkness. This is one of the basic teachings of Christianity. "He who loveth not his brother whom he hath seen, cannot love God whom he hath not seen." That is the cause of much ill health to-day. People try to love God and hate their brothers, and the conflict of conscience is so nerve-racking that the body suffers. Two musical notes out of harmony make discord, and where discord remains unresolved, music is killed, and the development of symphony becomes impossible.

What glory could be greater than this of which St. Paul writes:— the approval of conscience which is sincere and pure before God and men! What do we make the basis of our judgment about right and wrong? Is it the "fleshly wisdom" of those about us, or the principles of Jesus Christ? Is our standard "Everyone does it" or are we free spirits choosing what our inner spirit tells us is best? In freeing ourselves from an enlightened conscience do we enslave ourselves with the common standards of the crowd? How much is a good conscience worth? Jesus asked once, "What doth it profit a man, to gain the whole world, and forfeit his life?" (*Mark 8 : 36*). Our conscience is the high water mark of life. Jesus said, "I come that they may have life, and may have it abundantly." (*John 10 : 10*) Life to the full: that is God's purpose for us, and the purpose for which Jesus died. If we regret that gift of life we abide in moral darkness, and we cannot expect peace, or health. Life is all too short in which to raise its level by the education of a conscience. There are many values yet to be appraised. Let us begin at the point where we are now to make decisions in the light of eternal values.

> "Make us of quick and tender conscience, O Lord; that understanding, we may obey every word of Thine this day, and discerning, may follow every suggestion of Thine indwelling spirit. Speak Lord for Thy servant heareth, through Jesus Christ our Lord." *Amen.*
>
> *C. Rossetti 1830.*

THE BATTLEGROUND OF PRAYER

JESUS' TEACHING ABOUT PRAYER

Although men have always in all ages made their prayers to the heavenly powers, they lived a life of fear because they were not sure of the nature of that which they worshipped. When Jesus came He said three things about God which open to all of us the possibility for joy, and peace, and power, and free us forever from fear, and anxiety, and helplessness. The first assurance Jesus gave was that "God is Spirit, and they who worship Him must worship Him in spirit and in truth." If God is spirit then there is no spot where He is not, and it is possible for Him to possess the human spirit and control it. The most important part of us, then, is this inner spirit.

The next assurance we have from Jesus is that God, the Infinite Spirit, is Father, with all the meaning that word contains. It carries with it a relation of birth, an infinite caring for His children, a relationship of love, a protection from harm, a tender understanding of weakness, and a training for future position. "When you pray, — pray to your Father," said Jesus, and later when He talked about the elemental needs of our human life; — food, shelter, clothing, etc., He said, "Your Father knoweth that ye have need of these things: — be not anxious."

The third teaching was in harmony with the thought of Fatherhood. "If ye being evil know how to give good gifts to your children, *how much more* will your Father who is in heaven, give good things to them that ask Him?" As one thinks of all those in ages past whose hearts did fear and quake because they did not realize these truths about God, it is impossible to estimate what Jesus has done for humanity in making us know God as a Father. Even now, after two thousand years, there are countless folk who live utterly oblivious to this marvellous truth. How it would transform the lines in human faces and lift the weight of fear from our hearts if we would enter upon each day with the glad consciousness of a Father, adequate for all our needs, always accessible to our spirits and ready to release the power of heaven in response to prayer. Let us stop here, now, and let our minds dwell on this teaching until some new feeling stirs in our hearts. We must live with an idea, not merely catch it, if we would know its creative power. Any idea lived with long enough, fathers enough dynamite to shake the world. The Fatherhood of God is one of those transforming ideas. Test it out now. Another teaching of Jesus is equally dynamic if we will receive it. "When we pray say, *Our* Father." Spirit cannot limit itself. If it blends with God it must blend with all other human spirits, for the life is one indivisible life. It is like the imagery that St. Paul, the great believer in Jesus, uses. He speaks of the body, and many members, each dependent on the others and needed by the others, with the common life holding all together. There could be no enmity, no wars, no cruelties, no malice if we believed this word of Jesus. The severest words He utters concern those who make it hard for others to believe in a Father God; who forget that they are one with all life; who refuse to forgive men; who do not love even their enemies; who do not pray for them. It is the discovery of this truth which will make over the world and bring in the reign of peace. Peace shall indeed be on earth "to men of good will" and we hasten that time in proportion to the degree in which we are under the influence of this teaching. Not until we are vibrating in rhythm with God and all humanity can we expect to release power through our prayer.

Jesus also shows us the method by which prayer is answered. The Spirit of God, who has access to the humble spirit, uses all the resources within us to show us how to discover new paths to power. He works in our memory and from the forgotten experience of the past, reminds us of truth that will deliver us out of our present quandaries. He brings back to our remembrance some word of Christ's which lifts us above the influence which otherwise would pull us down. He selects from all the conflicting experiences which are latest in our subconscious minds, certain combinations which create a new possibility for peace, and health, and power. All those subconscious experiences are like the letters of the alphabet mixed up in curious combinations. Our spirit may call forth a combination of letters, spelling some idea which enervates and breaks down our moral reserves. The Holy Spirit of God delights in working out combinations which inspire us and help us to be more than conquerors in this world. Prayer is the time of inner stillness when we can hear the suggestions of the all-knowing, all-wise Spirit of God.

The process of finding the quiet inner room where only God's voice is heard is often mistaken for prayer itself. With some of us, the effort of detaching ourselves from the distractions of the outer world is so great that we have no strength left for prayer when we reach the threshold of God's presence. Therefore we ought to create some environment, at least for the period of intercession, which will help us to get quickly into touch with God. Each of us must work it out in his own way, but in some way, our dull spirits must be helped to the utmost concentration of which we are capable, in order that we may not miss the limitless possibilities which are ours if we really pray.

> "When the worldling, sick at heart,
>   Lifts his soul above;
> When the prodigal looks back
>   To his father's love;
> When the proud man from his pride,
>   Stoops to seek Thy face;
> When the burdened brings his guilt
>   To thy throne of grace;
> Hear then in love, O Lord, the cry
> In heaven, Thy dwelling place on high."
>
> *H. Bonar 1866.*

FOR STUDY AND THOUGHT

If any of you lacketh wisdom, let him ask of God, who giveth to all liberally and upbraideth not; and it shall be given him. But let him ask in faith, nothing doubting: for he that doubteth is like the surge of the sea driven by the wind and tossed. For let not that man think that he shall receive anything of the Lord: a double-minded man, unstable in all his ways. *James 1 : 5–8.*

The Comforter, even the Holy Spirit, whom the Father will send in my name, he shall teach you all things, and bring to your remembrance all that I said unto you. *John 14 : 26.*

If ye abide in me, and my words abide in you, ask whatsoever ye will, and it shall be done unto you. *John 15 : 7.*

Again I say unto you, that if two of you shall agree on earth, as touching anything that they shall ask, it shall be done for them of my Father which is in heaven. For where two or three are gathered together in my name, there am I in the midst of them. *Matt. 18 : 19–20.*

And they came unto a place which was named Gethsemane: and he saith unto his disciples, Sit ye here, while I pray. And he went forward a little, and fell on the ground, and prayed that, if it were possible, the hour might pass away from him. And he said, Abba, Father, all things are possible unto thee; remove this cup from me: howbeit not what I will, but what thou wilt. Watch and pray, that ye enter not into temptation: the spirit indeed is willing, but the flesh is weak.

Mark 14 : 32, 35–36, 38.

Wisdom is a gift we may have from God through prayer. In having that we have most things we desire. Note the condition, however: "Let him ask in faith nothing doubting." While we are in the turmoil of an inner argument, double-minded in our thinking, the voice of wisdom cannot be heard. It is when "the tumult and the shouting" have died away that God has our complete confidence and attention. Later on St. James describes the qualities of the heavenly wisdom which explains why it cannot come to a debating mind. He says that "the wisdom from above is first pure, then peaceable, gentle, easy to be entreated, full of mercy and good fruits, without partiality, without hypocrisy." (*Jas. 3 : 17*). With many folk the prayer for wisdom is mere petition that their own opinions may be victorious. They seek a divine sanction of their own point of view. If we tested our views by the adjectives St. James uses we might gain a spirit of humility which would win for us the secret of God.

A mind which is stored with the teachings of Christ, is more likely to recognize answers to prayer when they come. There is no joy equal to those moments when the mind becomes suddenly inspired with the remembrance of something which answers the search for light. Some people have very little material in their memories which the Holy Spirit can use for our help. We cannot recall what we have not previously learned. We need spiritual thought-forms to understand the mind of God just as we need a vocabulary to understand a foreigner. As St. Paul so clearly says to the Greeks, "The natural man receiveth not the things of the Spirit of God for they are foolishness unto him: and he cannot know them, because they are spiritually judged: (*I Cor. 2 : 14*).

There are two of our Lord's promises concerning prayer which seem to be unlimited in possibilities. One concerns only those who are living in as close a union with the spirit of Christ as a branch is united to the vine. Asking what we *will* then implies what God wills, because the will of the branch and the vine are one. The other promise is in harmony with the same spirit, for here it suggests that oneness with our brothers brings down the blessing of heaven. Harmony, a continuity of life with God and others, completes the circuit of power. The prayers which include both Christ and our brothers are never selfish and are always answered.

Even Jesus faced occasions when it was difficult to put God's will and human need first. Those sacred moments in the Garden of Gethsemane show us how even He was tempted to save Himself instead of saving others. We have a Christ who was faithful to us, and to God, even unto the death on the cross. He could have summoned legions of angels to His rescue; but, instead, He bore the strain of uniting humanity to God. Whenever we put God and others first and lose our lives for their sakes, we, too, find a deathless life of radiance and power.

Prayer is a battlefield. We strive not to release the power of heaven, but to bring ourselves to the point of being willing to be the channel through which God can do beyond what we ask or think *"according to the power that worketh in us."* (*Eph. 3 : 20*).

> O Faithful Lord, grant to us, we pray Thee, faithful hearts devoted to Thee, and to the service of all men for Thy sake. Fill us with pure love of Thee, keep us steadfast in this love, give us faith that worketh by love, and preserve us faithful unto death; through Jesus Christ our Lord. *Amen.* *C. Rossetti 1830.*

OVERCOMING THE EARTHLY NATURE

So long as we are incarnate in human flesh there will be an earthly nature, dogging our footsteps and laying claim to our full attention. There is a perpetual struggle between the desires of the flesh and desires of the spirit. We form high resolves that the earth shall not enthrall us, and straightway a fight is on.

> "When the fight begins within himself,
> A man's worth something. God stoops o'er his head,
> Satan looks up between his feet, — both tug —
> He's left, himself, i' the middle: the soul awakes
> And grows. "Prolong that battle thro' this life!
> Never leave growing till the life to come." *Browning.*

There is nothing static within us; everything is a process of growth or deterioration. We cannot stand still. The restless life energy of God within us pushes us on to new aspiration just as the sap flows through the tips of the branches of trees, pushing off the dead clinging leaves and reaching out to new life. If we arrest this push of life energy within us, we die; if we struggle on we achieve a higher, freer, broader life.

The earthly nature is so obvious, and clings so closely, and is so plausible that we recognize it as a legitimate possession and are usually not ashamed of it. We go occasionally into the realm of the spirit and get glimpses of a great undiscovered country and then we come back again to the comfortable desires and wisdom of the flesh.

> "And oftentimes, to win us to our harm,
> The instruments of darkness tell us truths;
> Win us with honest trifles, to betray us
> In deepest consequence." *Shakespeare.*

It is not easy to follow the gleam when earthly interests bulk large in our experience.

Here again we see the supreme triumph of Jesus Christ. He lived in the power of the Spirit and triumphed over the demands of the flesh until His being was so transfigured by the Spirit that even His garments shone with light.

It was natural that He should ascend into the realm above the plane of earthly experience, for He had burst through the trammels of fleshly desires. And when He spoke with His friends about His going away He left them thrilling with a new hope. "Let not your heart be troubled — where I am *there ye may be also*."

Jesus Christ is the great reinforcement to our spirits. He has proved to us that the realm of the spirit is the only one for us, and even if we have to go through toil and tribulation, the end is worth all the struggle. We, too, may know, here and now, the truth that the followers of Jesus learned: that "the law of the Spirit of life in Christ Jesus 'makes us' *free* from the law of sin and death. (*Rom. 8 : 2*).

The freedom and triumph of our spirit over our flesh comes usually through prayer. Freedom is largely a matter of responding to a great magnetic centre of control so that the smaller magnetic centres all about us shall not pull us hither and yon at their will. Jesus and his Father God were so one that no earthly urge could bring them into bondage. He was free as God Himself is free.

We, too, need this poise, this God-centre of perfect freedom. There is no limit to the obedience we could exact from our bodies, from our minds, and from other living forces in the world, if we were utterly willing to make God's will our own. Without this full commitment to an endless war against our earthly nature we can never hope to see God working wonders in us and through us. Some of us are beset now by struggles with weaknesses of the flesh in which we may still gain mighty victories to the glory of God. We shall never win out, however, until we, too, like Jesus Christ, live consciously in the presence of God.

The real use of an earthly nature is to serve as the gymnasium of our spiritual life, where we may strengthen our moral muscles and develop power to overcome handicaps. We gain strength through the conflict. Not every one of us is strong enough in spirit to lift the heaviest weights. We go from strength to strength. There are some victories we may win to-day that we were not able to win last year. Our bodies obey the command of the spirit better now than they did when we began to exercise our moral muscles. As we go on in a life of prayer we shall be able to work out our salvation more completely as God works in us to will and to do His good pleasure.

Perhaps our faith in the power of prayer has been failing because results for which we have longed have not come. Does not the reason lie in our unwillingness to undergo the daily discipline of our wills and desires in *small* issues as well as in larger ones until we attain that measure of self-control which will enable God to use us as a well-tempered steel instrument for His delicate and difficult working.

There is no way of escape from this struggle. Just as a garden of flowers, if left to itself for a number of years, will run to waste and revert to the original type, so the soul which is uncultivated and which follows the line of least resistance will revert to degeneration. It is this downward pull in life which necessitated the revelation of the victorious Christ to redeem us through a re-birth into a life in which the Spirit of God is dominant.

Spiritual character is the product of self-denial, and self-discipline according to the laws of life which Jesus Christ has taught us. We can grow away from the earth as the flower stretches up from the soil. We speak of the garden as nature, — the work of God. In the same way when we see ourselves growing silently but surely away from the earth nature, in spite of the winds of temptation, we know that a work of God is going on within us, that He has marked out the destiny of our soul and we are being transformed into His image from character to character.

> "Pray that he may prosper ever
> Each endeavor,
> When thine aim is good and true;
> But that he may ever thwart thee
> And convert thee,
> When thou evil wouldst pursue.
>
> Only God's free gifts abuse not,
> Light refuse not,
> But His Spirit's voice obey;
> Thou with Him shalt dwell, beholding
> Light enfolding
> All things in unclouded day."
>
> *F. R. L. von Canitz 1654.*

FOR STUDY AND THOUGHT

I know that in me, that is, in my flesh, dwelleth no good thing: for to will is present with me, but to do that which is good is not. For the good which I would I do not: but the evil which I would not, that I practise. But if what I would not, that I do, it is no more I that do it, but sin which dwelleth in me. I find then the law, that, to me who would do good, evil is present. For I delight in the law of God after the inward man: but I see a different law in my members, warring against the law of my mind, and bringing me into captivity under the law of sin which is in my members. O wretched man that I am! who shall deliver me out of the body of this death? I thank God through Jesus Christ our Lord. So then I myself with the mind serve the law of God; but with the flesh the law of sin. *Rom. 7 : 18–25.*

St. Paul has given us a graphic picture of the inner struggle of the human soul which is torn by opposing forces, the desire to do good and the downward pull toward evil. Every human being has this experience more or less. If the tension is acute there is hope for deliverance, but if the soul gives up the battle and goes to sleep, indifferent to the issues of life and death, the condition is tragic.

Even though we, in common with every organism, reach out for completeness, and self-realization we may refuse to respond to these higher desires and yield to lower desires. There is so much in the outer world to appeal to the earthly side of our nature that we are tempted to turn against our highest good.

> "The deep hath calm: the moon hath rest, but we
> Lords of the natural world are yet our own dread enemy."

There is a common attitude which assumes that following the highest ideal is like cultivating a hothouse flower which is not adapted to real life. We look at the life of ordinary men and ask whether it is really necessary to toil on in pain to attain a level of life which we cannot hold without a perpetual struggle. The modern Epicureans would have us eat, drink, and be merry, for tomorrow we die. That would be comparatively simple if we were sure that we *do* die; but with scientists to-day, like the renowned Flammarion and Sir Oliver Lodge, assuring us that there will soon be scientific proof of the immortality of the spirit, the Epicurean counsel is foolhardy. We cannot stand still. Life is like a winding road up a mountain. If a traveller ceases to climb, he slips back down into gorges where there is no horizon and no light of the sun. Out of the past we have come to use this earthly incarnation as a means of releasing our spirit for the perfect freedom of eternity. If we slip back into degeneration we shall be worse off than we are now, because we shall *remember* our high position and the glimpses of mountain tops and suffer tortures of remorse.

Therefore we must fight for the peaks of vision. The battle is not against us because "the law of the Spirit of life in Jesus Christ made us free from the law of sin and death;" St. Paul shouts in triumph. (Rom. 8 : 2). The discovery of that law of the Divine spirit is worth so much to every human being that the wonder is that any Christian can occupy himself with any other service except spreading abroad the good news of the gospel of Jesus.

Henry Drummond once wrote: "The Christian is a unique phenomenon. You cannot account for him, and if you could he would not be a Christian." He is the ordinary man, or woman, or child who sees in Jesus and the principles of His life the goal of perfection and clings to Him as the Redeemer of life. He proved Himself worthy of trust by laying down His earthly life on the cross, and bursting into the triumphant realm of the Spirit. Through Him we are born into a new life where, reinforced by the Spirit of God, we become new creatures and are "more than conquerors," in the struggle with the desires of the flesh, "through Him that loved us."   (Rom. 8 : 37).

> O God, Who for our redemption didst give Thine only begotten son to the death of the cross, and by His glorious resurrection has delivered us from the power of the enemy, grant us to die daily to sin, that we may evermore live with Him in the joy of His resurrection; through the same Jesus Christ our Lord.   *Amen.*
>
> *St. Gregory A.D. 590.*

THE CROSS AND HUMAN EXPERIENCE

Pain and suffering are universal facts of human life. Why this is so we do not know. Some people try to live in a fool's Paradise and deny the reality of suffering; others ignore it; many resign themselves to it. A few dauntless souls use it to release higher powers that lift them above suffering. There is pain of body because we have consciously or unconsciously broken the laws of health. There is that mental suffering because our spirit tauntingly accuses us of our stupidity in falling below our highest ideal. There is pain of spirit because we have been deaf to God's voice and have followed the desires of our earthly nature. There is untold pain, too, for which we are not at fault: pain because of enemies; the suffering of masses exploited through selfishness; sorrow through death, frustration of hopes and ambitions, unrequited loves, wars, convulsions of nature and last but not least, the spirit of evil, which is dead set against righteousness.

Some of this suffering we can avoid through experience, and divine common sense; especially if we are bent on living utterly in God's power. Most of it, however, we have to live with, and struggle with, and perhaps in the end it may lead us to the same place where it led Jesus Christ. That end was a cross. The Lord of all, who perfectly pleased His Father, was face to face with the hostile forces of the world from the moment He became incarnate in human flesh. There was no room where He could be born. The King sought to kill his infant life. His brethren did not believe in Him. There was no escape from start to finish. Suffering ever shadowed the Christ. At last He was killed by the treachery of an intimate, and deserted by His closest friends when He was led away by the mob of soldiers. He was nailed on a wooden cross like the lowest criminal even though the judge had said he found no fault in Him. Why could not the most triumphant human spirit save Himself from such a career?

There are several answers to this. In saving others He could not save Himself. The Cross of Jesus Christ is the historic symbol of the only way in which man may be free from that adverse energy which defeats our holy desires. We call that energy, "sin". God is an eternal will against sin, and there is no possibility of friendship with Him unless in some way we can become free from its power. It lurks in our earthly nature; so we must be clean from this earth mire that clings to us.

Jesus shows us how to rid ourselves of it. He took it upon himself
to solve the problem. As we see Him on His cross we realize that God
and sin met there and that there sin lost its power, and eternal freedom and life became possible for us. This is no theological dogma.
Even such a man as Oscar Wilde, burst into words like these:

> "O smitten mouth! O forehead crowned with thorn!
> O chalice of all common miseries!
> Thou for our sakes that loved Thee not hast borne
> An agony of endless centuries;
> And we were vain and ignorant, nor knew
> That when we stabbed Thy heart
> It was our own real hearts we slew."

"Jesus died for all that they who live should no longer live unto
themselves, but unto God."

There is also another reason why Jesus made Himself one with the
experience of suffering humanity. He shows us how to make suffering
an open door to power and love. People learn this slowly. A memorial
tablet at Hull House in Chicago reveals the very heart of service in
the lines of the poet:

> "As more exposed to suffering and distress,
> Thence also more alive to tenderness."

By the use of higher laws we overcome suffering and transform it
into spiritual energies. Thus Jesus shows us how to live in triumph
now and to buy back our wrecked humanity.

It is useless and unworthy to try to dodge suffering; sooner or
later it overtakes us. It is courageous to be a stoic, and die fighting;
but mere resistance does not always bring victory, because the combat
may be too much for our strength. Jesus' way is the best. He accepts
the cross as a method of pouring out sacrificial love. Then the cross
becomes the gateway to glory, and illumines the mysteries of life. It
is the sublime victory of the selfless principle over the self-principle;
or finding life by losing it. Not every soldier who dies is a hero. Some
merely die because the opposing forces are too great; but a hero is one
who has risked life because of some compelling loyalty which is so
dear to him that suffering counts for nothing in comparison with his
ideal. And a hero is more likely to come through, because his ideal
has released latent powers which help him.

There is a subtle connection between the shadow of a cross, in our
human experience, and the Cross of Jesus. He is the only one whom
we can follow in implicit trust. There is no other more worthy. Therefore when He bids us follow in His steps and take up our cross and

deny self the right to live, we dare not falter. We lay down our self-interest, our self-ambition, all our selfish nature in the same way that the seed gives itself up in the ground to die. Then from us, too, shall come a vital new life multiplying itself a thousandfold in power and fruitfulness. "He that loseth his life *shall find it*."

The reason why so many of us are hobbling about with limitations of spirit, mind and body is because we seek every other way to power save the one divine way that Jesus trod; — the way of the cross. There are countless people who could be well if they would lose themselves for others. There are thousands living in fear; so terrified by their own weakness and inability to cope with the cosmos, that all their strength and attention is absorbed by their fears. If they would relax and let go, accepting this cross, they would find themselves possessed by a power beyond their imagination. To be absorbed in oneself is sin. Sin is whatever separates us from God. The highest revelation of God we know is the Christ who laid down self for others. If we are to have oneness with God, we, too, must be free from self.

All prayer that avails must have this sacrificial spirit within it. It is "not my will, but thine be done" which opens the soul to all influences and powers of God. It is this which gives us the listening mind, free from insistent little demands, ready to detect the loving purpose of the heavenly Father.

There is a vast difference between falling back on oneself and falling back on God. To fall back on oneself is to crumple up in weakness and despair. To fall back on the loving purpose of God is to find everlasting arms of strength beneath one and the realization of all one's hopes.

Why God has put a cross in the heart of human experience we do not know, any more than we know why he made the grass green. We accept it as a fact of life. Instead of quarreling with the facts, the wise folk are they who, looking at the transcendent personality of Jesus, see in Him the divine method for the perfect release of the spirit, and for oneness with God.

> "Lord Jesus, when we stand afar,
> And gaze upon Thy holy cross,
> In love of Thee, and scorn of self,
> O may we count the world as loss!
>
> Give us an ever-living faith,
> To gaze beyond the things we see:
> And in the mystery of Thy death,
> Draw us and all men unto Thee,"   *W. W. How 1854.*

FOR STUDY AND THOUGHT

From that time began Jesus to show unto his disciples, how that he must go unto Jerusalem, and suffer many things of the elders and chief priests and scribes, and be killed, and the third day be raised up. And Peter took him, and began to rebuke him, saying, Be it far from thee, Lord: this shall never be unto thee. But he turned, and said unto Peter, Get thee behind me, Satan: thou art a stumbling-block unto me: for thou mindest not the things of God, but the things of men. Then said Jesus unto his disciples, if any man would come after me, let him deny himself, and take up his cross, and follow me. For whosoever would save his life shall lose it: and whosoever shall lose his life for my sake shall find it.

Matt. 16 : 21–25.

I came to cast fire upon the earth; and what will I, if it is already kindled? But I have a baptism to be baptized with; and how am I straitened till it be accomplished! *Luke 12 : 49–50.*

For the love of Christ constraineth us; and he died for all, that they which live should no longer live unto themselves, but unto him who for their sakes died and rose again. Wherefore we henceforth know no man after the flesh: even though we have known Christ after the flesh, yet now we know Him so no more. Wherefore if any man is in Christ, he is a new creature: the old things are passed away; behold they are become new. *II Cor. 5 : 14–17.*

The teaching of Jesus was so unlike the natural human point of view that even His closest friends could not understand Him. In the conversation with His disciples the human instinct of self-preservation is contrasted with the divine principle of self-sacrifice. When Jesus began to speak of going to Jerusalem in full knowledge that there He would suffer and be killed, Peter the most courageous of all His followers challenged Him at once. Another conviction was also shattered. If a man lives according to the highest ideal, why should suffering come to him? It was the historic problem of Job.

The severity of this rebuke to Peter shows the nature of what the Christ was facing. He was going in the teeth of all the natural urge of the world, and turning from the things of men to the things of God. From all time people have sacrificed unto God; flocks and herds, gold and precious possessions; in an effort to gain the approval of the Deity. But to lose one's own life in order to find it; to enter into the law of life as the lily bulb enters through losing itself in the dark earth, this was the supreme revelation of Jesus. The Jews looked for a Messiah to reign as King, but a Messiah, — to die; this was incomprehensible. Those are solemn words,— those words of Jesus, challenging anyone who would follow Him into resurrection life to take up his cross also. The way of Jesus divides all men into two groups: those who save themselves, and those who lose themselves. It was infinitely harder for Peter and the other friends of Jesus than it is for us to see that death unto self is the way to life. We can look back to the triumph of Jesus and the overwhelming victory of His method as the centuries show it. We know that the great ones of the world, the potent spirits, are those who dared to go the way of Jesus.

It is not easy to die to self. It was not easy for Jesus. He knew He could never kindle the fire of enthusiasm and conquering life in the world until He was baptized into the death of the Cross. "How am I straitened," He cries, "until it be accomplished!" Does this explain our inability to move men to seek divine life? Can it be possible that even in us the principle of self-preservation is working? Are we, like Peter, reluctant to go to Jerusalem?

St. Paul points out the motive which will make us brave in following the way of the Cross. It is "the love of Christ" which "constraineth us." His transcendent beauty is too appealing to refuse.

> "For Oh the Master is so fair,
> His smile so sweet to banished men,
> That they who meet it unawares,
> Can never rest on earth again."   *Barbara McAndrews.*

Therefore, because Christ died for us, we pour out our devotion to Him, to live for Him alone.

A strange miracle is wrought. The man becomes a new creation. The old laws of life, the old downward principle of reversion to type inhibit His spirit no longer. "The old things are passed away; behold they are become new."

> O Lord, Jesus Christ, our merciful and loving Saviour, Who didst bear Thy cross for us, help us to take up our cross daily and follow Thee. O Thou Who wast lifted up for us draw us unto Thee, that we may love Thee better for Thy great love to us. Lord, we love Thee; help Thou our want of love. O heavenly Father, make us to bear in our body the marks of the Lord Jesus by a pure and holy life. O Saviour of the world, Who by the Cross and precious blood hast redeemed us, save us and help us, we humbly beseech Thee, O Lord, both now and evermore. *Amen.*
>
> *Dean Goulburn 1818.*

PRAYER AND BELIEF

Experiences and emotion which move the heart are more responsible for our beliefs than most of us imagine. The fixed idea and conclusions which make up our intellectual beliefs are like iron filings clinging to the magnet. They collect under the influence of dominant desires.

When a man is moved by love, he finds it easy to believe in the beauty and attractiveness of the girl of his choice, even though others may not see these qualities in her. When a citizen is moved by loyalty to his country he finds it easy to believe in its laws: if oppressed by the government of his native land he is suspicious of any new country. When we are stirred by the feeling of hatred we find it difficult to believe in any evidences of good. If a child has had a cruel human father, he finds it hard to believe in a loving heavenly Father. In short, our beliefs take on the color of the predominant emotion which has been created by some experience. Therefore in order to change the beliefs of people we must influence them through new experiences.

In the atmosphere of prayer the strongest, purest, and highest emotions are created. There is no more powerful stimulus than the influence of the Spirit of God upon the heart. Most of our sorrows come because some unworthy emotion has so gripped us that the whole outer world becomes the personification of that emotion. We hate, and the whole world is hateful. We are stirred by love and everything responds in lovely harmony. We are happy and the world was never so bright. We are moved by a great loss and all the earth is empty.

If for no other reason than to control the environment in which we live, we ought to cultivate a daily habit of prayer. Our happiness depends upon it; for if we are not swayed by God-given emotions we shall be under the power of the demoralizing influences which touch us through our earthly nature.

Prayer moves us to reverence, and the reverent soul always receives the largest measure of life. "He makes me feel as though I were somebody, and I would do anything for him," said a workman of his employer — a man noted for his consideration of the sacredness of personality. Reverence toward God always works its way out into all the rest of life and belief in holiness comes as a natural result. That master of all apostles of Jesus understood this psychological fact. He wrote to one of the churches, "With the *heart* man believeth unto righteousness." He also listed the great emotions that come directly from the heart of God to us. That which grows like fruit from the life of God within us, he says, is "love, joy, peace, long-suffering, gentleness, goodness, meekness, and self-control."

In this list we see at the beginning the three highest emotions that can stir the heart. Love, the unselfish will toward others; joy, the perfect freedom of a triumphant spirit; peace, the deep content, — born of perfect oneness with God which drives away all fear. To be mastered completely by these divine fires would be to possess all we need of creative power to remake life on the spiritual plane. We would then resemble Christ and be able to do mighty works. "If any man be in Christ," says the same apostle, "he is a new creation; old things have passed away: behold all things are become new." This is not a future state, but a present possibility if the fire of God's Spirit burns in our hearts in prayer. We do no mighty work, because we do not pray; and yet this secret of power is available for anyone who will use it.

The other qualities of spirit, listed by Paul, are those which affect our relationships and the experiences we meet in life. Love, joy, and peace flame out in long-suffering, and gentleness with others; and in goodness and meekness as we come in daily contact with conflicting elements in our human relationships. Above all we attain to self-mastery, to self-control; to a poise which cannot be disturbed by the strife of tongues.

Out of all these dominant forces within our hearts, beliefs will come, mighty convictions will be born, which will remake the whole world; and a faith that may remove mountains. In the end we shall discern the heart of God and grow to be like the man whom Wordsworth describes:

> "One in whom persuasion and belief
> Had ripened into faith, and faith became
> A passionate intuition."

Many of us are incapable of a profound emotion because all our strength has been spent in restraining evil tendencies or frittered away in small desires. We have become hardened, too, by our experiences. Many people deplore all feeling because it may bring pain or hysteria. The Spirit which is not poised in God dare not be swayed by deep emotion unless it is sublimated in service for others. With God as a centre we find in prayer an emotional control which fits us to use these creative powers of soul and have dominion over our environment instead of becoming the victim of it. Childlike prayer is the great safety valve for that excess of emotion which strains the health of the body and brings tension to the mind. The more we use it as a habit of life the more we know and believe in the hidden connection between ourselves and God. Our faith becomes reinforced by the life-giving power by which we are renewed in spirit, mind and body. Therefore as St. Luke says of Jesus, "He spake a parable unto them to the end that they ought always to pray, and not to faint."

> " O Thou, by whom we come to God,
>   The Life, the Truth, the Way;
> The path of prayer Thyself hast trod,
>   Lord, teach us how to pray."
>
> *James Montgomery.*

FOR STUDY AND THOUGHT

For I know the thoughts that I think toward you, saith the Lord, thoughts of peace, and not of evil, to give you hope in your latter end. And ye shall call upon me, and ye shall go and pray unto me, and I will hearken unto you. And ye shall seek me, and find me, when ye shall search for me with all your heart. *Jer. 29 : 11–13.*

He that turneth away his ear from hearing the law, even his prayer is an abomination. *Prov. 28 : 9.*

Moreover as for me, God forbid that I should sin against the Lord in ceasing to pray for you. *I Sam. 12 : 23.*

Simon, Simon, behold, Satan asked to have you, that he might sift you as wheat: but I made supplication for thee, that thy faith fail not: and do thou, when once thou hast turned again, stablish thy brethren.
Luke 22 : 31–32.

Rejoice in the Lord alway: again I will say, Rejoice. In nothing be anxious; but in everything by prayer and supplication with thanksgiving let your requests be made known unto God. And the peace of God, which passeth all understanding, shall guard your hearts and your thoughts in Christ Jesus. *Phil. 4 : 4, 6–7.*

When we are convinced that God is love, we find it easy to believe that He can reach us with that love. A God who has thoughts of peace toward us will not rest until He has communicated those thoughts to us. Therefore it is natural that the inference should be "Ye shall call upon Me, . . . and I will hearken unto you." Love always finds some way to bridge the distance between it and the loved one. An unresponsive God of love is unthinkable, for love is responsiveness.

There is a relation between answered prayer and obedience to what our conscience knows to be the teaching of God. It is strange that so many people whose lives are far from obeying the principles of the spiritual life, look upon prayer as a mere business transaction, unrelated to any other law except supply and demand. People seek healing for their bodies in answer to prayer without the slightest intention of living for the glory of God. This is why so-called proofs of prayer cannot be used for argument. So large a part of the proof lies in those hidden values of character which cannot be weighed and measured. Availing prayer exacts complete surrender of the spirit.

If it is true that one spirit in full union with God can release spiritual energy in response to prayer, then *how much more* may a group of persons fired with the desire to lift the lives of others to a higher plane be able to produce a spiritual effect! Jesus speaks of His immediate presence being where two or three are together in harmony with Him, and says that they shall "ask what they will and it shall be done unto them." It is for this reason that small groups of people meeting for corporate prayer centered on someone whom they would bless with health of soul and body should be formed. Each must have complete trust in the others; and all must have one supreme desire. Silent concentration in fellowship with a group is all the more powerful because it is unselfish. All unite on something which is a common good for all or a special good for someone who needs help. We have not yet measured the influence of thought vibration between spirit and spirit. We know that it exists but do not yet understand its laws. One thing however is certain. The thought-form which is in harmony with the nature of Christ is bound to be more powerful than any other. The example of Jesus in praying for others gives fullest sanction. Therefore we may well enter into intercession; — that most selfless service that our soul can render another; and God will not disappoint our faith.

A spirit which *rejoices* in the Lord is one which is full of faith. Joy and thanksgiving are the atmosphere in which faith abounds. It is well to prepare our hearts in this way as an aid to effective prayer.

> "More things are wrought by prayer
> Than this world dreams of. Wherefore, let thy voice
> Rise like a fountain for me night and day."

> O Lord Jesus, teach us to pray. May Thy will be done so completely in us that we shall be free to serve others in the ministry of intercession. *Amen.*

THE IRRESISTIBLE LAW OF LOVE

THE CREATIVE ENERGY OF LOVE

Love is the mightiest unused force in the world. Everybody wants to be under the influence, and to bask in the sunshine of its presence. We all desire to consume it, but are loath to produce it. It cannot be stored up as a commodity; it is distilled from the human spirit through a process that puts to death the life of self. It is the most costly, vital energy that a human can create. The world cannot stand without it and yet it cannot be bought. It is produced only by the voluntary offering of oneself to be consumed and transformed into the glowing heat of love, even as the wood gives itself to the fire.

The reward of giving up one's life to love is a gift of creative power which is second only to the power of God. Indeed it is His power distributed through us to others. It gives health to the body, peace to the mind, and freedom to the spirit. It ends strife, softens enmity, outruns evil, never fails in strength. The more it spends itself the richer it becomes. Whatever it gives, comes back one hundredfold. It is the master key which unlocks every heart, is trusted with every secret, inherits everything. Love creates whatever it desires and is never in want; it holds all hearts in friendship; it achieves what is humanly impossible; it upsets all worldly calculations and is victorious in all things.

It will do us no good to sit down supinely and sigh for love. Only the heroic will to throw into the divine fire everything in our hearts which prevents love from being created within us will release this energy. The walls of pride, selfishness, prejudice, self-consciousness, fears of consequences, must be battered down by determined efforts, so that the waters of love may no longer be dammed up, but flow on into the mighty ocean of God's creative power. Who among us is brave enough to give himself to a life of love — whatever it may cost?

It is doubtful if anyone ever attained the fullness of his powers without the influence of love. The very conditions which are necessary to growth are created only by love. It is the great, positive energy which gives all who feel the effect of it, that unconquerable elixir of life. We have all had some experience with love. It brought us a relaxation from strain which meant freedom. It gave a rest which meant unimpeded action. It replaced fear with trust, and all the bodily functions worked for health, because nerves were not depressed by worry.

One of the most beautiful gifts of love is the faith that it creates: faith in God, faith in humanity, faith in the purpose of life, faith in the possibility of a career. Love brings a new sense of value, a conviction of the vast importance of one human life, and we begin reverently to ask, "Lord, what wilt Thou have me to do?" as we go on to discover hidden powers in ourselves that we scarcely expected. We are amazed at what love brings forth in us.

There is also no joy or pleasure apart from love. Without joy we dwindle and die. Joy is the oxygen of the soul, and is itself love in the act of exulting over that which is beloved. All our appreciations of beauty in God's world, or in people, or in books, are born of love. Without love Nature is dull and uninteresting, people are boresome, and books uninspiring.

Love also creates unity — that blending together of varied creative power which, like skilful workmen, construct the beautiful temple to the glory of God. Without love no community of interest could survive, no common cause be promoted.

We have often watched love at work in the creation of personality. Everyone of us has felt that moulding power calling out new desires, greater achievements, heavenly visions, and more abundant life. Love has led us forth, away from our baser selves, into those spacious realms where our spirit stretches and grows. Few of us suspect the latent powers that are called out in response to someone who has faith in us. Love is like the sunshine and shower which calls out the fragrant flower from the brown seed. When St. John writes about the love which the heavenly Father has bestowed on us, he adds: "it is *not yet* made manifest what we shall be." The full creative work of love will be finished only when we shall become like the God who loves us. With a goal like that, who can resist purifying himself in order to grow up into that likeness?

Love cannot be divorced from God and His holy purposes without turning to lust and burning out in ashes of hate. It is a fearful experience to be without love. If we sacrifice self voluntarily to be possessed by love we never die. If we shrink from the pain of self-crucifixion, the sacrifice of self will be exacted by the world just the same, but we shall die impotent and inglorious.

"O Love, that wilt not let me go,
I rest my weary soul in Thee;
I give Thee back the life I owe,
That in Thine ocean's depths, its flow
May richer, fuller be." *George Matheson.*

FOR STUDY AND THOUGHT

If I speak with the tongues of men and of angels, but have not love, I am become sounding brass, or a clanging cymbal.

And if I have the gift of prophecy, and know all mysteries and all knowledge; and if I have all faith, so as to remove mountains, but have not love, I am nothing.

And if I bestow all my goods to feed the poor, and if I give my body to be burned, but have not love, it profiteth me nothing.

Love suffereth long, and is kind; love envieth not; love vaunteth not itself, is not puffed up, doth not behave itself unseemly, seeketh not its own, is not provoked, taketh not account of evil; rejoiceth not in unrighteousness, but rejoiceth with the truth;

Beareth all things, believeth all things, hopeth all things, endureth all things.

Love never faileth: but whether there be prophecies, they shall be done away: whether there be tongues, they shall cease; whether there be knowledge, it shall be done away.

For we know in part, and we prophesy in part: But when that which is perfect is come, that which is in part shall be done away.

When I was a child, I spake as a child, I felt as a child, I thought as a child: now that I am become a man, I have put away childish things. For now we see in a mirror, darkly; but then face to face: now I know in part; but then shall I know even as also I have been known. But now abideth faith, hope, love, these three; and the greatest of these is love.

I Cor. : 13, 1–13.

When people seek for power they long for greater talent, or great possessions, in order to secure for themselves unusual advantage. We are not born with equal gifts. It would be a disaster if we were, for then all inter-dependence on one another would be unnecessary and we would lose interest in one another. If all were great actors there would be no audience. If all were qualified to teach there would be no schools. If all had everything they wanted in material possessions there would be no incentive to scientific growth or industry. It is the inequalities in endowment that keep the sense of need alive in us.

There would be a sense of helplessness in humanity if there were not some way in which everyone could qualify for lasting influence. These words of St. Paul point out the way. "Set your hearts on the higher talents. And yet I will go on to show you a still higher path." This way of life is the life of love. Everyone may qualify for love. The old man, and the baby, the rich and the poor, the wise and the ignorant.

Each of us has at hand a power that is greater than any other power in the world, because it does not stop with the one who loves, but lives in the hearts of men. We know St. Paul is right in his teaching because Jesus won His place in the hearts of men by this simple power of love.

Is not much of the pain of the world due to the exercise of talents without love? How often have people suffered because people of faith have had no tender consideration for the human heart which could not see what the prophet saw. How many little children have been hindered from coming to God by the righteous, but *unloving*, compulsions of men of faith. What slavery in the world is exacted when love is wanting! What broken hearts there are in families where untiring service is rendered with no reward of love! What satisfaction is there in building up mighty institutions if they are impersonal machines in which no love dwells. How barren are gifts which are mere material things with no glow and significance which love alone can give! Everything in life becomes hard, or bitter, or crucifying without the power of love. Therefore we do well to yearn for this power.

The works of love show it to be the very essence of self-sacrifice. We often pray for love when what we really mean is that we wish to be the object of love; as though we had the right to expect that we should be enriched in the manner of a miser who does not realize that gold is valueless save as a medium of exchange. "We love God *because* He first loved us," says St. John and the law of love is the same for us all. We are loved by others because we love them. Self-forgetful love calls forth love because our love has been planted in the soil of other hearts. Love never fails when we remember that our present knowledge is imperfect, that as St. Paul says, "We only know bit by bit" and that at present we see things as in a mirror and are puzzled. Most of the afflictions of love come because we discover it to be human and not divine, we expected in it the perfection of God and cannot be patient with broken human reflections.

> "All loves are shadows cast
> By the beautiful eternal hills
> Of Thine unbeginning past."

We long for more than shadows; but we are not yet what we shall be. We can only press on, experiencing in ourselves the longings of all creation to gain some day the glorious freedom of the children of God.

O God, we have known and believed the love that thou hast for us; may we by dwelling in love dwell in Thee, and Thou in us. May we learn to love Thee whom we have not seen, by loving our brethren whom we have seen. Teach us, O heavenly Father, the love wherewith Thou hast loved us. Fashion us, O blessed Lord, after Thine own example of love. Shed abroad, O Holy Spirit of love, the love of God and man in our hearts; for Thy name's sake. *Amen.* *Henry Alford 1810.*

TRUE AND FALSE LOVE

Love, like money, is continually being counterfeited, by those who desire it without having to pay its price. Therefore, one should know the marks of the genuine spirit in order to detect that which is false, although it be a close imitation. There are so many who deal in counterfeit love that some people never see the true coin and often deny its real existence. With their lips they say there is no divine love, while their hearts are crying for it. Self, however, refuses to pay the price, and strives for the effect apart from the cause. While the eternal struggle between flesh and spirit is waged, it may help on the victory if we have the common sense, born of wisdom, to respond only to true love and to turn away from what is false.

True love swings in a limitless orbit around God the Creator of all life. False love spins like a top around itself as a centre. It lives for itself and its own gratification, while true love lives for others. False love is always asking, "How much can I get?" while true love sighs with its longing to give freely to others. True love is like the living ozone which sets the circulation tingling with new energy. Its counterfeit is like a leech drawing the life from our veins until we are exhausted with weakness.

Perhaps the genuine ring of true love is more easily detected by its effect upon the growing personality. New powers, new capacities, and new freedom are some of the marks of divine love. We find it easier to do our duty and to make our contribution to the work of the world. We love others more; we are more conscious of all beauty and joy, we forget ourselves, and our comforts, in the exhilaration of living. If, however, we come under the influence of counterfeit love, we become stunted in our development, and life's horizon becomes contracted. We stand aloof from others, and become the satellite of one magnetic centre. Soon health breaks down under the strain. Many men and women are suffering from nervous prostration, or anæmia, and countless kindred weaknesses, because they have encountered a love which was a blight instead of a tonic; a ball and chain instead of wings.

One of the most subtle distinctions between true and false love is the important line between self-mastery and self-indulgence. Love must be master of self in the elemental passions of the flesh, in the imaginations of the mind and in the desires of the spirit. It knows well the difference between license and freedom. It never burns itself out in feeling, but rises through feeling to a high sense of its responsibility. We never needed to understand this more than we do to-day. So many are seeking love for the pleasure of it; the thrills it gives to the senses. They care not for its cost and its sacrificial nature. Then, some day, they want it to create for them a temple of life and discover, too late, that what they thought was love was only a passing state of feeling. There is always feeling. It is the *"infinitely more"* that proves its genuineness.

There is a quiet, deep faith which is the very breath of true love and one of its most creative qualities. "We are always at our best when anyone has faith in us." After wandering about in the wilds of South America for fifteen years, a wreck of a man boarded a steamer for North America, — "I am going back to my old mother," he said, "My brother cabled that she still believes in me. If I can only get back to her!" There is nothing more divine on earth than a love that draws one like that. It builds the waste places, and redeems lost years. Everyone of us has someone in the close circle of his friends who will never be re-created in the image of God unless we have a love that burns with a steady flame of faith. It is a fearful responsibility to begin a relation of love; because it must *never* fail.

The difference between true and false love is shown by its loyalties. No one can discern those loyalties all at once; it takes time to know them. But as the days go on we shall find out whether the loyalties of the lover are those of self-interest or those which are true to the great purposes of the relationship. True love brings together those who feel the divine urge to create something worthy of love.

> "Meseems it renders God great joy to see
> Hands stirring after His creatively,
> Yea, that He even left a part undone
> That we might finish that by Him begun,
> And help Him with our efforts to erect
> His house, as masons help an architect.
>
> .   .   .   .
>
> If this be true, that He of us hath need,
> Oh, then are we the sons of God indeed."

Bonds of loyalty to some creative purpose like this can never be broken. It is a fair question to put to love, "what is the burning loyalty of thy heart to which thou wouldst also have me be true?" If there is no call to a purpose worthy of our devotion we do well to mark time a little longer until we know what we are following.

"O Love of God, how deep and great,
Far deeper than man's deepest hate;
Self-fed, self-kindled like the light,
Changeless, eternal, infinite.

O wide-embracing wondrous love!
We read thee in the sky above,
We read thee in the earth below,
On seas that swell, and streams that flow."

H. Bonar 1861.

FOR STUDY AND THOUGHT

Ye have heard that it was said, Thou shalt love thy neighbour, and hate thine enemy: but I say unto you, Love your enemies, and pray for them that persecute you; that ye may be sons of your Father which is in heaven; for he maketh his sun rise on the evil and the good, and sendeth rain on the just and the unjust. For if ye love them that love you, what reward have ye? do not even the publicans the same? And if ye salute your brethren only, what do ye more than others? do not even the Gentiles the same? Ye therefore shall be perfect, as your heavenly Father is perfect. *Matt. 5 : 43-48.*

But love your enemies, and do them good, and lend, never despairing; and your reward shall be great, and ye shall be sons of the Most High: for he is kind toward the unthankful and evil. Be ye merciful, even as your Father is merciful. *Luke 6 : 35-36.*

People have always thought of love as something which could be turned on or off as one turns a water spigot. We classify people according to those we like and those we dislike. We exercise love according to our tastes and prejudices. We love our intimates but not strangers; we love our country but not other nations; we love those who have our religious training but not those who differ from us in custom and point of view. We have not advanced very far from the attitude of the Jews in the days of Jesus who loved their own nation and hated Samaritans and Gentiles. Such an attitude toward life arises from a false conception of love. Two opposing forces cannot stream from the heart at the same time. The apostle James asks, "Does a fountain pour out fresh water and brackish from the same hole?" Nor is it possible for the vital energy of life to be benevolent and malevolent at the same time, without denying the rule of the spirit.

Therefore when Jesus says, "I say unto you, Love your *enemies*," He is not giving an arbitrary command, but is stating a moral necessity. How can anyone be in harmony with the heavenly Father and not be swayed by His spirit which is love! Who can limit the outflow of God from a life? If we are really the *children* of God how can we

have a spirit alien to the Father? "A good tree *cannot* bring forth
evil fruit," said Jesus. How then can our Father bring forth children
who hate.

Note the two appeals that Jesus makes to show the reasonableness
of the command of love. He cites the common facts of life. God the
Creator of all who knows intimately the life of people, sends down
the necessary blessings of rain and sun alike on all; — His enemies
and friends. Men scoff at God and He does not strike them down.
Every good gift is from above, "coming down from the Father of
lights, with whom can be no variation, neither shadow that is cast
by turning." (*Jas. 1 : 17*). Could there be any wars and national
selfishness if we were like unto our Father? Love would indeed then
be the fulfillment of the law.

Then, too, any human being loves the one who loves him. Even a
dog responds to a kind master. Even our enemies, and the despised
nations, love those who love them. What then is our claim to super-
iority? A fuller control by the Spirit of our Father. Notice that Jesus
says we are to *be* superior; not to take the attitude of the Pharisee
who *thinks* himself superior. The only high circles in life are the levels
of love. We are to be perfect as the Father is perfect.

That is the climax of true love; to be like unto the Father. Does it
seem an impossible standard? "*perfect as*," not in *degree* — that would
be a depressing command, but in *kind*. To have the same quality of
love as the Father, — that is possible for every child. Is there harmony at the heart of things? Is there any strife of opposing forces
that is keeping us from wholeness of life? Have we pet aversions which
prevent our drawing on God's power? We cannot expect peace,
health, or power until there is clear right of way for the law of love.

> O God, fountain of love, pour Thy love into our souls,
> that we may love those whom Thou lovest with the love
> Thou givest us; and think and speak of them tenderly,
> meekly, lovingly; and so loving our brethren and sisters
> for Thy sake, may grow in Thy love, and dwelling in love
> may dwell in Thee; for Jesus Christ's sake. *Amen.*
>
> *S. B. Pusey 1810.*

THE COURAGE OF LOVE

It is not difficult to be brave when we have full understanding of a situation. It is the X in the equation which terrifies. The danger which lurks in the dark brings fear. One of the sublime qualities of love is its courage. Why should it not be so? It has already crucified itself in order to live, therefore what more can it fear?

We are face to face with the ultimate test of our sincerity. Is there any real love in us? "There is no fear in love: perfect love casteth out fear;" writes the one who knew Jesus Christ most intimately. How this contradicts our daily life! We have fears of what the future may bring; fear for our friends, fear of poverty, and want, fear of sickness and death. Most of the physical disturbances which end in disease are a result of the spirit of fear. We have tried to rid ourselves of this haunting spectre, but no mental reassurance comes. What is the trouble? It is because we do not love and trust the purposes of our Heavenly Father, by whose will we came into life, and by whose will we are held in life. If we love all the gifts of life which God showers on us, why should we not love more dearly the Giver of all good gifts. "We love Him because He first loved us," says the close friend of Jesus again. There is evidently some hindrance within us which prevents the spirit of love from being perfect, and freeing us from all fear. Why not take the path God meant us to walk in, and break down the barriers between us and self-forgetful love? It will displace fear as surely as the rising sun dispels the mists in the valleys. We shall begin to feel the difference in our bodies and minds and new health will be ours.

When fear is routed, courage comes, and grows from strength to strength. When we are gripped by fear, our vision is narrowed down to the object of our fear and we become blind to everything else except our obsession. When love casts out fear, we are able to take a long look ahead. That which loomed so big in our sight seems ridiculously unimportant in the light of future happenings and past events. A courageous love ransacks all of life to find reassurance, and is never disappointed. That is why a vacation from work does one so much good. It helps one to detach himself from the anxieties of work and the new perspective brings courage; and courage creates health of mind and body. It is easy then to see the relation of our experiences to God's far-reaching purpose. "*All* things work together for good to *them* that *love God*." If He is supreme in His world and is our loving Father, no evil can befall His children. All must be right even though it seems to be wrong.

Courage is the essence of sacrificial love. The battle for truth could never be won without it. It is only by struggle that we lift ourselves to higher planes of living and thinking. It is not possible to call off the fight without becoming effeminate. There is always some truth, dimly discerned, which shines brightly only when we love it to the extent of laying down our lives for it. Every truth which has pushed the world on to higher achievement has risen from the sacrifice of multitudes.

> " 'Twas out of time thou camest to be ours,
>   And dead men made thee in the darkling years;
>   .   .   .   .
> And all thy virtues spring like flowers
>   Thick on the field of some forgotten fight."

It takes courageous love to face the discipline of life. Courage feeds on difficulty. Obstacles become the challenge to courage and call out valiant strength; a football team needs an opposing team to bring its powers into action. Pain calls forth the prayer of faith. If we were not ill there would be no way of proving the skill of the Great Physician. The discipline of daily life is God's chosen way of building character. In reacting from something we do not like we lay hold the more firmly on the ideal love has created. We loath selfishness when we have to live near some selfish soul. It is by the law of contrasts that our appreciations develop. We realize whiteness only by contrasting it with gray. The blue sky brings out the green fields. If the world were colorless there would be no artists; if life had no conflicts of ideas we would never discern the truth. We stretch our souls and grow by the daily choices we have to make between ideals. If we choose high ideals, we will need all our courage in the struggle to grasp them.

Therefore we should expect obstacles to be the normal condition of life. If we say, as we often do, "I am weary of struggling," it is because we are resisting the outflow of sacrificial love and courage and are sinking down to the lower levels of self-desire. Instead of quarreling with this inevitable law of life we must accept the situation, and find through ceasing to resist, a new consciousness of God's strength which can only manifest itself in our weakness. There is a strength which comes when we allow ourselves to be carried on the river of God's power and cease going against the stream. If we fall back upon Him

in confident love and courage, we find that all things *do* work together
for good for the carrying out of a purpose beyond anything we could
plan for ourselves.

> "Thus would I live; yet now
> Not I but He
> In all His power and love
> Henceforth alive in me."
>
> *Latin.   W. L. Caswell 1858.*

FOR STUDY AND THOUGHT

So when they had broken their fast, Jesus saith to Simon Peter, Simon,
son of John, lovest thou me more than these? He saith unto Him, Yea,
Lord; thou knowest that I love thee. He saith unto Him, Feed my lambs.
He saith to him a second time, Simon, son of John, lovest thou Me? He
saith unto him, Yea, Lord; thou knowest that I love Thee. He saith unto
him, Tend my sheep. He saith unto him the third time, Simon, son of
John, lovest thou me? Peter was grieved because he said unto him the
third time, Lovest thou me? And he said unto Him, Lord, thou knowest
all things; thou knowest that I love thee. Jesus saith unto him, Feed my
sheep.   Verily, verily, verily, I say unto thee, When thou wast young, thou
girdedst thyself, and walkedst whither thou wouldst: but when thou shalt
be old, thou shalt stretch forth thy hands, and another shall gird thee,
and carry thee whither thou wouldest not.   Now this he spake, signifying
by what manner of death he should glorify God.   And when he had spoken
this, he saith unto him, Follow me. Peter, turning about, seeth the disciple
whom Jesus loved following; which also leaned back on his breast at the
supper, and said, Lord, who is he that betrayeth thee? Peter therefore
seeing him saith to Jesus, Lord, and what shall this man do? Jesus saith
unto him, if I will that he tarry till I come, what is that to thee? follow
thou me.   *John 21 : 15–22.*

Some days earlier in the life of Jesus, when He told his intimate
followers that He was going away and that they would not be able to
follow Him much longer, Peter, burning with devotion for the Master,
asked impatiently, "Why cannot I follow you, just *now?* I will lay
down my life for you." Jesus replied, "Lay down your life for me? . . .
before the cock crows you will have disowned me thrice over" (*John
13 : 37–38*).

We all know the history of Peter. His love, which was an intense
emotional expression, could not stand the test when the Master he
loved was in trouble, and unpopular with the multitude. It takes
courage to love. The saying goes that trouble comes, then one discovers his real friends. "The friend in need is the friend indeed."
The joyous emotion of love is a health-giving elixir of life. Everyone
loves the feeling of love; but there is a time when love and thrills
part company and the true sacrificial character of love is revealed.

How much of our love is based on feeling, or on the approval of an observing world? Can it live in the dark? Can it give itself freely even unto death? Is love only possible when it seems worth while to love? Peter learned these truths in sorrow. He discovered that love has to be a courageous thing.

Now after his disappointing experience with himself, Peter had an unexpected meeting with his Master. He had gone back to the common avocation of fishing in reaction from the tumult of emotion; and the love of the Master finds him there. Jesus showed him that no experience, or denial, can cut off the life of love. Peter wanted so much to retrieve his past disloyalty that he plunged into the water to get quickly to his Master. Then they talked it over.

Peter might have forgotten the word of Jesus if He had not emphasized three times the only proof of love. Service, service, service! All the declarations of devotion are meaningless unless there is service. Love remembers, too, that the helpless little lambs, and the foolish sheep belong to the one that is Lord, and the care is all the greater because love is expected to be faithful. It was the sin of Judas that he took advantage of his intimate knowledge of Jesus' whereabouts to betray Him to enemies. The man who robs the orphan of his intimate friend is lowest in the scale of robbers because he has reviled love.

It takes courage to carry the burdens of love. That is why so few of us cultivate the spirit of hospitality. "Don't get involved in friendships or you will get into trouble" is the counsel of the world which lives on emotions, but is afraid of service. We may follow this counsel when we are strong and self-sufficient, but sooner or later we, too, shall need love. Happy is that man or woman who receives full interest on what has been given in sacrificial service to their friends. But if it does not come, what then? Untold treasures are ours in the life that is just beyond the vision of our mortal eyes, because our love has been like that of Christ who went calmly to His Cross, with the courage of God, deserted by those same foolish sheep whom He had served, but living in the conscious approval of God who said, "This is my beloved Son, in whom I am well pleased."

> O God, who hast commanded all men to love Thee, and hast drawn them to Thyself by Thy mercy and goodness; fill our hearts with the love of Thee. We are weak and sinful, and cannot love Thee enough without Thy help. All our desire is to give Thee the service of loving hearts all the days of our life, and to love Thee throughout the ages of eternity; through Jesus Christ our Lord. *Amen.* (*The Narrow Way, 1869*).

THE RELATIONSHIP OF LOVE

It is significant that the most courageous and militant of all the apostles of Jesus should have written that immortal classic on love. In his efforts to describe it Paul rises to height after height until at the end he exclaims breathlessly, "Love never faileth." How then dare anyone suggest that there are limitations in the life of love!

There are no limits in the expression of love; in the relationships of love there are inevitable bounds. There is no point in experience where true love fails in its expectant faith. It may have to forgive seventy times seven the same sinner, but it always says to itself, "while there is life there is hope. Perhaps this time he will not fail me." Where would any of us be if we did not know that this unending, hopeful faith is the kind of love God has for us! We would be desolate if we were not sure that His mercies fail not in spite of our many offenses. Love dare not fail in its faith or there is no hope for us, and no hope for those whom we love. Much of the sorrow in this world comes because we love others conditionally while beseeching God to love us unconditionally.

Love never fails in its protecting influence. The one who is loved may wander far away and voluntarily choose to separate himself from the shelter of love, but time and space are not realities. A living spirit does not regard them. Wherever the wanderer may be, he is never beyond the reach of love, nor can he shake off its protecting influence. Love must have this quality if it comes from the heart of God.

Love can never fail in patience; it has no time element. If it has limits it is not divine.

> "I count no time the Shepherd gently answered
> As thou dost count and bind
> The days in weeks, the weeks in months,
> My counting, — is just until I find."

There is also another sense in which love never fails: its honesty and truth abide forever. There is very little human love which rises to this divine height, because it entails the utmost of self-sacrifice. The kind of love we know is too often silent or sinks to the level of criticism, which is discernment without love. God never fails us in the love which longs to free us from all blemish so that we may shine in radiant glory in His presence. The great reason why we fail others in honesty and truth lies in our unwillingness to apply the same standards to ourselves that we expect of others. Thus we stand silent, and fail in our love for others because it condemns ourselves. He who is not honest toward God cannot be honest toward his friend.

Love indeed never faileth, but it is limited often in its relationships. It is never perfect unless there is complete oneness between two spirits, because love always has a goal: — the heart of another.

If there is evil in the heart of the one who is loved, the creative power of love is inhibited. Light and darkness cannot mingle. What does it avail to know that God's love does not fail so long as we fend it off with an unworthy spirit. When love becomes degraded to passion it also loses its divinity and in the end turns to hatred. An evil heart cannot know love.

There are also the inexorable standards of love which must be maintained if the divine energy is to continue. Love must be able to respect the standards of the loved one or the relation of love ceases, and pity takes its place. This is the great reason why love at first sight cannot be trusted. It takes time to know those standards and loyalties of heart which condition unfailing love. When we fail to live up to the highest ideals of the heart that has sacrificed itself in our behalf, we cut the connection between ourselves and the limitless resources of strength in our friend.

True love can be limited by cowardice of heart. It may degenerate into sentimentalism if it does not hold itself under discipline and self-control. It cannot follow blindly the leadership of another unless that leadership is true to the laws of God. Free lance love which does not move in conformity to those principles of life which have been revealed to us by Jesus Christ will turn to lust; and, in the end, to death.

It is because of all these limitations that our ideals of the life of love are blurred and we miss the miracle of its creative power. There is no limit to what God can do through a life that loves to the uttermost. It becomes a channel for infinite good to others. It is like the river bed through which the waters flow bringing life to the parched ground and quenching the thirst of many a traveller. Everything it touches lives in new vigor; the waters flow from the spring of God's love and never fail in drought. They give themselves to everything that has need. Such a life is never in want; it is never lonely, for multitudes bless it and believe in our God who is love.

> "My heart is weak and poor
> Until it master find:

It has no spring of action sure,—
It varies with the mind:
It cannot freely move
Till Thou hast wrought its chain;
Enslave it with Thy matchless love
And deathless it shall reign."   *Matheson.*

FOR STUDY AND THOUGHT

Hereby know we love, because he laid down his life for us: and we ought to lay down our lives for the brethren. But whoso hath the world's goods, and beholdeth his brother in need, and shutteth up his compassion from him, how doth the love of God abide in him?   *I John 3 : 16–17.*

There is no fear in love: but perfect love casteth out fear, because fear hath punishment; and he that feareth is not made perfect in love.
I John 4 : 18.

Love not the world, neither the things that are in the world. If any man love the world, the love of the Father is not in him. For all that is in the world, the lust of the flesh, and the lust of the eyes, and the vainglory of the life, is not of the Father, but is of the world.   *I John 2 : 15–16.*

If a man say, I love God, and hateth his brother, he is a liar: for he that loveth not his brother whom he hath seen, cannot love God whom he hath not seen. And this commandment have we from him, that he who loveth God love his brother also.   *I John 4 : 20–21.*

For this is the love of God, that we keep his commandments: and his commandments are not grievous.   *I John 5 : 3.*

All the relationships of love follow the ideal of our great relation to Jesus Christ. When He laid down His life for us, He transfigured the meaning of love for the whole world. Since then all lower forms of love have had to hide themselves under other names, or be lifted up to the spiritual standard of Jesus. At the heart of the relationship is the sacrificial principle; living not for our own desires, but for the good of others. Ourselves and our goods for the good of the world. We brought nothing into the world and we take nothing out of it save the flame of love, therefore we are mere stewards of temporary resources for the needs of others. We are distributing centres for the love of God, in order that men may see through our life with them what life with God is like.

The life of love is a life without fear. Very few of us know what this is by experience because so much of our conception of love is concerned with what others feel toward us instead of what we feel toward them. When love is feverish desire for self-satisfaction there is well grounded fear lest it be denied us; but the perfect love which gives without thought of return can have no fear. We may ask ourselves whether our love is an anxiety or an asset.

In a closer sense the love of the Father and love of the world can have no fellowship. It is not the material world that is meant, — the handiwork of God; but the devotion to the things of sense, what our eyes covet, and the worship of position and power. These deaden the life of the soul and enslave it with the absorbing interest of the passing show. Love is turned to lust and the relationship with God is broken.

Our human connections with our brothers are the laboratory tests of our spirit. If love is real, it will be mirrored in those about us. What we are will be reflected back from human hearts.

> "A love that gives and takes, that sees the faults
> Not with flaw-seeking eyes like needle points,
> But loving, kindly, ever looks them down
> With the o'ercoming faith of meek forgiveness;
> A love that shall be new and fresh each hour,
> As in the golden mystery of sunset,
> Or the sweet coming of the evening star,
> Alike and yet most unlike, every day,
> And seeming ever best and fairest *now*." *J. R. Lowell.*

An utter committal to the life of love is the only possible course for those who want the friendship of God. "This is my commandment," said Jesus, "that ye love one another as I have loved you. . . . . Ye are my friends if ye do the things which I command you!" There is no choice open. We either are or we are not in harmony with heaven. If we are, all things are possible; if we are not, nothing can come to fruition.

> O God, who has taught us to keep all Thy heavenly commandments by loving Thee and our neighbor; grant us the spirit of peace and grace, that we may be both devoted to Thee with our whole heart, and united to each other with a pure will; through Jesus Christ our Lord. *Amen. Leonine Sacramentary A. D. 440.*

FINDING OUR WAY IN LIFE

INEVITABLE LIMITATIONS

A human being cannot be at peace with God or himself if he has nothing to do but to satisfy his own desires. Health also is at stake. There is a lingering sense of importance in everyone. We are happy and well only when we know that we are needed for some purpose.

The reason why many older people lose their health so rapidly is because the career which demanded the strength of a man in his prime is no longer possible and he fails to find another field of service which furnishes scope for his riper powers. The wise person foresees that critical moment and plans for it so that his sense of vocation is never lost. The peril of wealth lies in the fact that it frees people from the necessity for work. Then things may become so absorbing that inner resources are neglected and health breaks down. It does not occur to many such people to use their resources for great service. Many people are ill to-day who would be well to-morrow if some big responsibility dropped down upon them and there was no one else to carry it.

To realize that we are necessary for some important service is the greatest tonic for health. A drifting life runs downstream and is a perversion of God's purpose. He never brought anyone into life without some clear intent. Some of us, however, are like children, stopping along the way to play marbles, forgetful of the errand on which we were sent. Some day we shall have to render an account of ourselves.

We may be willing in spirit to go anywhere or do anything, but when we begin to think of what we *may* do, we find certain inevitable limitations with which each of us must reckon. So many of us lose time by refusing to accept our limitations, only to find in the end that we *have* to accept them. Meanwhile we have lost our running start for success. What baffled hopes we would spare ourselves if we had faced the moral situation in the beginning and weighed all the facts!

The law of cause and effect works inevitably in the making of our career. Two children start in school; one does faithfully the daily task, the other cares more for fun. Slowly but surely, the conscientious student develops a taste and a capacity for brain work which will guide him to some career only possible for trained minds. The fun-loving comrade will be far removed on another trail which leads to work of a different sort. In the same way one who has interests and resources within himself will be puzzled to know which way to take because there are so many alluring paths. It is as inevitable in the mental world as in nature that we reap as we sow; that our possi-bilities or handicaps in work are the natural results of the small choices we have made.

Most of our air castles and day dreams are unrelated to our present circumstances. The lure of the unfamiliar holds us under its spell, and we are sure that somewhere, anywhere, — save where we are now, — we shall find our heart's desire. It is right to cherish a vision, but let us look at that vision in the perspective of to-day, with the oppor-tunities God gives us now. In other words a vocation will be the outcome of past preparation and background. Even now I am forging another link in the chain of my vocation. "To-day if ye shall hear his voice, harden not your hearts." It is not our circumstances them-selves but that part of them to which we pay attention which deter-mines our future. A career or ill-health hangs in the balance with some of us. Let the imagination center about the possibilities of to-day rather than the hopes of to-morrow. To-morrow grows out of to-day. Most of the daily events will be small and seem insignificant, while the big ones will be few and far between. It is good that this is so; for through small events we can be masters of our destiny.

We see this truth so clearly in lives like that of Abraham Lincoln. No one would have envied him his chance in life when he lived in the little log cabin; but every one would indeed be proud to hold the place in the hearts of the world, which he holds. It was not the call of the war which made him great, but the unfaltering obedience to his highest instincts, and "the next thing," from his boyhood up, that determined his future.

No one can realize his ideals by a single leap. If we set our hearts on a certain goal, we must count the cost of attaining it; and then be willing to conform the last detail of our daily living to that end. The attainment of our heart's desire means utter sacrifice and the uniting of all our powers in the quest.

It seems absurd to suggest that any service we choose should be big enough to compel all our enthusiasm. One cannot go about casu-ally, when God's plan is to be carried out. Such modern Micawbers lose the whole meaning of life. "Waiting for something to turn up" usually means following our wandering desires. We need to see ourselves in the perspective of eternity. It will help to steady our thinking if we ask ourselves this question, "What difference will this make one hundred years from now?" Some things that we think important will dwindle to a vanishing point in the perspective of a century. Other purposes will deepen, and be more satisfying as the years go by. We need to ask also, "Does this life which I am living now satisfy only one side of my nature, or does it stimulate and call out my latent powers and ideals?"

As we grow older, it takes more to satisfy us; and we revise our scale of values. Therefore, if we want joy to come with the years, we should not take any path which does not lead to higher levels, and further views, and clearer air. If any one who reads this, says sadly — "It is too late. I have lost my opportunity," remember that to-day is still ours and we can redeem it and start new influences working in our behalf. Now is the day of our salvation. We can yet say of God, "He restoreth my soul."

> "Thou art my Way; I wander, if Thou fly;
> Thou art my Light; if hid how blind am I!
> Thou art my Life; if Thou withdraw I die."
> *Francis Quarles.*

FOR STUDY AND THOUGHT

Is not this the fast that I have chosen? to loose the bonds of wickedness, to undo the bands of the yoke, and to let the oppressed go free, and that ye break every yoke? Is it not to deal thy bread to the hungry, and that thou bring the poor that are cast out to thy house? when thou seest the naked, that thou cover him; and that thou hide not thyself from thine own flesh? Then shall thy light break forth as the morning, and thy healing shall spring forth speedily: and thy righteousness shall go before thee; the glory of the Lord shall be thy rearward. And if thou draw out thy soul to the hungry, and satisfy the afflicted soul; then shall thy light rise in darkness, and thine obscurity be as noonday: and the Lord shall guide thee continually, and satisfy thy soul in dry places, and make strong thy bones; and thou shalt be like a watered garden, and like a spring of water, whose waters fail not. And they that shall be of thee, shall build the old waste places: thou shalt raise up the foundations of many generations; and thou shall be called The repairer of the breach, The restorer of paths to dwell in. *Isa. 58 : 6–8, 10–12.*

There is no more beautiful description in literature than this unfolding of the path which leads to life. It begins in unselfishness. It is the spirit of St. Paul, who said, "we that are strong ought to bear the infirmities of the weak and not to please ourselves." (*Rom. 15 : 1*). Social service is the Christian program. It is not the way of the unregenerate world. That is ruled by the law of the survival of the fittest. The Prophets preached a God who meant the unfit also to survive. The old supremacy was based on physical strength and material possessions. There is much of that pagan point of view still left, even among cultivated people. The new supremacy, based on mind and spirit, is independent of material advantage, and may be stronger without it. Jesus saw in every human spirit, the image of God; and therefore each had a claim on every other child of God.

The magnitude of the program of service is enough to furnish a career for every Christian. Nearly two thousand years have passed since Christ walked the earth and yet the larger majority of the human race are in bondage of one sort or another. The hungry, the poor, and the naked, abound. Even some of the so-called "service" is founded on selfishness and greed. The superman, the composite of countless folk whose oneness is the desire to gain rights by the old law of might, stalks through the land. There are great careers waiting for those who will follow the narrow road which leads to life.

Many of us seek in our inner life the presence of our Lord and forget that the promise is for those who are going out into the world to work among their fellows. We cannot hide ourselves from our own flesh and expect a private illumination of the face of God for our enjoyment. *"If* thou draw out thy soul to the hungry, . . . then shall thy light rise in darkness . . . and Jehovah shall *guide thee continually."* "God so loved the world that He gave" — and we too must give to the world if we would have the privileges of sonship and love.

The logical reward of service is an endless supply of the means of service. To be a spring of never failing water, — the refreshment of all thirsty souls, without effort! There is something wrong about the service that drains one dry. Perhaps we cut our connection with the Source while we are occupied with "many things." Only life can beget life.

To find one's own path, by restoring paths to others is the perfection of a career. What a constrast to the end of the exploiter whom Isaiah describes a little later! They who "made them crooked paths." Their end is a cry of remorse. "We grope in the twilight; we are in dark places like the dead": — the logical end of moral atrophy. If people mean to live in darkness, eyes are superfluous: therefore Nature takes them away. Neglecting to choose the path of light, the soul inevitably walks into darkness. "I am the real and living way," said Jesus: "No one comes to the Father except by means of Me." *John 14 : 6* (*Moffat translation.*)

Lord Jesus Christ, who alone art wisdom, Thou knowest what is best for us; mercifully grant that it may happen to us only as it is pleasing to Thee and as seems good in Thy sight this day; for Thy name's sake. *Amen.*

Henry VI, A. D. 1421.

MAKING DECISIONS

Sometimes a remark overheard on the street tells a whole life story. A man on the street was replying to some mental anxiety in his friend, "Come on, be a sport; life is only a gamble and you jump in the dark. Take your chance without so much thinking and you will come out all right." As they turned the corner, questions suggested themselves. "Is it true that life is so full of surprises that it is a gamble? Are careful decisions useless? How is one ever to know that he is on the right track?"

The answer to these questions will make a vast difference to some of us. Even if we are so purblind in vision that we cannot reckon with certainty upon the next hour, we should be without sense if we did not have some principles by which to steer our course.

People face their responsibility for making decisions in different ways according to their temperament. There are some like jellyfish with no backbone, who go with the tide. They follow the crowd wherever it chances to go. Their happiness depends upon the will of someone else who plans their life for them. This flabby attitude is often developed in a child by a parent who never lets him think for himself because he might do something foolish. He probably will; but how is he to learn except through experience? Failures are blessings in disguise if they lead us to wisdom. Some of us are still missing the will of God for us because we find it easier to lean back upon some *venturesome person* who says without a moment's hesitation, "Yes, this is the thing to do."

Others feel keenly the need for making choices, but are in a perpetual state of indecision. Sometimes this results from sheer mental laziness, but oftener it is because they lack courage to face consequences. Nothing reacts on the nervous system more than anxious uncertainty. We may be losing our health from this cause, imagining that outer circumstances, and not our own divided minds, are to blame. The apostle St. James said of the double-minded man, "Let not that man think that he shall receive anything of the Lord."

Some of the most unhappy people are those who have the type of mind which always regrets the decisions of the day before. "I wish I had not promised to do that," or "I should have chosen this." Such an attitude denies the guidance of God. Decision of character in the light of all possible wisdom at the time, is essential to peace, health and power. There is sufficient wisdom for the needs of the day if we ask in faith. God did not make us omniscient. We attain more and more through the honest use of our discernment.

Why should we have been given brains, and the power of thinking, if life is merely a gamble and we cannot make choices which will in the end control circumstances? The creative power in each of us has never been tested to the full. God works within us. His guidance of our days is the result of His Spirit working through the mental processes of our brain.

It is never possible to see the results of our decisions at once. If we did see them we would be divinities. We walk by faith. We always have enough light to see the next step. What is that light? It is the consciousness of what is true, beautiful, good; like unto the character of God, in harmony with what we know is His will. We follow that gleam, that standard, which we know is His, and we never have to regret such decisions.

The guidance is not always the same for everyone, because we all have different gifts and desires, and no one can work our life out for us. We ought, though, to be able to defend our position to reasonable people. If so, it may be for our good to oppose the inertia of our friends. There are many human tragedies lived out by men and women who have been prevented by their families from making choices which affect their whole life. A brilliant lawyer destined his only son to succeed him in his profession. The boy had not the courage to disappoint him and labored on with his studies. To the public, he seems like a mediocre half-awake son of a successful man. Some of his friends, however, know the real truth. They are invited to his home where he entertains them with his violin. When he gets it into his hands, he is a man of power. He still follows monotonously the career of his father; but the world has lost a great musician.

Our ability to make wise choices depends upon our power to think. To hold in our mind all the points in a situation, and to look at their worth and then decide which shall be our chief concern, this is the highest art. We cannot prove our power to think until we can see clearly that there are always two sides to a question. No one can get far in thinking who forgets this. And yet there are thousands of people with fine minds who never get beyond their original opinion. They depend on what they experienced in the past and have no hope and faith for the future.

Some people can transform their whole lives if they form a large unselfish purpose. If we are clear in our minds about the chief end of our desire, then quite naturally, many things are settled for us. This is illustrated in the history of countless people. A boy who had been unstable in his ways, suddenly faced the duty of caring for his widowed mother. He found a job and went at it with a new purpose. In a short time all his life was organized around this central idea. His purpose brought poise, business success, and a reputation for steadfastness.

A purpose will not go beyond the stage of a day dream, unless it is backed up by our will power — as soon as we begin to use this we shall find a great wall of inertia rising up to prevent us from reaching our goal. Until we push through we shall never find freedom.

There is some moral decision every one of us needs to make. God waits for us to take a new step away from the fears and discouragements of the past and turn our faces toward a new future, bright with hope and faith.

> "The trivial round, the common task
> Will furnish all we ought to ask,
> Room to deny ourselves, a road
> To bring us daily nearer God."

FOR STUDY AND THOUGHT

The LORD is my shepherd; I shall not want.
He maketh me to lie down in green pastures:
He leadeth me beside the still waters.
He restoreth my soul:
He guideth me in the paths of righteousness for his name's sake.
Yea, though I walk through the valley of the shadow of death,
I will fear no evil; for thou art with me:
Thy rod and thy staff, they comfort me.
Thou preparest a table before me in the presence of mine enemies:
Thou hast anointed my head with oil; my cup runneth over.
Surely goodness and mercy shall follow me all the days of my life:
And I will dwell in the house of the Lord forever.   *Psa. 23.*

There are people, even in this age, who read the opening words of this Psalm and would accuse King David of sublime egotism. Jehovah, the Creator, who inhabits eternity and sets the stars whirling in space, the Mighty God, becoming *my* shepherd, guiding the infinitesimal footsteps of little *me* who am less than an atom in contrast with the universe! The conception is so stupendous that, even after centuries of Christian teaching, many minds laugh at its absurdity. Nevertheless the faith of David has been more than justified by the prayer of Jesus when He said, "I pray for them — that — even as Thou, Father, art in me, and I in Thee, that they also may be in us:

that the world may believe that Thou didst send me" (*John 17 : 21*).
If we are thus as close to God as Jesus was, then David's confidence is
not absurd egotism.

What a contrast to the din and confusion of modern civilization
are the experiences of a spirit led by God. "Green pastures," "waters
of quietness": A strange conception for a life like David's which was
outwardly far from restful. He was hunted down like an animal by
Saul; enemies and troubles beset his reign; there were wars and strife
on every side, and yet he says exultantly, "He leadeth me beside the
still waters." Evidently there is a possible experience where the
human spirit can be at rest even though there is no outward warrant
for it. If we could learn David's secret, what peace and health would
be ours. Medical men write long articles about the menace of modern
life with its turmoil and anxieties. They urge men to return to a
simple life to avoid nervous breakdowns. Much of this counsel is
beside the mark because few of us can regulate the cosmos. Why
not urge people to seek a spiritual experience such as David's. The
weight of a depressing past with its failures and mistakes takes the
heart out of us. We settle down in disillusionment and middle-aged
stodginess, when what we need is a spiritual bath to restore our soul.
That is the gift of God in answer to a humble, contrite heart.

One reason why we are not more conscious of God's guidance is
because we are not sure whether we *want* to walk in paths of righteousness. We insist on reaching the goal of our desire if we have to cut
across someone else's property to arrive there. The ways of right living
are too slow for some of us. Clean living is as dull to us as it was to
the small boy who longed to buy candy when his mother had told
him to buy soap. The real trouble is with our hearts. We do not want
God's guidance; we want to adventure: so we do, — and suffer for it
in our minds and bodies.

Even death itself is not a blank wall. It is only a shadow and as
harmless as shadows always are. We walk *through* them, without fear,
with God. Note the change from the personal pronoun "He" to the
more intimate "Thou" as David walks into troubles. God draws
nearer. If we are lost in the storms of life, the Good Shepherd searches
and finds us and brings us back on His shoulders rejoicing. (See *Matt.
18 : 12–14*). Life cannot balk the resourcefulness of the God who is
our Shepherd. The marginal reading of "surely" is "*only* goodness
and loving kindness shall follow me." The Shepherd God ahead of us
and loving kindness behind us — what greater protection could there
be! What do we want when we seek guidance? Is it that we shall

have what our eyes covet, or that we may know the right path and follow it?

> O Lord Jesus Christ, Thou Good Shepherd of the sheep, Who camest to seek the lost, and to gather them to Thy fold, have compassion upon those who have wandered from Thee; feed those who hunger, cause the weary to lie down in Thy pastures, bind up those who are broken in heart, and strengthen those who are weak, that we, relying on Thy care and being comforted by Thy love, may abide in Thy guidance to our lives' end; through Jesus Christ our Lord. *Amen. Ancient Collect.*

EXPERIENCES ALONG THE ROAD

The adventurous spirit of Christopher Columbus does not appeal to most people. We like novelty and new experiences, but do not care to pioneer into the unknown. The way has to be opened by others. We like to be safe and sure.

When we decide to walk in God's ways and follow His purpose, we picture our ideal of the right path, as a straight, sunny highway, level and smooth, with no fog or overhanging clouds. So long as our experiences in life correspond with the ideal, we voice our confidence in God's sure guidance. If other kinds of experiences come, we are likely to feel that there is something wrong and that God is withholding this loving care. Therefore we become a prey to fears of the future and wrestle with anxiety until the spirit is enslaved and health begins to feel the effects of worry. Many a sincere Christian loses the sense of the heavenly Father's nearness and is mentally depressed merely because his ideal of the path of life is not true to the facts.

What then is the normal experience of all who start out upon the road of God's purpose? What have we a right to expect from the teachings of Jesus? What ideal will keep us in that perfect peace which is essential for the health of body, mind, and spirit?

At the outset we need to remember that the open road of God's purpose is to be travelled by faith rather than by sight. We do not discern the end nor the beginning. The Divine reasons why we were brought into life are veiled in mystery: and the end and purpose of our incarnation is yet to be revealed. All we really know is that we are here on the road. Our chief business is to follow the Christ because we know He walked with God towards a glorious destination. We pin our faith to Him and are content to go on. If the beginning and the end are inscrutable, why should we be troubled because some of the shorter distances are beyond our present sight?

We shall find, too, that progress is made by taking the next step that is immediately before us. It takes courage to concentrate on the present moment and leave the outcome of the next hour, or day, or month with God. There is no way of predicting what a day may bring forth, because we are dealing with life, and life is ever moving and changing. It is never static. Time and space are imaginary concepts like the lines of latitude and longitude. They are convenient for describing locations, but are not real goals. We are always shown how to use the next moment and to make the immediate decision. That is really all we need to know. The past step has been taken, the future is yet beyond us. All we have is the present step. The true attitude is voiced in the prayer of Newman:

> "Keep Thou my feet, I do not ask to see
> The distant scene;
> One step enough for me."

We might be able to meet this test of faith if it were not for the challenges of other people on the road who are sure we are going the wrong way. They would have us turn aside to walk with them and the pressure of their influence is hard to withstand. It is one of the strange facts of life that there are always head winds opposing our progress in the path of faith. "Woe unto you when all men speak well of you," is the warning of Jesus to His followers. It is unlikely that any of us would win spiritual victories save through a conflict with human opinion. Perhaps this is what keeps us true to our purpose and makes us depend more fully on the strength of God. Happy are we if we are not turned aside by the plausible arguments of those who are unwilling to lose their lives in order to find them. The sacrificial spirit is born out of the struggle between the Spirit of God and the spirit of the world. It will be a struggle to the end, as it was in the life of Jesus. This is the normal experience of those who press on in the life of faith.

We can understand the human influences that oppose our progress better than the uncertain character of the road itself. Instead of walking in the light we often find ourselves headed toward darkness. Light and shade come in tantalizing succession and unless we know our God we shall waver in our quiet trust. Upgrades, downgrades, roughness and smoothness are likely to come at any moment. And yet it is all God's highway and we are in the path of His power, guided by the same spirit who led Jesus. "This is the victory that overcometh the world: even our faith," writes the chief pioneer who followed Jesus. If we could once fix our minds on the faithfulness of our Father's love rather than on the changing scene, we should be freed from such a weight of anxiety that we could triumph over anything. Paul in his lonely pioneering for the Christian faith was able to shout in triumph loyally because he could say, "None of these things move me — Looking unto Jesus, I press forward." As for us, we lose our strength because *everything* moves us with disappointment and doubt.

There are sharp turns in the road, too, which shut off our vision.

It is the normal experience. Those corners are the supreme test of faith, but they serve a useful purpose. If it were not for them, the road would be a long stretch of plodding monotony. A stone wall or the seeming end of a trail, is the signal for new discovery. Some fresh revelation of God's power is about to happen. When we come to the last step before we turn, we shall get a new glimpse of God's loving guidance and go on in greater faith, because the crooked place was made straight. Think of what Israel's deliverance from the Red Sea meant to their faith!

Following the road of God's purpose brings us the companionship of all true souls. There in no kinship like that between those who are following the same path of God's purpose. Closer than brother and sister is the understanding of two hearts burning with devotion to the way of Jesus. "How these people love one another," was the comment of the pagan historian writing about the early Christians. And John wrote, "we know that we have passed from death to life because we love the brethren."

> If thou but suffer God to guide thee,
> And hope in Him through all thy ways,
> He'll give thee strength whate'er betide thee,
> And bear thee through the evil days:
> Who trusts in God's unchanging love,
> Builds on a rock that naught can move.   *Neumark.*

FOR STUDY AND THOUGHT

He clave rocks in the wilderness, and gave them drink abundantly as out of the depths. He brought streams also out of the rock, and caused waters to run down like rivers. Yet went they on still to sin against him, to rebel against the Most High in the desert. For their heart was not right with him, neither were they faithful in his covenant. But He, full of compassion, forgave their iniquity and destroyed them not: Yea, many a time turned He His anger away, and did not stir up all His wrath. And He remembered that they were but flesh; A wind that passeth away, and cometh not again. How oft did they rebel against Him in the wilderness, and grieve Him in the desert! And they turned again and tempted God, and provoked the Holy One of Israel. They remembered not His hand, nor the day when He redeemed them from the adversary.
Psa. 78 : 15–17, 37–42.

This Psalm is a long recital of human fickleness and unsteadiness of purpose in contrast with God's faithfulness. Most of the reason why we do not find our way in life is due to this vacillation. We tend to be opportunists and point the bow of our boat in whatever direction a favoring wind blows. We are like the tramp in a recent English book who, when asked how he knew which way to go, replied: "I always go with my back to the wind." That is the trouble with most of us in our spiritual life; we follow the urge of the moment and the line of least resistance. We do not love anything hard enough to suffer for it. Our fundamental desire is for a smooth road and we are willing to endure hardness as good soldiers having a cause.

Nothing short of a fixed religious purpose will steady our thinking. We waste years playing about and seeking the traditional pot of gold at the foot of the rainbow. Not till we discover that there is a divine purpose for human life shall we be free from haunting anxieties.

We have all had marvellous escapes from trouble. Somehow at the very moment when we were about to be overwhelmed by circumstances, a deliverance came. God had His eye on us, and led us through the fire so that we were not burned. We may not have seen His hand in our life, but that was due to our blindness; not to His absence. "I will gird thee, though thou has not known Me," came the word of God through the prophet Isaiah.

Spiritual stupidity is a common weakness. Perhaps some of it is due to our inability to see beyond, or behind the present moment. Only those to whom God is very real dwell much in the past or future. Our arc of vision is tiny when we remove the sense of eternity from it. God takes this into account for, as this Psalm says, He remembered that they were "a wind that passeth away and cometh not again." This does not excuse disloyalty when we make great promises during our troublesome times and forget to pay our vows after we are delivered. It does not excuse also the remembrance of past experiences. The real reason for our disloyalty is the ancient spirit of *fear* which is always looking out for trouble. So long as we are guided by our fears instead of by our faith we shall see only the terror of the night and the arrows that fly in the day. Fear fixes the attention on what is fearful. Faith sees what is faithful and that is God. There are two possible ways of judging the character of the world; looking at it by night or looking at it by day. Both are facts of experience, but the day rules the night and we really live from day unto day.

What if my job vanishes, and my garden fails to mature, or my future is unknown and I see only waste places ahead of me, I can depend upon the same God that Isaiah found, who reassures His people with those matchless words, "I will bring the blind by a way that they know not; in paths that they know not will I lead them: I will make darkness light before them and crooked places straight; these things will I do and I will not forsake them."

O God, who hast commanded us to be perfect as Thou
our Father in heaven art perfect; put into our hearts,
we pray Thee, a continual desire to obey Thy holy will,
teach us day by day, what Thou wouldst have us do,
and give us grace and power to fulfill the same. May
we never from love of ease, decline the path which Thou
pointest out, nor, for fear of shame, turn away from it;
for the sake of Christ Jesus our Lord.   *Amen.*

Henry Alford 1810.

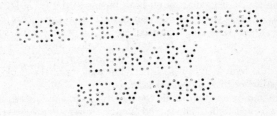
GEN. THEO. SEMINARY
LIBRARY
NEW YORK

THE LIBRARY FOR THE EDUCATION OF THE SPIRIT

A student once tried to defend his indifference to religion by declaring that the life of the spirit was too intangible and speculative to be taken seriously. "In law, medicine or chemistry there are intellectual resources for the student, but in religion one has to go by his inner consciousness. How are you to know you are on the right track?"

It is strange that so many should be seemingly unaware of the great deposit of wisdom gathered from the religious experiences of the centuries, and contained in that great collection of books we call the Bible. It is not a text book written for propaganda, but a library of sixty-six volumes collected during a period of more than fifteen hundred years. The average student is staggered by the multitude of books by which the growth of modern education has developed during the past two or three hundred years. It is doubtful how much of it will survive the next ten centuries. Time sifts all things and, like a fire, burns up the thoughts of men. Much of what was written two hundred years ago has already disappeared forever, and has ceased to influence men. But to have survived fifteen hundred years and then to have been collected in a library and to sway fifteen hundred more years of thinking — this may well command the reverence of every scholar. And in the realm of modern publishing business, the Bible is still the best seller, — far beyond the most sensational literary success of the day.

Sixty-six books on spiritual education which have survived the closest analysis of the brains of centuries, are worthy of respect; especially if we are looking for guidance in the life of the spirit it would be foolish indeed to ignore the wisdom of the Bible, which has proved wiser than the wisest man.

In finding our way in life the past religious experiences of humanity give us clear light. The sacred library traces the progressive development of all humanity in the knowledge of God. Every phase of human experience, every mental attitude is traced to its logical end through the lives of men and women who reached out toward the spiritual world. All the wisdom they gained through failure and success is there plainly told. And the amazing unity in the conclusions of fifteen hundred years of living makes us sure that we are dealing with basic laws of life and not with theories about it. We are not likely to follow the wrong trail when we work out our lives in harmony with those same laws which were worked out in the lives of characters in the Bible.

The spiritual instincts and hopes which drew people on and up out of darkness became vivid realities with the coming of Jesus Christ.

> "All thoughts that mould the age begin
> Deep down within the primitive soul,
> And from the many slowly upward rise
> To one who grasps the whole." *Lowell.*

The transcendent personality of Jesus was the great amen to all the spiritual yearnings of the world. We know that the old prophets and teachers were on the right trail. The world was ready for the full truth which would forever set us free. The Bible was not completed until more than two hundred years of living in the power of Jesus' teaching had demonstrated what could be done, when the spirit in man was free. Since then countless other folk have come near to the life of Jesus through the study of the Bible and found their way also, to peace, health and power. The church through all the centuries has been the great training school in the religious life and has held the mind of men to the degree that it has been true to the laws of the spiritual life as revealed by Jesus Christ. "I am the light of the world," said Jesus; "he that followeth me shall not walk in darkness, but shall have the light of life." How foolish of anyone to think that he can guide himself without the clear light of Jesus' life as we know it through the Bible! As well might one expect to analyze the properties of gold without a knowledge of chemistry.

We save much time and many regrets if we use the wisdom of the scriptures before we make experiments in life. Our days here on earth are few and precious and we have so far to go before we enter the heavenly realm that we have no time to waste on wrong theories. It is only common sense to start right so that we shall not have to use so much energy in finding the right road that we are not free to enjoy the companionships and beauties along the way. Nor do we want to lag behind others in our purposes toward God.

The Bible is the great guide for daily living. Some of us have wise friends who help us by their counsel and keep us from making mistakes. The perplexing questions which come up in our relations with others and the need for discernment call for wisdom beyond our experience. The wisest human friend may fail in judgment, but the guidance of the Bible is sure. It shows us the right principle to follow and how to apply it. It is like a mirror in which we see ourselves as well as the heavenly reflection.

If we use the Bible casually, opening it for some magic direction we may wrest its meaning to our own destruction. It is not a book of rules, but a progressive revelation of God's dealings with men, and man's experience with God. If we bring to this library of books the same intelligence we use in other fields of knowledge we shall be rewarded beyond our fondest hopes.

Some people use the scriptures to confirm their own theories rather than to receive its full teaching with humble hearts. There is only one way to use this spiritual wisdom of the ages. The character and point of view of Jesus is the gauge for all that is recorded there. He is the fulfillment of the law and the prophets and the Lord and master of all His followers. Everything in the religious experience of the Bible is of spiritual value only as it reflects the heart of Christ.

The expression of all this wealth of religious experience helps our soul to wing its way into the very presence of God. We learn how to pray — we find the memory of those teachings, and visions, and, experiences of human hearts, coming back to us again and again, nerving our will to follow the same path of life. " Thy word have I hid in my heart that I might not sin against thee."

> "Word of the everlasting God,
> Will of His glorious Son;
> Without Thee how could earth be trod
> Or heaven itself be won?
> Lord, grant us all aright to learn
> The wisdom it imparts;
> And to its heavenly teaching turn
> With simple, childlike hearts."

FOR STUDY AND THOUGHT

Think not that I came to destroy the law or the prophets: I came not to destroy, but to fulfil. For verily I say unto you, Till heaven and earth pass away, one jot or one title shall in no wise pass away from the law, till all things be accomplished. Whosoever therefore shall break one of these least commandments, and shall teach men so, shall be called least in the kingdom of heaven: but whosoever shall do and teach them, he shall be called great in the kingdom of heaven. *Matt. 5 : 17–19.*

Ye search the scriptures, because ye think that in them ye have eternal life; and these are they which bear witness of me. *John 5 : 39.*

And he said unto them, O foolish men, and slow of heart to believe in all that the prophets have spoken! Behooved it not the Christ to suffer these things, and to enter into his glory? And beginning from Moses and from all the prophets, he interpreted to them in all the scriptures the things concerning himself. *Luke 24 : 25–27.*

For whatsoever things were written aforetime were written for our learning, that through patience and through comfort of the scriptures we might have hope. *Rom. 15 : 4.*

But abide thou in the things which thou hast learned and hast been assured of, knowing of whom thou hast learned them; and that from a babe thou hast known the sacred writings which are able to make thee wise unto salvation through faith which is in Christ Jesus. Every scripture inspired of God is also profitable for teaching, for reproof, for correction, for instruction which is in righteousness: that the man of God may be complete, furnished completely unto every good work.

II Tim. 3 : 14–17.

Most of the reformers in the world have been in opposition to all that has gone before and have tried to turn people from old established ways to some new path which they are blazing out. Jesus Christ, however, rooted His unique message in the religious experience of the past. He never discounted the spiritual verities which had been wrought out through the age-long search for God. He came to fulfill, not to destroy. The mid-day sun does not deny the pale yellow and rosy beams of the sunrise. The truth of the dawn shines brighter and brighter into the white light of perfect day. We know Jesus is the truth because He gathers up Himself all the bits of truth which were wrought out through the experience of men with God.

Jesus knew the writings of the Old Testament and expected people to judge Him by them. There could be no greater testimony to the divine authority of the scriptures than this. Anyone is likely to err unless he knows the truth which has been revealed, and the power of God. It takes an appreciation of the nature of God to understand the significance of what has been written, just as the character of our President gives peculiar meaning to his words.

It is important to note that in the conversation with the mystified disciples, after His resurrection, Jesus pins their faith to the eternal truth of the Old Testament for an understanding of Him rather than to the great events through which He had just passed. They were to see Jesus as the climax of all the religious yearnings of the past. The supreme proof to them of His presence was the way their heart burned within them as the old mountain peaks of truth were illumined by a new glory. What they had we too can have as we search those same scriptures with an open heart.

How many of us keep our hope in God living and ever present? If it grows dim it is because we are neglecting the wisdom which would give us patience and comfort. The truth of God as revealed to men is as great as the heavens and comes out of the universal experience of the human heart. It is because Jesus is rooted in the past that we can trust Him for the days to come. He is not the exotic blossom of a single generation, but the inevitable flower born of the common hope and yearning of mankind.

We enter into the life of a great university for the culture of our minds, and count years of study a necessity that we may understand the wisdom of humanity. Of how much more importance is it to live in the vast library of the Bible for the education of the spirit. One hundred years from now the wisdom of men will have ceased to be important to us, but the word of God's truth shall abide.

> "With my whole heart have I sought Thee:
> O let me not wander from Thy commandments.
> Thy word have I laid up in mine heart,
> That I might not sin against Thee.
> Blessed art Thou, O Lord:
> Teach me Thy statutes." *Amen. Psa. 119 : 10-12.*

HEALTH AND SPIRITUAL LAWS

THE RIGHT TO BE WELL

When God chose the body in which to incarnate the human spirit. He designed it to be the best possible means for expressing the life of the soul. Jesus Christ in His teachings emphasized God's concern for the body as well as for the mind and spirit of man. A large part of the ministry of Jesus was devoted to the healing of people's bodies so that the spirit might be released for a life of service on earth. There is some high and holy purpose for the life of the body or we would not have it. Everything that God has made is good, and serves His divine purpose. When He would reveal Himself to men He incarnated His Spirit in human flesh in the person of Jesus. If for no other reason than this, we do well to revere our bodies. They are meant to help and not to hinder.

It has been a long hard struggle for the world to accept the body as a divine gift to be governed by the spirit and mind. It is the interpreter of the outer world, and is the necessary instrument for self-expression. It is like the mighty organ which reveals the soul of the musician. Without it he could not express the harmony within him. It may be used to suggest unworthy emotions, but that is not the fault of the instrument. In the same way our body may prostitute our soul because our physical senses may appeal to some evil desire within us and drag us down. If high desires control our heart those same bodily senses may be the means of exalting us.

Many people seem to be quite content to go on for years "enjoying poor health," or "complaining of feeling well," as the honest negro mammy put it. They neglect the body and with a curious kind of resignation live meekly with numerous ailments and disorders. A discerning man once said that he made it a rule never to greet any acquaintance with the usual, "How are you," because that was a signal for an inglorious recital of pet bodily ills. Many people fall back on their bodily weakness as their only method of attracting attention to themselves and getting sympathy. Why should we pride ourselves on a run-down body, when we would not think of boasting about shiftless housekeeping and bad sanitation, or reckless expenditures.

There are many, too, who think that giving thought to the body degrades the idealism of the soul. In exalting the life of the spirit they deny the claims of the body and ignore its protests and warnings, refusing to recognize it. Sooner or later the body collects everything that is due it with interest. We never live the complete life when we leave out of consideration any important fact in experience. Jesus recognized the perfect unity of body, mind, and spirit and always began to help people at the point of their greatest need. His concern for the health of those about Him has been too long unnoticed by those who follow Him.

Our states of mind leave their mark upon our bodies. We have watched lines of care etched on people's foreheads by anxious minds. We have seen shoulders bent by discouragement and faces paled by fear. We now are beginning to see, even more clearly, the effects of our thinking on diseases, and weakness which lays us aside for years. We long to be well, but we are in such bondage to our mental states that we cannot change our condition.

For some of us the battle for health has been made hard by our parents. They took the line of least resistance and yielded to our childish clamor for late hours, unwholesome food and uncontrolled living, until our bodies got the best of us and have forced their attentions upon us with pain, nerves, and helplessness. Our right to be well has been taken from us by those who were responsible for our training in earthly experience.

It is God's will that our spirit should control our mind and body and use them for the carrying out of God's purposes. Therefore if we give into God's hands the mastery of our spirit and train ourselves to be skillful in using the laws which control the mind and body, we have the right to expect an ever larger measure of health.

The right to be well lies largely in our hands, like the right to be a musician. My spirit may love music and desire it intensely, and have an ear for it; but unless I am willing to study the laws of harmony and train my fingers to respond to my desires, I cannot have what I have a right to have.

We know that Jesus was so perfectly one with the Father of all life that power vibrated through Him, giving health to those who were sick and helpless. He expected His disciples also to heal the sick because He told them explicitly to do so when He sent them out. Jesus Christ is the elder brother of a new race of men and women who are to be victorious over the flesh and live by the laws of the spirit.

What the full achievements of the spirit are to be we know not now, but we may expect larger results in proportion to our intelligent faith and our determination to meet the condition.

God has given us the priceless privilege of working with Him in the creation of our spiritual powers. Most of us would like to sit down and see God work wonders for us without any effort on our part. Many blessings of life come that way, like the rain and sunshine. It is through the prayer of faith, plus our best effort, that the great personal gifts come. A father's money will not give his son an education without years of study by the boy himself. My right to be well is a sacred trust; but I am responsible for acting upon all the wisdom God has already given through past experience. God can only work miracles for people who are doing their utmost to bring about an answer to their prayer. The laws of health cannot be ignored. If I put my hand into the fire, its consuming energy will warn me through pain, and recovery will follow the orderly process of nature's laws, and will take time. The world is not fool-proof. We are put in the midst of forces which may destroy us or be used to work out weighty destinies. The part of us that is material must conform to the laws of the material world and its perfection depends upon the wisdom with which our living spirit controls the situation.

We are finding that our spirit can govern the health of the body much more fully than we have ever supposed. What the limit is to be, no one knows now, but we may be sure that a perfect union with God will do more than a skeptical world imagines. At least we dare not settle down in despair over any bodily condition, for perhaps through it God waits to reveal Himself to us in answer to our trust. "The things which are impossible with men are possible with God."

FOR STUDY AND THOUGHT

Know ye not that your body is a temple of the Holy Ghost which is in you, which ye have from God? and ye are not your own: for ye were bought with a price: glorify God therefore in your body. *I Cor. 6 : 19–20.*

But put ye on the Lord Jesus Christ, and make not provision for the flesh, to fulfil the lusts thereof. *Rom. 13 : 14.*

But if the Spirit of him that raised up Jesus from the dead dwelleth in you, he that raised up Christ Jesus from the dead shall quicken also your mortal bodies through his Spirit that dwelleth in you. *Rom. 8 : 11.*

"The secret of perpetual youth is the power of growth," writes Dean Bennett of Chester Cathedral. The tree lives as long as it puts forth new branches. Its power to do so lies in the roots of its life. It does no good to treat the bark and wood of the tree if its roots and leaves no longer draw life from the earth and air. In human beings also, the health of the body depends on the life of the mind and spirit. If, as modern science suggests, our body is a universe of whirling electrons held together by the life spirit, then there is the greatest significance in these words of Paul about our body being the temple of the Holy Spirit of God.

The phenomena of physical youth and growth cover only one quarter of our earthly experience. During the other three quarters, the life of the body is largely controlled by the growth of the mind and spirit. If we disregard the laws which control this inner life, the life of the body will deteriorate far more rapidly than Nature meant it to do. The great battle of life consists in an incessant struggle between the mind and the flesh in order that the mind may keep its supremacy and control the life of the body. The body tends to pull downward, to degenerate, to be a drag on the life of the mind and spirit. The only hope for it lies in the strong control of the mind which can hold it to its best. When the limitless power of God's Spirit comes into us to reinforce our mind and spirit, the body is held in a central control which keeps the billions of electrons from becoming chaotic and manifesting their riots in the disturbance of physical functions; thus bringing on disease.

If this is true why then, asks someone, are Christians as liable to illness as others? Because for many generations Christians have been centered in their faith on heaven rather than on realizing the truth of these words of St. Paul. They have regarded the body as a limitation rather than an opportunity for the practice of spiritual power. We have been like a man who reads books on athletics and rejoices in them but dies of tuberculosis because he has never exercised or rejoiced in the outdoor athletic life. The life of the spirit related to the life of the body is the great teaching which is needed by the mass of those who glory in the triumph of Christ and yet never think of using the same power which He gave us to do mighty works in that physical realm.

The situation is worse than mere failure to relate the indwelling Spirit of God to the life of our bodies. We deliberately disobey the basic moral laws by which the health of the body is safeguarded and set up an opposition to the rule of the Spirit. Living in compartments is not possible. From the centre of the heart to the periphery of the skin there is one continuous life interrelated and interdependent. The control must come from within.

The word is clear: if the Spirit of Jesus Christ is living within us why should it be thought strange that our mortal bodies should be quickened to health by this presence of God within us. It may take time for the spirit to overcome the long years of neglect for which we are responsible, but every sufferer in the flesh ought to make *sure* that in no way he is short-circuiting the current of power in his life by strengthening the hold of the flesh. It takes time, too, to train the mind in faith and to educate our soul in the discovery and use of the Spirit. It will never be any easier to begin than to-day. Some of us may be hoping for some supernatural trick which will "cast a spell" for us over any " ill that flesh is heir to."

There is no magic phrase; there is something far more wonderful — a possibility to realize in ourselves the promise of Jesus, "He that believeth on Me, the works that I do shall he do also." Is belief credulity or the conviction which results from understanding and experience? Let us begin now to understand and live, in all smallest details, the conscious Christian experience.

> O God, Thou art indeed the Guardian of our life, the Giver of strength and health. Help us to reverence the body for Thy sake; may we keep it a sacred house for Thy Spirit. Refresh us daily with Thy mercies so that we may use all our powers to glorify Thee. *Amen.*

THE HUMAN ELEMENT IN ILL-HEALTH

Most of us are personally responsible for the beginnings of our ill-health. Through our habits of thinking and ways of life we have set influences at work which slowly but surely lower the tone of the body and cripple its powers of resistance to disease. We all have our pet points of view which have grown up with us and are such an intimate part of our personality that we cannot see ourselves as others see us. We have so many good reasons for thinking as we do, and living as we do, that we are quite likely to feel that there is little use in attempting any fundamental change in our temperament. It will be our loss if we do not take ourselves in hand seriously and make sure that nothing in us hinders our abundant health.

First let us ask ourselves whether we tend to the negative in our viewpoint on life. What is the natural attitude toward new suggestions and ideas? Do we say, "It cannot be done! I don't believe it! It doesn't appeal to me. I am sure I never could do that. I am sure I shall fail." In other words, are we more inclined to see difficulties than opportunities in our daily experience? If we have this kind of negative temperament we shall soon discover that we have become incapable of enthusiasm and that the fires of vitality are burning low. Suspicion, cynicism, doubt and despair will creep into our hearts before we are aware of it, and our physical health will slump. Some people with negative minds will read these pages and say to themselves, "There is nothing in it; it's pure poppycock." Watch out, those of you who think this — for before long you will lose the vigor in your step and the light in your eye and you will remind your friends that you are utterly worn out. Begin now to change your temperament. Let your spirit be lifted up and not dragged down by every small experience! See what a difference it will make in your relation to others.

Our false standards undercut our health. We feel that we must keep up with the demands of others, even though we have no honest right to do so. Many of us have a false sense of pride which pushes us to the breaking point. We then spend sleepless hours in anxiety about how we shall meet our obligations. Living beyond our means, undertaking more than we can do well, appearing to be what we are not, create a state of insincerity which hides the face of the Christ from us and leaves us a prey to worry. Many chronic diseases come on the heels of worry, and all the doctors and best cures will avail nothing unless we face our double life and begin to live in truth and honesty. It takes courage, but it is the price of health.

There is also a vicious circle connecting a worried mind and a sensitive body. Anxiety causes disease and disease in turn causes more anxiety. Each makes the other worse. Then we act and react upon ourselves until we are helpless. Unless the shock of some new experience takes our attention from ourselves, there is no hope save in God. It is He who holds us in life and all our future is in His keeping. His mercies fail not. There is no relief save to go to Him as a little child in the loving confidence that Jesus taught us and let Him take away anxiety from us. Faith in God's word will release us from depression and give nature a chance to build up health again. In any case, however, we need to strengthen the connection between ourselves and God, for He is the one fact with which we must reckon, both on earth and in the realm beyond.

There is yet another element in the situation. The greatest force which undermines health is the spirit of fear. Most of us live in bondage to it in some way or other, and yet it takes from us all mental vision and creative ability, and keeps the body from functioning in health. Fear is the most terrible slavery. Some of us fear lest disasters will overtake our loved ones. Some mothers live in such constant fear for their children that they are incapable of any intellectual growth or achievement. Men grow old before their time because of their fear of poverty. Many men live in such fear of losing their jobs that in the end they do lose them through consequent ill-health. Diseases often become epidemic because people fear them. There is no doubt that much of the nervous depression of later middle age is due to a fear of approaching disability and death.

The spirit of fear is really a distrust of the loving purposes of God. For countless generations those who have lived closest to God have all had the same experience of the prophet who said, "Behold God is my salvation. I will trust and be not afraid." They knew that conscious sin was the only enemy of peace that they needed to recognize. If they were rebellious against the divine laws of God which were written in their hearts, they knew they had everything to fear because they had cut themselves off from their source of help. Sin always separates the heart from God and His love. When sin enters, fear enters also. Through the life and death of Jesus we know what the heart of God is like and may draw near in full confidence that God forgives and restores us to Himself in a relation of love. When He thus saves us from ourselves, we too can trust, and fear nothing.

The truth is, we do not believe sufficiently in a loving heavenly Father. What new health might come to us if at the beginning of each day we should repeat the words of the Psalms audibly and thoughtfully ten times, until we sense the meaning in every fibre of our being.

"Bless the Lord, O my soul;
And all that is within me, bless His holy name.
Bless the Lord, O my soul,
And forget not all his benefits;
Who forgiveth all thine iniquities;
Who healeth all thy diseases;
Who redeemeth thy life from destruction;
Who crowneth thee with loving kindness and tender mercies;
Who satisfieth thy mouth with good things;
So that Thy youth is renewed like the eagle." *Psa. 103.*

> "For the love of God is broader
> Than the measure of man's mind,
> And the heart of the Eternal
> Is most wonderfully kind.
> If our love were but more simple,
> We should take him at his word,
> And our lives would be all sunshine
> In the sweetness of our God."
>
> *Frederick William Faber.*

FOR STUDY AND THOUGHT

I beseech you therefore, brethren, by the mercies of God, to present your bodies a living sacrifice, holy, acceptable to God, which is your reasonable service. And be not fashioned according to this world: but be ye transformed by the renewing of your mind, that ye may prove what is the good and acceptable and perfect will of God. *Rom. 12 : 1-2.*

Now therefore hear ye the word of the Lord, O remnant of Judah: thus saith the Lord of hosts, the God of Israel, If ye wholly set your faces to enter into Egypt, and go to sojourn there: then it shall come to pass, that the sword, which ye fear, shall overtake you there in the land of Egypt, and the famine, whereof ye are afraid, shall follow hard after you there in Egypt; and there ye shall die. *Jer. 42 : 15-16.*

That ye put away, as concerning your former manner of life, the old man, which waxeth corrupt after the lusts of deceit; and that ye be renewed in the spirit of your mind, and put on the new man, which after God hath been created in righteousness and holiness of truth. Wherefore, putting away falsehood, speak ye truth each one with his neighbour: for we are members one of another. *Eph. 4 : 22-25.*

As far back as the time of Solomon the proverb runs: "The curse that is causeless cometh not," (*Prov. 26 : 2*) and Eliphaz reminded Job that affliction cometh not forth out of the dust, neither doth trouble spring out of the ground, (*Job 5 : 6*). There are causes in the spirit of fear, which is the herald of many diseases. Dr. Hadfield says in one of his books, "If fear were abolished from modern life, the work of the psychotherapist would be nearly gone." The mental states of fear include general pessimism, nervousness, despondency, worry, irritability, indecision, restlessness, cowardice, suspicion and a host of other kindred ills. Some of these states of mind we may recognize in ourselves; others may be so habitual that they are subconscious and almost intuitive.

St. Paul strikes the nail on the head when he pleads, "Be ye transformed by the renewing of your mind;" by getting a new point of view of life. In other words he is counseling us to cultivate those states of mind which are the exact opposite of the manifestations of fear. Every mental state under the reign of fear distorts sensations. We undervalue normal sensations and exaggerate abnormal sensations. Every mental power suffers. The imagination is filled with emotions and images which are diseased. Even the memory becomes unreliable and untrustworthy. Some of the people who read this book will be unable to take its suggestions seriously because their minds are incapable of mental assimilation after long years steeped in fearfulness. What many a man and woman needs is a *new* way of looking at everything. If this were not so the religious message of the centuries of Old and New Testament wisdom would not have reiterated *ad infinitum* the words," Fear not." It is significant that we are told to offer our *"bodies* a living sacrifice," as a "spiritual worship" because the body is the wax on which the thoughts of the mind are imprinted.

Fears have a habit of materializing and bringing to pass in experience what has been dreaded in the mind. Even so long ago as in the days of Jeremiah the prophet this truth was recognized. Notice that the culmination of their fears was to come, "if you wholly set your faces to enter into Egypt;" that is if one decides to go back on all the life of faith and return to the bondage of fear. Egypt represented to the Jew, fear, slavery, despair. Our Egypt is the settled depression into which we sink when we decide that there is no use in venturing out in faith; that our condition is "peculiar" and we are tired of struggling. Fear is really a faith in what we *do not want,* and as such has a positive power to bring that which we do not want to pass. We have it in our power to decide whether we will create what we do not want or what we do want.

The only way to be delivered from fear is to practice faith. When the weathervane points to the clear west it cannot point to the rainy east. The laws of the mind which many people hail as new are as old as the human race. Deceitful desires are our undoing. Our fearful minds fool us with suspicion, prejudices, and anxieties, until we cannot think straight, and an enfeebled body in turn holds our mind in bondage. We need to put away our old thought forms and get a new point of view. We do not have to change our bodies geographically, though sometimes that makes it easier for our minds to change; the real victory comes through attention on new goals, new ways of looking at old things, new courage to take ourselves in hand and venture everything on the stake that the wisdom of God and His point of view is the only right way of life.

God of my life: what time I am afraid I will put my trust in Thee.
Amen.

THE WAY TO HEALTH

Our particular bodily needs may vary from time to time, but there are certain attitudes of mind which must become habitual before we can expect any help. We have certain responsibilities to fulfil before we can exercise intelligent faith. Chief among these stands honesty in facing our situation. We must be governed not by our fears, but by our actual knowledge. There are so many things we suspect to be true without knowing them to be so.

> "Some of your hurts you have cured
> And the sharpest you still have survived;
> But what torment of grief you endured,
> From evils which never arrived."

All of us have had experiences like this. We are so afraid of what we may have to meet that we do not face facts. A haunting fear of some possible bodily condition is far harder to bear than the actual truth. There is a therapeutic value in truth which often rallies all our latent powers and restores us. An intelligent understanding of our body and its mechanism prevents many a disaster. A competent engineer knows his engine and knows its power and limitations; whereas we who are in command of a far more complex organism often presume to direct it in ignorance of its laws. Even though God meant our spirit to control our body, He has established certain methods and laws which we dare not ignore without woeful results.

When we begin to study these laws we shall discover that there are causes back of all effects, and that we cannot deal with conditions until we know what caused them. God has placed us in an orderly world where things do not happen by chance. If we would have perfect health we must deal with the source of our troubles. Some causes may yet be hid from our knowledge, but in most cases they can be traced back to some way of living in which we are the chief cause of our undoing.

It is at this point that the work of the physician comes in. The years of experience with disease have yielded much wisdom which is a sacred trust handed down through medical training. The man who discovers in the laboratory the natural laws of health is discovering God's purposes as much as another who discovers the laws of the mind and spirit. God does not need to work a miracle to feed us,

117

because we have learned wisdom in the use of what nature has provided for our nourishment. Neither does He need to work wonders when there are means of help for us in the medical knowledge available for the world's use. What we now need is to learn how to coöperate with the wisdom and the laws of health by giving the full assistance of a mind and spirit which can voice the suggestions which our bodies will obey. We must prepare the way for God to work by utilizing revealed wisdom and doing all in our power to help Him. "Working together with Him, we intreat that ye receive not the grace of God in vain." There are prophets of God in the medical realm just as in the realm of prayer and the preaching of God's truth, and they give themselves sacrificially for truth that will bless humanity. When Walter Reed gave his life in the discovery of the cause of yellow fever he preached a truth that has saved the health of untold thousands, and he is only one of many who have loved truth more than life and have cheerfully accepted martyrdom that we might live. However, like all men, they are limited in wisdom and can only lead us as far as human power can take us. There yet remains all the limitless power of God which can do beyond what we know to do, in accordance with our faith and His purpose for us.

In training ourselves in faith we have other preparatory work to do. Our past experiences have so often meant defeat instead of victory that we do not have much hope that the present or future will be any better. We therefore lose our enthusiasm and settle back in stodgy indifference or rebellion. Such a condition makes faith impossible, and "without faith it is impossible to please God" or work out our salvation. There is no reason why the past should prevent new experiences now. Every day is a new day; every week we change, and new conditions arise. Why then should we not keep our minds in an expectant attitude, and be alert for new manifestations of our Father's love. Expectancy is the atmosphere in which faith grows. We can change indifference to expectancy by our act of will: then we shall be awake and ready to lay hold on the power of God.

Faith is confidence in a loving Father who is concerned for the good of his children. We can count on Him as the ever-watchful friend waiting to bless us. An intelligent faith is a trust which is based on the knowledge of God's purposes and methods of work and on the relationship we have to him. This springs not from our desires, but from the teachings of Christ and the experiences of His disciples. The human mind can make powerful suggestions to the body which will influence it toward health, but the same mind filled with living faith in the power of Christ can do infinitely more. The scientific world has proved the power of mental suggestion as a healing force, but the realm of faith goes beyond scientific proof and is dependent upon our intimate connections with the heart of God. No one can reduce mother love to a formula; its powers vary with the need. No more can we compress the free heart of God into a law: it transcends all reason.

Therefore, in coming to God for health, we are coming to a Father who has our whole life in mind and knows what will fit us for the special work he sent us here to do. It is not His will that our body should limit the spirit, or the spirit limit the body. He sees the end from the beginning and we can trust Him to set us free. It may take time to work out the necessary changes in us in order that we may use rightly the health we seek. Mary prayed that she might find the dead body of Jesus in order that she might anoint it. Her prayer was denied because there was something better in store for her — the vision of a living Lord.

FOR STUDY AND THOUGHT

And Moses said unto the children of Israel, See, the Lord hath called by name Bezalel the son of Uri, the son of Hur, of the tribe of Judah: and he hath filled him with the Spirit of God, in wisdom, in understanding, and in knowledge, and in all manner of workmanship; and to devise cunning works, to work in gold, and in silver, and in brass, and in cutting of stones for settings, and in carving of wood, to work in all manner of cunning workmanship. And he hath put in his heart that he may teach, both he, and Oholiab, the son of Ahisamach, of the tribe of Dan. Them hath he filled with wisdom of heart, to work all manner of workmanship, of the engraver, and of the cunning workman, and of the embroiderer, in blue, and in purple, in scarlet, and in fine linen, and of the weaver, even of them that do any workmanship, and of those that devise cunning works. *Exodus 35 : 30–35.*

What doth it profit, my brethren, if a man say he hath faith, but have not works? can that faith save him? If a brother or sister be naked, and in lack of daily food, and one of you say unto them, Go in peace, be ye warmed and filled; and yet ye give them not the things needful to the body; what doth it profit? Even so faith, if it have not works, is dead in itself. *James 2 : 14–17.*

Most of us have been trained to divide life into two mutually exclusive compartments; the religious and secular. We have been taught to believe that the Spirit of God was especially with those who were engaged in prayer, preaching and Christian service, while outside of this favored group, people struggled on as best they might by the unaided light of their minds. This has an immense significance when we discuss the way to health because it has seemed impossible to relate the power of God to bodily need apart from some miracle performed in answer to prayer. Thus many people depend upon the direct act of faith in God according to some religious system as the only legitimate way of caring for their bodies.

We are beginning to see now, what Moses knew thousands of years ago, that the Spirit of God is the direct inspiration of *all* creative work, gold work, stone cutting, wood carving, embroidering, and all manner of skilful workmanship. The reverent search of the scientist, in astronomy, physics, medicine, and surgery, is directed and inspired by the self same Spirit Who also reveals the truth of the Bible and the sense of God in His church. The sincere scientist knows he is being illumined and aided by inspired ideas, but he has not dared to call them religious because the world has labeled his vocation a secular pursuit.

The work of the universe needs the honest coöperation of all of us to reveal the manifold wisdom of God. The man who searches out patiently the orderly processes by which God administers the life of the body has divine wisdom to reveal to those of us who do not know it. He may be as much the voice of God for the body as the clergy may be the voice of God to the soul. As far as the mind and spirit control the body, the counsels of religion are bound to be effective for those diseases which come from the spirit of fear, anxiety, etc. There remains, however, a realm of organic trouble which is controlled, in so far as it can be, by medical skill. In this realm the mind is thus reinforced by the wisdom revealed through other experienced minds.

The questions which St. James asks are pertinent to this subject. He teaches us to believe that the prayer of faith will save the sick, and at the same time links up faith with works. God does not treat us like tiny babies to be taken up and cared for in answer to our inarticulate cries, nor does He make us so omniscient and powerful that we can live independent of the help of others. He makes us dependent on one another and expects our faith to be reinforced by every bit of help we can summon to answer our own prayers. To pray for the poor and not share our abundance with them is mockery. To expect God to heal our body and refuse to use the abundance of help at our disposal is presumption.

There will come times when all we can do, and all that others can do for us, will fail to help. When that limit is reached, we yet have the right to go to God with a faith that He will meet our need in our way, if that be His way. Otherwise He gives us the insight into His far-reaching purpose, which will satisfy our heart.

> Our Father, Thy loving kindness doth not fail, nor dost Thou forget us in our weakness. Help us to dwell so near to Thee that our strength may be renewed and our anxiety swallowed up in peace. Show us Thy purpose and help us to trust Thy love even though we walk in darkness. Through Jesus Christ our Lord. *Amen.*

THE SECRET OF SELF-MASTERY

So long as we live, we have to struggle for the mastery of self. It is an endless fight, but there are certain methods of warfare which insure success in keeping the mind and body in health. Chief among these is our responsibility for keeping up the normal life of our body. This involves eating, drinking, sleeping, and exercise. These primitive requirements are vital to self-mastery, for they tone up the body and give it poise. Many diseases come because we are careless of these elemental needs. We overeat or undereat, turn night into day, let our muscles become flabby, and then wonder why we have ill-health and over-wrought nerves. We cannot break the laws of health and then expect God to set us right by supernatural power. If these four daily needs of the body are supplied intelligently, we shall prove our ability for self-control and find it easier to fix the mind on the important work of life. Indigestion, fatigue and poor circulation have ruined many a promising career and wrecked health. It is no wonder that Paul said "whether, therefore ye eat, or drink, or whatever ye do, do all to the glory of God."

One of the beautiful laws of life concerns effort and relaxation; the divine way to free us from all strain. It is the rhythm of activity and rest, work and play to which the body is adapted. The intervals of rest and play are the precious moments when what we have striven for in activity becomes a part of us. It is said that we learn to skate in summer even though the actual performance occurs in winter. We solve our problems in sleep after the struggles of the day. It is foolish indeed to think that, in our feverish haste, we can change the rhythm of life by extending the work and omitting the rest. We cheat ourselves of all mental growth and break the harmony in the body until it turns against us and compels us to heed it. It is the fever of getting, the fever of outdoing others, the fever of ambition, that defeats itself in the end, and kills the spiritual nature. We know it is wrong because it contradicts the divine plan. It will be hard for some of us to swing back into the rhythm of peace, health, and power, but unless we do so there will be no possibility of lasting self-mastery.

There is another secret, too, which will help us in this fight for self-control. The more we think of ourselves and consider ourselves seriously the more self-centered we become. Instead of mastering our ego, it masters us. It demands more of our attention and before we know it we have an ingrowing sense of our importance. Some remedy must be found to divert us from ourselves. It is most often achieved through service for others. If we can enter heartily into the sorrows and experiences of others who need us, we shall find new powers of self-control. A man who was sinking into melancholia because of his pity for his own sorrows was induced to assist at a big Christmas dinner for poor newsboys. The sight of those children, who were facing life gaily in spite of poverty and rags, absorbed his attention and he decided to help them through some social service. Before the winter was over he had found peace and health, and his old mental powers. He discovered the eternal truth that our health depends on our having some interest outside of ourselves. Then our self-control becomes perfected through unselfishness.

There are times, also, when a change of environment helps us to master ourselves. This does not necessarily mean a geographical change, but a mental change brought about by study, and the use of leisure to create new interests. Health requires enthusiasm and if our present situation does not create it, we must add some new element to it. A new line of reading, a new training in some unfamiliar work will give us the mental buoyancy we need and solve our health problem. We dare not settle down in boredom lest our spirit lose its control over the mind and body. An environment which is too perfect is boredom. We need contacts in life to keep up courage.

All of these secrets of self-mastery are overshadowed by the supreme method of simple childlike prayer, and study of the Bible. The deepest suggestions are made to the mind when we are quiet and alone in the presence of God. Egotism melts away and the mind unburdens itself of its anxieties. There is nothing like the habit of prayer to bring health and power and a sense of relaxation.

When we come into the presence of God our thought must be centred on Him and not on ourselves and our petty little experiences. They will melt away in the light of His countenance. One great need in prayer is that God's love should come into our heart and fill the mind with holy suggestions which will lift us up above our weaknesses. Let us make a genuine experiment in prayer and as often as possible each day become quiet within while we breathe rhythmically and relax as we pray.

> Every day and every hour,
> Father, I breathe in Thy life-giving power —
>> Power to love,
>> Power to be pure,
>> Power to be well,
>> Power to endure.

As we consciously breathe in the vital life of God, let us in the same consciousness let go of our enmities and prejudices and breathe in love; let us turn from earthly desires, and breathe in purity, let us also relax until the vitality of God reaches the limit of our bodily need; then let us renew our strength in God until we are well able to endure whatever may be His purpose for our day.

If we are faithful in this prayer and surround it with the atmosphere of the thoughts and truths of the Gospels, a new power and victory will surely be ours.

> Father in Thy mysterious Presence kneeling
> Fain would our souls feel all Thy kindling love;
> For we are weak, and need some deep revealing
> Of trust, and strength, and calmness from above.
>
> *S. Johnson 1846.*

FOR STUDY AND THOUGHT

All things are lawful; but all things are not expedient. All things are lawful, but all things edify not. Let no man seek his own, but each his neighbour's good. Whatsoever is sold in the shambles, eat, asking no question for conscience sake; for the earth is the Lord's, and the fulness thereof. If one of them that believe not biddeth you to a feast, and ye are disposed to go; whatsoever is set before you, eat, asking no question for conscience sake. But if any man say unto you, This hath been offered in sacrifice, eat not, for his sake that shewed it, and for conscience sake: Conscience, I say, not thine own, but the other's; for why is my liberty judged by another conscience? If I by grace partake, why am I evil spoken of for that which I give thanks? Whether therefore ye eat, or drink or whatsoever ye do, do all to the glory of God. *I Cor. 10 : 23–31.*

Therefore let us also, seeing we are compassed about with so great a cloud of witnesses, lay aside every weight, and the sin which doth so easily beset us, and let us run with patience the race that is set before us, looking unto Jesus the author and perfecter of our faith, who for the joy that was set before him endured the cross, despising shame, and hath sat down at the right hand of the throne of God. For consider him that hath endured such gainsaying of sinners against themselves, that ye wax not weary, fainting in your souls. Ye have not yet resisted unto blood, striving against sin. *Heb. 12 : 1–4.*

Know ye not that they which run in a race run all, but one receiveth the prize? Even so run, that ye may attain. And every man that striveth in the games is temperate in all things. Now they do it to receive a corruptible crown; but we an incorruptible. I therefore so run, as not uncertainly, so fight I, as not beating the air: but I buffet my body and bring it into bondage: lest by any means, after that I have preached to others, I myself should be rejected. *I Cor. 9 : 24–27.*

The good is often the foe of the best. There are countless things which are right in themselves but wrong for us if they defeat the main purpose of life. It may be right to read a book, but wrong to do so if it interferes with a responsibility which I have undertaken. Self-mastery consists in making decisions which will further the realization of life's ideal.

Every detail of life hangs on its purpose. Eating and drinking become religious acts when our faith is reaching out for God-like powers. Nutrition builds up the cells of the body and creates the nervous energy by which we live, and achieve our career. There is a right standard for each one of us. Malnutrition causes disease and mental weakness, and gluttony also causes disease and spiritual degeneration. Even sleeping and exercise influence the spirit. There is no possibility for victorious faith unless the whole self is organized as an ally with our spirit. Chronic liver trouble creates a brown soul. "Prepare ye the way for God: make His paths straight" might well be applied to our daily habits of bodily living. We must learn to part with our pet ailments and indulgences or our spirit will be enslaved. With women the temptation to be subnormal in weight, and anæmic to boot, will sooner or later take its toll from mental and spiritual powers.

The remembrance of all the men and women of the past who have won victories through faith, ought to be an incentive to self-mastery for everyone of us, as it was to the writer to the Hebrews. Before we can rise to heights of faith there are remembrances and pet sins to be laid aside though they cling to us. The sacrifice of these things is easy because of the joy which is before us. Self-denial for the sake of self-denial has no virtue; but the scientific ordering of our life because of a greatly desired goal is a rewarding experience. Everything that loosens the hold of the earthly pull makes one that much more able to possess the powers of Christ.

The world is full of air beaters who fight to no purpose. They are the nervous invalids whose thoughts revolve uncertainly around themselves, aimless and self-indulgent. They are also the lazy souls who are not in the race for *anything*. They put off self-mastery until it is too late. They are permanent losers.

Too much cannot be said about the importance of fixing one's eyes on the character of Jesus. It is not enough to be familiar with the historic facts of His life: what this generation needs is to study the significance of His life in the light of our mistakes in thinking and living. The psychology of His teaching is far richer in wisdom than anything yet written. He is the only hope, and the way out of all our difficulties. When we pray we know that we are lifted up into companionship with Him. If we make Him our ideal, we shall be in unity with all others in the world who see in this human incarnation an opportunity to "fashion anew the body of our humiliation that it may be conformed to the body of His glory, according to the working whereby He is able even to subject all things unto Himself." (*Phil. 3 : 21*).

> O Thou victorious Christ whom death could not hold grant us Thy strength that we too may live in triumph. Thou hast been tempted in all points as we are, and art touched with the feeling of our infirmities; help us in coming to Thee to find strength for our weakness and shelter from temptation. May the power which dwells in Thee quicken our bodies and our minds that we may glorify Thee on the earth; and this we ask for Thy name's sake. *Amen.*

GOD'S WAYS OF WORKING

THE LAW OF FAITH

There are few subjects which inspire as many differences of opinion among religious people as the spiritual law of faith; and yet it is fundamental to every relationship with God. We are told that "without faith it is impossible to please God," therefore it is important that we know how to possess it and how to use it.

There are several ways of describing faith. If we apply the word to the realm of intellectual convictions we mean belief: if we apply faith to persons we mean trust. One is an intellectual process, and the other is a personal relationship. When we are dealing with faith in God, both processes are involved. In the relation of our spirit to Him in loving trust we use faith, and as we observe the laws by which He works in the world we create a faith which becomes part of our intellectual belief; — these beliefs become guides for our conduct; rules for living and a standard by which we measure values in the world. Everyone has a set of beliefs which are law and gospel to him. Faith in those mental conclusions represents what we call, broadly speaking; an education.

The word conclusion suggests a certain characteristic of faith; viz., — its freedom from unrest. When truths are being argued within our minds, we do not know whether or not to believe in them. Our faith is replaced by doubt, and unrest. Perfect faith predicates always a quiet confidence and comes after the battle is over.

There is also another important aspect of faith. It is that fact of the mind or spirit which greets the unseen with a shout. It is that part of us which really gives the victory. It is that which enjoys the reward before we actually have it. In other words faith determines the perspective of the soul.

Without faith we would have no great perspective in life. It is an impressive fact that as one works in the world, one sees very few who could be called men of faith. Most folk work with a very narrow perspective of faith. It is a venture into the unknown, in confidence that the future will justify all expectation.

It takes courage to live a life of faith because while one end of the ladder rests on the tangible ground, as Jacob saw it in his vision, the other end reaches up to heaven far beyond our power to see. Faith involves a scale of values which are beyond the near-sighted vision of most people, and widens our horizon.

Faith also acts upon the mind as a dynamic. This is a familiar truth. We have all seen people depressed and hopeless in the midst of anxieties and perhaps a few hours later we have seen those same people, with no change in circumstances, buoyant and hopeful. The only cause for the change was the faith which helped them to grasp future certainty even though the present warranted no such hope. The point to emphasize is that the change of spirit brought by faith enabled them to change the circumstances. It is usually ourselves and not our environment that must be changed if victory is to be won. It is well this is so, for thus we become independent of circumstances and superior to them. Faith is the power which gives wings to our spirit and lifts us above the world of stress and change.

Perhaps some of us imagine that this quality of spirit is a special gift not meant for any but chosen souls. Because it is so rarely found we may argue that it is difficult to obtain. This is far from true. Its rarity comes more from our stupidity than from our lack of capacity. It is so simple that we stumble over it.

Christian faith involves taking Jesus at His word and accepting the fatherhood of God as a blessed fact. We put our trust in Him and believe that as He has been a real Father to millions in the past, so He will be to us. We take the position of a little child in simplicity, and teachableness and find that this simple trust is in itself an act of faith.

There is a real connection between faith and love. When we love, we have faith. It is natural to trust the one we love. It is natural, too, to believe in the point of view of the loved one, and to revise our mental conclusions in the light of love. One who really loves Jesus does not find it hard to believe in Him and to have faith in His teachings. There is a belief which is as impersonal as 2 x 2 and affects our lives as little as the multiplication table. Many religious folk put great value upon this kind of reasoned belief in facts and call it faith. This is why so few mountains are removed at a word. The true faith is a living, aspiring spirit, piercing clouds of doubt and reaching heaven at a bound. A little child may have it and all men and women of humble heart may use it. Faith unlocks the mysteries of God. "Lord, increase our faith."

"Turn you to the stronghold, ye prisoners of hope; even to-day do I declare that I will render double unto Thee." *Zech. 9, 12.*

FOR STUDY AND THOUGHT

Now faith is the assurance of things hoped for, the proving of things not seen. *Heb. 11 : 1.*

Ye men of Israel, why marvel ye at this man? or why fasten ye your eyes on us, as though by our own power or godliness we had made him to walk? The God of Abraham and of Isaac, and of Jacob, the God of our fathers, hath glorified his Servant Jesus; whom ye delivered up, and denied before the face of Pilate, when he had determined to release him. And by faith in his name hath his name made this man strong, whom ye behold and know: yea, the faith which is through him hath given him this perfect soundness in the presence of you all. *Acts 3 : 12-13, 16.*

And when he was come into the house, the blind men came to him: and Jesus saith unto them, Believe ye that I am able to do this? They say unto him, Yea, Lord. Then touched he their eyes, saying, According to your faith be it done unto you. And their eyes were opened.
Matt. 9 : 28, 29, 30.

The way of faith is the way to health. Faith is that faculty which refuses to believe in chaos and which knows that at the heart of the universe is a Fatherly God who works, without shadow of changing, according to beneficent laws. Faith stakes everything on this conception of God and thus knows in advance that what it hopes for is really true. When people believed in a chaotic world in which one could never be sure of anything there could be no assuring faith. Dean Bennett describes faith as "our faculty of dynamic, anticipatory thought." The laws of the universe are so orderly and so sure that we can anticipate them in advance and adjust our life according to them.

Faith is not a religious faculty alone; it is in all of us and we use it all the time. We have faith in our bank as well as faith in God and we have the same peace of mind when we exercise this special gift. It is our most powerful faculty and therefore best enables us to reach out to God. Psychologists have discovered that when faith and optimism dominate the mind, the brain and nervous system function normally. Physicians have found that faith is a health-promoting faculty, whether the object of faith be God, or a pill. The usefulness of the pill is limited to one kind of disorder; so that it is not a permanent object of trust. If we really believe in a Fatherly God of love, He becomes an object of faith in *all* experiences of life and our faith is justified through the precise working of the laws by which health of spirit and body is possible.

Our faith ought to be a stronger faculty now than in generations ago. Physical science has opened up vast mysteries through the exercise of faith because, even with more confidence than we religious folk show, it resolutely refuses to believe in a chaotic cosmos. The further it proceeds in faith, the wider becomes the application of the laws of God to the detail of our entire life.

Through faith we are able to say, as never before, to the lame, "Rise up and walk." When religion and science really join hands in the quests of faith then will be unfolded such wonders as have never entered into the imagination of man.

Jesus Christ was in fact what we hope to be by faith. His powers become actually ours according to the intelligent reach of our faith. Prof. J. T. Simpson in his "The Spiritual Interpretation of Nature," says, "Christianity gave a new direction to human history. For in Him (Jesus) there came to light and actuality for the first and only time, that for which the whole process from the beginning had evidently been planned, and He is the fulfillment of all that went before." If this be true, then there is no limit to what our faith can bring to pass if we measure up to the completeness of His surrender to the Spirit of God. He asked the blind men if they believed He was able to open their eyes, their faith anticipated His power and accordingly it worked in them.

Faith, then, is a health-producing faculty. It grows by trust in a benevolent universe and especially by confidence in Jesus Christ. Whatever power the mind has over our body to that extent by that law may we have health. If we are consciously or unconsciously breaking other laws which affect our bodies, we shall suffer until we discern them We dare not say that they are beyond the reach of faith for we have not yet measured its height. It is for us to follow the Christ very closely for there is none other to whom we may go.

> Choose for us, God! — nor let our weak preferring
> cheat our poor souls of good Thou hast designed.
>
> *William Henry Burleigh 1868.*

FAITH AS A WAY OF LIFE

There are two ways in which we may go through our years on the earth. We may look upon life as one long struggle to satisfy human desires, or we may look upon our human incarnation as a special commission to accomplish some divine purpose. We may go through all the motions of living, or we may walk by faith. Without faith life is merely a series of disconnected acts. With faith, life is like the close-woven threads of a tapestry revealing a beautiful design.

Faith works both in the realm of the possible and the impossible. In the realm of the possible it becomes a way of daily living. Faith creates all personal relationships and all the higher planes of living. It orders the daily program. You go to the city in faith that the engineer knows how to run his engine, and in faith that your friend will be at the appointed place of meeting. You start your children to school in faith that the teacher will instruct them. Without faith all society and comradeship would disappear and we would be lurking in caves with our hand against every other man.

In the same way we do not live a day without a childlike faith in things. We push a button believing that electricity will light the room, because we have intellectual faith in certain facts which have been discovered. No one lives only on his own experience. We have faith not only in what we have discovered but also in what others have found true. We take their results on trust. Every meal we eat, we eat in faith that people whom we may not know — the milkman, and farmer and manufacturer — are honest. Without fear, we take what they provide.

The scope of faith is constantly widening by experience. The older we grow the more we depend upon our confidence in the relationships of life. The margin of possibility is widened constantly for us. Fifty years ago we put the art of flying in the realm of the impossible. Now we know that the faith of countless men who pushed on in spite of ridicule has been justified in experience and we perform our own miracles as a result of the persistent faith of the pioneers. Through coöperation with faith we do mighty works beyond our full understanding. It brings the zest of adventure, the thrill of creation into our lives.

It seems strange that the spirit of faith which we accept and use in every phase of human experience should be resented by many as a means of discovering God. We question the spiritual realities which faith creates, when we accept without question the human realities revealed by the spirit of faith. When we take faith as a way of life the greatest realities are created. Everything we do has significance, because it helps to make our dreams come true.

Faith makes all work worth while. The carpenter saws and planes the lumber not for physical exercise, but because he dreams of the house he is to create, or the possibilities wrapped up in the money he will receive. We believe in the destiny we desire for our children, or for ourselves, therefore we spend time and money in training and education for the joy set before us. We have faith in love and therefore we cultivate friendships and create a family life and sacrifice ourselves for the sake of it. We sense in some dim way the value of our human life and what it may grow to be; therefore we try out our powers in adventure and ambition and live by the faith we have in our own powers. In fact, without faith we could never know the highest experiences in life.

Why then should we not use this sixth sense in relation to God? There are great discoveries for those who will make a spiritual adventure. There are unexplored paths of power waiting for the feet of that one who will say, "I believe in God, and I believe that he rewards anyone who diligently seeks Him."

In the spiritual realm, faith brings results when we fulfil the necessary conditions. We must know, first, that we are in harmony with the character of God. Jesus taught us to pray "in His name" and therein lies a secret. A name is a symbol of personal identity. Most of us have two names: the name our parents gave us and the character name which the world applies to us. Character shouts the real name. "They say his name is John Smith but he is known around here as Old Grouch," said a boy to a stranger. The character of the man had won for him a new name which was a precise description of his dominant characteristic. The prayer of faith which is answered must be brought in the name of Christ; in the full appreciation of His character. We cannot expect results unless we hold in reverence all those qualities which make the Christ, the radiant outshining of God. He works with those who are in harmony with Him. An honest man will not coöperate with a dishonest man: no more can we expect the rewards of faith and trust unless we are truly one with all the ideals of the heart of God.

We must also know the purposes of God and what he desires us to accomplish. It is utterly foolish to build up our little scheme of life without reference to the great plan. His purpose is bound to be accomplished. It is not good sense to conduct my life as I see fit regardless of God's purposes. If I ally myself with what God wants, the whole pushing power of the universe is behind me and I cannot fail. When self-will rather than the purpose of God pushes us then faith becomes unreasonable wilfulness and cannot work wonders.

It is important that we understand this because our power to achieve results in faith and prayer is at stake. This is why we must go back again and again to the study of the teachings of Jesus. There is no better way in which to know the character and purposes of God. Sometimes we pray and strive to carry out certain ambitions which are dear to us. As time goes on we find that the plot thickens and we are baffled on every side, so that we cannot do what seemed possible. Perhaps we were working at cross purposes with God. If so we need to change our prayer from, "Lord give me this which I so desire," to "Lord what is *Thy* purpose for me?"

> If our love were but more simple,
> We should take Him at His word,
> And our lives would be all sunshine
> In the sweetness of our Lord.   *F. W. Faber 1854.*

FOR STUDY AND THOUGHT

For this cause I bow my knees unto the Father, from whom every family in heaven and on earth is named, that he would grant you, according to the riches of his glory, that ye may be strengthened with power through his Spirit in the inward man; that Christ may dwell in your hearts through faith; to the end that ye, being rooted and grounded in love, may be strong to apprehend with all the saints what is the breadth and length and height and depth, and to know the love of Christ which passeth knowledge, that ye may be filled unto all the fulness of God.

Now unto him that is able to do exceeding abundantly above all that we ask or think, according to the power that worketh in us, unto him be the glory in the church and in Christ Jesus unto all generations for ever and ever. *Amen. Ephesians 3 : 14-21.*

Faith is applied in any realm of life, but some of the objects toward which it is directed are not worth the expenditure of this soul energy. It is possible for faith to be mistaken in its sense of values. A man once said of another, "He believes so much that isn't *so*." Faith may degenerate into weak credulity unless the objects of faith are tested for their true character. Even in the scientific world men have to revise continually their major premises. They base their faith on certain facts and from these frame an hypothesis as a possible guide up the hill of difficulty to the next point of vision. Perhaps before they reach that point, other facts not before realized may necessitate a change in their hypothesis. It is the open-minded willingness to face *all* facts that makes their faith triumphant and opens up new fields of vision. A man of faith must also be a man of humility. A faith which does not widen and find room within it for *all* God's truth is likely to die and turn to prejudice.

When we make Jesus Christ the object of our faith, we have a goal which is worthy of *all* our aspiration. He towers, like the Alps, above the small hills of vision, and we can measure their true importance because their height is relative to that of the shining summit. Without Christ as the perfect standard, we are divided in our ideals and our sense of value becomes unreliable.

Even a faith in Christ which does not go forth in love is valueless. The illustration of the garden which St. Paul used makes this clear. Faith is the upreaching plant which is rooted in love and grows in love and penetrates to the length and breadth and height and depth of love. In other words, the God who is Love dwells in a universe of love and by faith we realize it. Faith gives us the analytical eye: but faith plus love functions with sympathy as well as discernment. Faith is power; but, combined with love, it is also protection.

The life of faith is a life of self-realization. The reason why so many of us fail to achieve satisfying experience is because we are guided by opinions rather than by faith. Opinions are based on a vision of future reality. The architect saw the cathedral in his mind before he drew the plans; Florence Nightingale saw the ministry of nursing before she began its work; Columbus saw land in the West before he set sail on the uncharted ocean. A mother sees the man she desires her child to be while he is yet an infant. Out of these visions of faith came the constructive discoveries of the world. Faith is the *only* way of life that is satisfying.

God meets our asking and thinking with the power to do. He is always urging us to go on beyond our present desires. The measure of accomplishment is not *what we think* but is determined by the *power* which is at work within us. Any business which measures its capacity by what it has done will soon be outstripped by another which *anticipates* the *future* as a present reality. "Where there is no vision the people perish" and faith itself dies. "When the Son of man cometh shall He find faith on the earth?" (*Luke 18 : 18*).

> Our Father, grant me, day by day, the courage to face facts; may I discover in them Thy will for my life, and knowing it, help me to devote myself utterly to its accomplishment regardless of cost o r consequence. Through Jesus Christ, our Lord. *Amen.*

FAITH IN THE REALM OF THE IMPOSSIBLE

The teachings of Jesus urge us continually to higher levels of faith. We were not meant to be content with doing only as well as we have done. We are to reach out to new possibilities like every living thing. Not one of us has exhausted our latent possibilities. We long to have God satisfy certain desires of our heart by the painless method of loving trust. We want Him to work in answer to our faith without our having to toil and suffer in bringing our desires to pass. We forget that "faith apart from works is dead."

It is strange that so many people prefer to degenerate into spiritual parasites, rather than to become creators with God. We are slow to learn the law of life as we see it in the world. We pray "give us this day our daily bread," and yet we know that prayer is not answered unless we plant the seed, cultivate the ground and gather the harvest. Bread is a coöperative gift. God's sunshine, rain and seed plus our cultivation, and mill-grinding, and baking bring the daily bread. It's a blend of what we can do and what we cannot do, God's power added to our work through faith.

As in bread so in other gifts, the possible and impossible are joined. We may never say, "This is my loaf which I made," for without the elements given by God our work would have profited nothing. So there is always beyond the limit of our effort, a realm of humanly impossible. There is that great margin between the limit of human strength and the bounds of God's strength. That margin is infinite and vast and is a place in which faith alone can work. Faith reaching out to the impossible is the only way by which we can reinforce our human strength, and draw from God's infinite resources.

Jesus invites us to enter this realm by faith. He says, "if ye have faith, all things are possible," so limitless are some of His assurances that the ordinary mind is staggered and falls back on the supposition that the age of wonders passed with the time of Christ, or that He never meant them to be taken literally. So many conflicting opinions sway people to-day that it is well to ask what kind of faith inherits the large returns Jesus promised.

It could not be an erratic faith which expects a fantastic display of power at the will of the one who prays. God is too faithful and just to allow his laws, which are His orderly methods of work, to be interfered with by the clamour of some insistent soul. We could not want such a possibility, for it would put us all at the mercy of capricious will. When we think about it we are glad that we live in a dependable world where results come from obedience to universal principles. God is not, however, in the position of the man who refused to let the eleventh guest sit down at a club dinner because his orders called for only ten plates. There are no such exigencies in God's ruling. He finds the way to answer our faith within His laws through our obedience to them. They are not like the traditional red tape instituted by government, but are the element in which we live and breathe and work. It would be a dangerous world for all of us if we could not depend upon God's established methods of procedure.

The same principles of life reach into the spiritual world. In the realm of the impossible it is even more necessary that I know God's purposes, because there God alone reigns. If I expect to do anything beyond my human strength, I must know those great purposes of God which are bound to be fulfilled.

God's infinite power joins our weakness whenever we need freedom of spirit; anything is possible if it really frees us from the enthralling power of our earthly nature. The results of faith may mean new life for body, soul and spirit. For example, fear keeps the spirit in slavery, and is not God's will for us. If we have faith in God's love so that fear is banished, far-reaching effects will begin to come. The mind will be clearer in its wisdom; the body will become more normal because the nerve centres are no longer paralysed by fear. Mighty cures have been wrought and will be again in perfect harmony with the law of trust and love. Whatever ill is caused by some outer circumstance, not beyond the disposition of the spirit, will obey the laws of life and compensate us in other ways for the loss of power in the bodily life. In this way the loss of a limb will give increased sensitiveness of spirit which may unlock the greatest possibility for a future career if it is used for discernment instead of irritation.

It is also God's purpose that we shall grow into his likeness. Anything which promotes this we may expect to receive through faith. Spiritual gifts do not drop down from heaven like the snow. They grow out of experiences in life. There is nothing impossible with God if it means more likeness to Him. This is one reason why many of our prayers are denied. We fix our minds on something which may make us more material in our desires and more satisfied with our spiritual poverty. On the other hand if we reach out in sincere faith for the carrying out of God's purpose, the material supplies will come flooding in to help us in our spiritual career. Let us be sure that we do not fool ourselves by imagining that God will not discern the thoughts and intents of the heart. He will answer the spiritual desire. Many times we do not strengthen that desire until a denial of the material blessing we longed for brings it to our attention.

If we expect our faith to avail in the heavenly realm where God reigns, we need to be sure that our prayer of faith comes from an honest heart. The limitless power of God will be ours if we are honest with ourselves and with God. There are spiritual enemies which must be fought and conquered: pride, vanity, sloth, selfishness, wilfulness. In the realm of the possible, God responds in exact ratio to our coöperation with him: in the realm of the impossible, God responds to the extent that our spirit is perfectly in accord with His character.

"If ye abide in Me and My words abide in you, ye shall ask what ye will — it shall be done unto you."

FOR STUDY AND THOUGHT

Then was Jesus led up of the Spirit into the wilderness to be tempted of the devil. And when he had fasted forty days and forty nights he afterward hungered. And the tempter came and said unto him, if thou art the Son of God, command that these stones become bread. But he answered and said, It is written, Man shall not live by bread alone, but by every word that proceedeth out of the mouth of God. Then the devil taketh him into the holy city; and he set him on the pinnacle of the temple, and saith unto him, if thou art the Son of God, cast thyself down: for it is written:

> He shall give his angels charge concerning thee;
> And on their hands they shall bear thee up,
> Lest haply thou dash thy foot against a stone,

Jesus said unto him, Again it is written, Thou shalt not tempt the Lord thy God. Again, the devil taketh him unto an exceeding high mountain and showeth him all the kingdoms of the world, and the glory of them; and he said unto him, All these things will I give thee, if thou wilt fall down and worship me. Then saith Jesus unto him, Get thee hence, Satan: for it is written, Thou shalt worship the Lord thy God and Him only thou shalt serve. Then the devil leaveth him; and behold, angels came and ministered unto him. *Matt. 4 : 1–11.*

When we see people under strain we see their true character. The testings of Jesus at the beginning of His service shed much light on His point of view concerning His relation to God. The three temptations are typical of what comes to us. When He was hungry and had no bread Jesus resisted the suggestion that He use His power to satisfy it by working for Himself a miracle which ordinary human beings could not work. It was like having a million dollars in trust and not taking one cent of it for one's own necessities. Jesus chose to be obedient to the laws of human life and refused to use His intimate relation to God for selfish purposes. His daily bread was to come in response to the ordinary methods by which our need is met. So many of us are like the Pharisees who were looking for signs and special manifestations. We are prone to think that something which comes to us unexpectedly is more an evidence of God's power than that which helped to bring it to pass.

It is dangerous to quote scripture as a warrant for our faith unless it accords with the laws of the spiritual life. Jesus refuses the evil suggestion backed up by the Psalm, that if He is the Son of God there will be no limits to what He may not do; that there are no situations from which He cannot come out unscathed. We often fail to measure up to our Master in this. How often are we dismayed because God does not rescue us from some cross by performing some miracle for us which will cause people to marvel, when the highest faith is that which takes up the cross knowing that it is in itself a gateway to larger life. Jesus met this same temptation in Gethsemane when He asked that the cross be removed *if it were possible*. When it was *not* removed, this faith was made equal to the strain, so that He triumphed over it in resurrection life.

In another temptation, Jesus refuses to gain power by compromise with evil, even for an end which is good. Such experiences test the purity of our motives. The life of faith does not mean easy victory for us. Those of us who have the most confident trust often have to sail into the teeth of an adverse wind. Faith does not always bring peace, it may be the herald of battle. Jesus had perfect faith all His life and yet miraculous deliverances did not always come. Enduring faith is sometimes a higher quality than victorious faith. Both come into our experience and God alone knows which is best for us. God *can do* for us what is humanly impossible and we have the right to ask it in faith. If the deliverance does not come now it is because the love of God has prepared something greater "*beyond* what we ask or think."

> As the hart panteth after the water brooks, so longeth my soul for Thee, O God. Send out Thy light and Thy truth, — let them lead me ever nearer to Thee. Make Thy holy will my only wish. Through Jesus Christ, our Lord. *Amen.*

THE LIMITATIONS OF FAITH

When we read that word of Jesus, "the things which are impossible with man are possible with God," it seems beside the mark to speak of limitations in the range of faith. We think of God's infinite power and wonder why we are not able to release it with our faith. Why do we not do it? What are our limitations? We do well to understand them.

The spirit of faith is limited by our experience in the Christian life. It takes time to know the purposes which God has for us. Sometimes our faith is ignorant because we have not made it wise by searching the scriptures to learn the secrets of Christ's faith, and to see what limited the faith of those men whose experiences with God are recorded for our benefit. We spend years studying the causes of victory or downfall in the life of nations, and in reading the thoughts of those who write books. Why should we expect to become expert in the use of faith toward God without studying diligently the history of man's search after Him. There are certain truths about faith which have been proved by countless experiences in the past. If we study philosophy we review the history of all that has been learned in the past and then add to it the wisdom of the present. Many of us are limited in faith because we are stumbling along without a text book to guide us. Life is too short to waste it in learning by personal mistakes only. We need first to profit by the experience of others.

We are also limited in faith by the generation in which we live. This is a hard saying for those who feel that the present age is the ultimate point of progress. We discount the worth of past generations who were reaching up to the highest that they knew. We forget too that after us will come other men and women who will pity our ignorance and wonder why our faith was not more perfect.

The development of the life of the centuries is just as much part of God's plan as the development of the individual from childhood to manhood. The individual repeats the history of his race, and the race repeats the history of the individual. It is humbling to our pride to think of ourselves as unable to go further than the general limits of our generation. Yet this is so in scientific development and in the realm of faith.

We are able to work with God more fully now than those of past generations. Our faith operates in a far wider field. This is true of the body as well as the mind. We have it in our power now to work miracles in our bodies through surgery and the therapeutic art which were impossible five hundred years ago. In the same way the people of the future will outstrip us in the use of that faith which connects human effort with divine power. This is also true of ideas and desires which will remake the world. We see the promise of the future now, for here and there are human spirits who are leading in the new generation. They are like the mountain peaks which glow with the light of the rising sun while the valleys and plains are still wrapped in gray shadows. The peaks rejoice in the coming day, but their faith cannot create light in the valley till the time has come.

Our personal faith is also limited by the necessity for unselfishness. We are like ships made for a cargo, weighted down by the load of our responsibility for this world. This slackens our speed but we rejoice in it because we "bear one another's burdens and so fulfil the law of Christ." Most of us spend far too much time lamenting over the burdens we have to bear; the social group which is deaf to the harmonies we hear; the opposition to progress from those who are bound up in the same bundle of life with us. Unselfishness is a willingness to bear the burdens of the group; a sacrifice of ourself for the good of those who were chosen as our companions in life by the purpose of God. Jesus gave himself for the life of the whole world. He said when you pray say *"Our Father."* Our faith will reach its mountain peak only as it rises out of the common need of the world. I cannot detach myself from others and expect to release resources of power for myself alone. Have you been wanting some "pull" with Heaven which will bring you special privilege? The question sounds irreverent, and it is; because like all selfishness it is out of harmony with the character of God.

This suggests another limitation for faith. The requirements of character are inexorable. There is no short cut to power. We pray for help when some painful calamity occurs and we want deliverance from our thorn in the flesh more than we want character. Sometimes this craving for deliverance becomes in a sense a thermometer which registers the degree of our idealism, and we find it has been falling with the years. In such a case, our "thorn" may be a blessing in disguise, if it wakens us to spiritual needs. We cannot live on a low plane of thinking and pray on a high plane of faith — we cannot ask God to restore the dying body when we have no concern for the living spirit. Character must be consonant with our faith, or prayer becomes a mocking. We can ask God to restore our soul through His forgiving love, but that will not fit us for mighty deeds of faith until we understand the character of God through personal experience.

The world is waiting to see us prove, by our understanding of the law of faith, that we surely do believe the teaching of Jesus Christ. If we seek *first* the Kingdom of God and his righteousness, all these other things that have to do with our eating, drinking, clothing, and bodily needs shall be added by the watchful love of our heavenly Father.

> Yes, Thou art still the life; Thou art the way
> The holiest know, — light, life, and way of heaven;
> And they who dearest hope and deepest pray
> Toil by the light, life, way which thou hast given.
>
> *Theodore Parker 1846.*

FOR STUDY AND THOUGHT

O Lord Thou hast searched me, and known me.
Thou knowest my downsitting and mine uprising,
Thou understandest my thought afar off.
Thou searchest out my path and my lying down,
And art acquainted with all my ways.
For there is not a word in my tongue,
But, lo, O Lord, thou knowest it altogether.
Thou hast beset me behind and before,
And laid thine hand upon me.
Such knowledge is too wonderful for me;
It is high, I cannot attain unto it.
Whither shall I go from thy spirit?
Or whither shall I flee from thy presence?
If I ascend up into heaven, thou art there:
If I make my bed in Sheol, behold, thou art there.
If I take the wings of the morning,
And dwell in the uttermost parts of the sea;
Even there shall thy hand lead me,
And thy right hand shall hold me.
If I say, Surely the darkness shall overwhelm me,
And the light about me shall be night;
Even the darkness hideth not from thee,
But the night shineth as the day:
The darkness and the light are both alike to thee.

Psa. 139 : 1–12.

There is no more beautiful expression of perfect faith in an omniscient God than in the lines of this Psalm. The all-seeing eyes of God may be a cause of terror to some who, like wilful children, long to get away from that watchful presence; but to all of us who believe in a friendly world, this conception of God brings a full assurance of faith.

Who of us has not had a haunting fear lest some day our friends will see us as we really are and cease to love us. We are in such a tumult of thoughts and opposing desires which we can never explain that often we do not have faith in ourselves. We are always being surprised by such unexpected revelations of weakness and cowardice, and fires of passion within, that we lose our confidence. Nothing restores our soul so quickly as this realization of David that God knows us *better* than we know ourselves. A great deal of inner distress of mind would disappear if we made it a habit to repeat the words of the Psalmist over and over until the rest of perfect understanding brought us peace. Try it as a method of relaxation before sleep at night and see how all the vagrant thoughts and anxieties come under the calm control of the spirit of God. Nothing will quiet the inner argument more than this.

The rest of the Psalm is breath-taking. It gathers up into the protection of God every possible experience in life. There are *no* problems anywhere in the heavens above or in the depths of the sea or in the dark spaces of life. Faith in an omnipresent God brings perfect rest. God saw us before we were born, so there is nothing surprising about us to Him. Much of our ill-health comes from lurking fears which skulk about in the dark corners of our mind. If we know that the wind of God's Spirit is blowing through all the corners of our life, we become free spirits.

So long as our attention is fixed on our sensations and emotions, our faculty of faith is chained. We must escape from ourselves. A spacious conception of God will develop a spacious soul. In other words the chief reason why our faith is limited is because our conception of God is limited. Meditation on such sweeping faith as this Psalm shows and upon countless other portions of scripture, will convince our heart as well as our intellect. It is "with the heart man believeth." Faith becomes limitless when a spacious conception of God grows from an ideal to an enthusiasm.

The reign of law in the spiritual world does not limit faith. Law is our description of God's ways of action. It is our witness to His reliability. "He's a great friend of mine," said one of another, "I always know where to find him," so it is with God; our faith in Him grows in proportion as we know where to find Him in all the expression of this life.

Grant us, Blessed Father, a courageous faith in Thy love, and a never-failing confidence in Thy great purpose for each of Thy children. May our service equal our capacity in Thy sight and truly express our devotion to Thee. Through Jesus Christ, our Lord. *Amen.*

THE CRYSTALLINE LENS OF THE SOUL

THE SPIRIT OF PURITY

Our world without is the counterpart of our world within. The old saying, "A man sees that for which he is looking," is truer than most of us realize. All the beauty in the world goes for naught if there is no love of beauty in the soul. Two friends were listening to a famous orchestra. One of them, unmindful of all else, sat enthralled by the harmonies. He was brought back rudely to earth by the voice of his companion: "O come along, let us get away from this noise." Music ceased to be, because the soul of music was not within him.

It is only the pure in heart who are able to see God. He is hidden from other eyes. If there have been no sacred moments in our lives when we have caught glimpses of His glory, it is probably because the springs of our heart have been so muddied by all the refuse that has been thrown into them that they cannot mirror the image of the sky. We ourselves control the situation, and cherish or destroy true purity of heart, according to what we are willing to receive within ourselves. Purity is to the soul what the crystalline lens is to the eye. It is the organ of vision, and should be guarded as a priceless possession. It is the window through which the spirit looks out and up. Many a soul lives in a dismal prison house because this window has been covered with dust of the earth. There will never be any understanding of God until, out of a pure desire, there is a personal cry: "Create in me a clean heart, O God, and renew a right spirit within me."

The fine gift of discernment is only possible to the pure in heart. It takes clean sight to appreciate spiritual values and to understand inner qualities. How can we appraise the true worth of anything unless we are able to see the perfect standard and estimate how closely each quality approaches perfection? How can we determine the curve unless we see the straight line from which it deviates! How can we know the true character of our desires unless we know what God is like and how far short we come in being like Him.

The ability to know right from wrong depends upon purity. The chief reason why we are so confused in our thinking these days is because our standards are blurred by our murky vision. We often say that seeing is believing. If we realized that what we see is that which leaps to meet our desire we would know the truth about ourselves. The old French phrase, *Honi soit qui mal y pense* expresses a profound spiritual truth. It is evil to him who evil thinks. The brown shadow which he sees is the dull reflection of the brown soul within. It is a simple matter to test the quality of one's soul by noticing carefully the quality of the first thoughts which come into the mind in response to the daily relationships with those around us. Do we discover shortcomings, and ulterior motives? Does envy, criticism, snobbery or censoriousness rise up within us? If so the fountain spring of our life needs cleansing. If joy, sympathy, appreciation and friendliness rise spontaneously within us as others come near us, we may be sure that the love of God has been at work creating purity in the soul.

This gift of a clean heart is a mighty protection against the mire of the world. It throws off impurities by the force of the life within, provided we renew its strength constantly by association with God. There are uncounted moments when the mind falls back upon itself in relaxation. Thoughts of some kind will rise to meet us. If we hold in reserve one of the matchless sayings of Jesus, or the poetic lines of a psalm, or recall the picture of some incident in the life of Christ, or some beautiful parable of nature, or revelation of God in a friend, we can make our idle moments pure and clean. Then when we return to the world we shall have new power with which to withstand the appeal of evil.

Is there anything more enviable than that experience of which the poet sings,

> "My strength is as the strength of ten
> Because my heart is pure."

Purity is always courageous. It has nothing to fear. It has no mixed motives, but is simple and direct. Most of us are not naturally this way. We plunge into strife and disunion without a thoroughly clean mind and accomplish nothing more than a compromise between opposing forces. The work of the Church, and the community halts because of this. Each group sees in the other the reflection of its own spirit. How much of this strife would be saved if every member of the group, or even a few rare souls, fought out first in his own heart the battle of mixed motives and came forth a pure-minded soul ready to be an ambassador of Christ, and to represent His name and spirit.

The political world and the varied groups of workers need the armor of crystal purity. It is the supreme quality for all leadership. People trust and follow gladly the men and women who meet this test. Never as now was there a time when the world needed such leaders. Who will pay the price in his own soul?

Purity of heart is essential for the life of the body. Every bit of the physical mechanism is sensitive to the darkness of the soul and wreaks its vengeance upon it. When purity is gone everything crashes to ruin. The window of the spirit is darkened, and the vision of God has gone. As Jesus said, "If the light that is in thee be darkness, how great is that darkness." No one can rise to the dignity of a human soul and neglect the clean heart. It was for the sake of this, that Christ died for the world, to wash away the stains of an evil conscience and make it possible for us to see God and be transformed from character to character, into His image.

> "Spirit of purity and grace,
> Our weakness pitying see,
> O make our hearts Thy dwelling-place
> And worthier Thee." *Harriet Auber.*

FOR STUDY AND THOUGHT

The lamp of the body is the eye: if therefore thine eye be single, thy whole body shall be full of light. But if thine eye be evil, thy whole body shall be full of darkness. If therefore the light that is in thee be darkness, how great is the darkness! *Matt. 6 : 22-23.*

And he called to him the multitude again, and said unto them, Hear me all of you, and understand: There is nothing from without the man, that going into him can defile him: but the things which proceed out of the man are those that defile the man. For from within, out of the heart of men, evil thoughts proceed, fornications, thefts, murders, adulteries, covetings, wickednesses, deceit, lasciviousness, an evil eye, railing, pride, foolishness: all these evil things proceed from within, and defile the man. *Mark 7 : 14, 15, 21, 22, 23.*

In a recent autobiography the writer says of the difference between herself and her sister, "I tell people the truth about themselves but L— made them feel it." That is how the quality of purity shows itself. It is felt more than it can be described. The purity of a pane of glass depends on the degree to which the glass itself is *invisible*, and the landscape beyond is visible.

There is a great cry among the rising generation for reality. "We want to see things as they are without any sugar-coating," said a young student. If sugar-coating means glossing over the ugly facts of life with deceiving whiteness, the impatience of youth is justified. If, however, it means actual *experience* with evil, the very reality that we seek will escape us because when the pure medium of vision is smirched we do not see things as they are. People who accustom themselves to vulgarity lose the power to see vulgarity in its true character, and also fail to see the beauty of delicacy. Experience may ruin the standards of generations and darkness of soul is the end. Someone may suggest that evil may enhance the beauty of good by contrast. That is true *if the love of good* is already the passion of one's life. How shall we love good unless we live with it and delight in it!

The spirit of purity is born *within* the heart. Environment does not create it. It only furnishes food for what is already within the heart. Beautiful and sheltered surroundings do not prevent vulgarity in the heart. Many a favored child of fortune has developed the soul of a savage.

The list of evils which Jesus said come out from within and defile the man begin with evil thoughts and end with foolishness. The spirit of purity develops from pure thinking. If children are brought up in an atmosphere where every motive of others is questioned and suspected, and ideals of life are looked at cynically, and if there is no responsibility for service given them, evil thoughts and foolishness and all that comes between are likely to become habitual when they are grown. The natural facts of life, when used with an evil significance, become impure.

All our appreciations of beauty, all true sense of values, all reality of God, all sincere experience are born of a pure heart, because they are reflected through this crystalline lens of the soul. A boy once said of his mother: "There is something about her that makes me feel clean; it is nothing she says: — it's just mother." Nothing can break the power of such a relationship. It has been expected of women that they should hold purity as their most cherished ideal. It has made them divinities to men. In this day when both men and women face the same experiences in life, the ideal of purity must be cherished by both alike. One half of society cannot retain its ideals when the other half esteems them lightly. Both are equally tempted, from different angles, to eat freely of the tree of the knowledge of good and evil, and unless the face of God is more precious than experience, both will again be driven into the outer darkness. "Blessed are the pure in heart: for they shall see our God." (*Matt. 5 : 8*).

Almighty God, unto whom all hearts be open, all desires known, and from whom no secrets are hid, cleanse the thoughts of our hearts by the inspiration of Thy Holy Spirit, that we may perfectly love Thee, and worthily magnify Thy holy Name; through Jesus Christ our Lord. *Amen.* *Bishop Leofric A. D. 1050.*

THE SPIRIT OF THANKFULNESS

A grateful heart is the surest sign that the soul is awake and alive to the glory of life. It is the line of separation between the instincts of the animal and the urge of the spirit. It is the first step toward a loving God. Browning grasped this truth in his pointed question:

> "For what are men better than sheep or goats
> That nourish a blind life in the brain,
> If knowing God they lift not thankful hearts in prayer
> Both for themselves and those whom they call friend?"

In spite of this, however, the spirit of thankfulness is rare. It is so easy to satisfy ourselves with the rich experiences of life which we take as our natural right that, before we realize it, a spirit of independent self-assertion has rooted itself in our hearts. "I do not care to be under obligations to anyone!" We often hear; "I prefer to stand on my own feet." This is a praiseworthy spirit if it means that we propose to carry our own burdens and bear our share of responsibility, but if it breeds in us such an indifference to God and to our fellow beings that we acknowledge no debt to them we kill within us the humble childlike heart. When we put that to death we have shut ourselves out of the kingdom of heaven.

In truth no one is freed from obligation to others. All the blessings of life which we take as an inherent right are ours only because of the countless services rendered us by others. The well-ordered country in which we live, whose protection we enjoy; the supply for all our daily needs, the chance to work, the very opportunity to be independent and self-reliant, — all involve us in sacred relationships which we may not ignore without reverting to the lowest plane of life. God has so ordered the world that we are dependent one upon another to the end that we may recognize it with thankful hearts and be lifted up into the realm of friendship with God.

Thanksgiving is not synonymous with smug satisfaction. There are thousands who congratulate themselves on their rich estate, that they were clever enough to get a running start of their fellows; that they are not like the poor unfortunates they see on the streets. Like beautiful birds pluming their feathers in the sun, they think their hearts are moved by the spirit of gratitude. They are only rejoicing in themselves. They are taking pride in themselves; little realizing that the spirit of thanksgiving is a relationship of love between two spirits when each has given to and received from the other. We can never be thankful with ourselves.

"The poor are so ungrateful," said a richly dressed woman one day. "There is no use in doing anything for them; they do not appreciate it." It was easy to see why there could be no gratitude. Even a little child could have discerned that the gifts were made because the giver wanted for herself grateful homage as an opiate for her conscience and she was willing to pay for it by making gifts. This is why Jesus counselled us not to sound a trumpet when we give, but to hide ourselves so that not even our left hand should know what our right hand has done. True gratitude is a spontaneous lifting up of the spirit in response to the blessing of love. Truly

"The gift without the giver is bare."

All thanksgiving runs over with the spirit of joy. We cannot help rejoicing when we appreciate the loving spirit of the heavenly Father who has given us richly all things to enjoy. A true appreciation of that which brings good to us is always a joyous experience. The reason why so many people find little joy in life is largely because they have their eye so fixed on some special joy which is not yet theirs that they do not see the other joys all about them. The real trouble with such people is not that their blessings are so few, but that they do not face the world as it is, and turn from reality to an imaginary realm. So long as they detach themselves from the actual relationships of life they cut themselves off from its joys.

We need to deepen our appreciation of the glory in the world and the expression of love in the lives of others, in order that we may be delivered from slavery to things and enjoy the contentment of a thankful heart. To have and to possess are two different experiences. One may have actual flowers in one's garden and yet live as though they were not there. The neighbor may possess them more really by appreciation. It is not necessary to own the woodland to enjoy it.

When people are wrapped up in themselves they look upon the rest of the world and the people in it as mere stage setting for their personal acting. They see people performing certain functions: selling shoes, cooking meals, teaching children, but they are impersonal so far as any relation to themselves is concerned. But if we once lose ourselves in the love of God, people become vivid and personal and we begin to appreciate them and to be grateful to them. A man who was overflowing with gratitude for the gift of a woman's love, found himself looking at all other men with a new interest, wondering if they too had such blessing and wishing that they too might have such joy as his; it is the natural expression of a thankful heart. True gratitude is a humble thing: it wants to share its joy with others.

There is a thanksgiving which is not necessarily pleasurable. In following Christ there are times when the road winds over hills of difficulty and the spirit loses its spontaneity as it squares its shoulders for the hours when courage is tested. Then we are grateful for the strong arm of God, for the chance to prove our devotion to Him, and for the sense of His nearness. Faith rather than joy is linked to our gratitude, and we rejoice in the victory which is yet to be. Whether we see the goal of our desire or not, we can rejoice in the faithfulness of God and give thanks for the Giver instead of the gifts.

Nothing separates us further from God than a thankless spirit. It brings discord into every relationship and into our whole being. Shakespeare describes such a spirit in a child as "sharper than a serpent's tooth."

> "Oh that men would praise the Lord for His loving kindness
> And for His wonderful works to the children of men!
> And let them offer sacrifices of thanksgiving,
> And declare His works with singing."

> Praise, my soul, the King of heaven,
> To his feet Thy tribute bring;
> Ransomed, healed, restored, forgiven,
> Who like me, his praise should sing?
> Praise Him, praise Him, praise Him, praise Him,
> Praise the everlasting King.   *Henry F. Lyte, 1834.*

FOR STUDY AND THOUGHT

I will give Thee thanks with my whole heart;
Before the gods will I sing praises unto Thee.
I will worship toward Thy holy temple,
And give thanks unto Thy name for Thy loving kindness and for Thy truth:
For Thou hast magnified Thy word above all Thy name.
In the day that I called Thou answeredst me,
Thou didst encourage me with strength in my soul.   *Psalms 138 : 1–3.*

And let the peace of Christ rule in your hearts, to the which also ye were called in one body; and be ye thankful. *Col. 3 : 15.*

In nothing be anxious; but in everything by prayer and supplication with thanksgiving let your requests be made known unto God.
Phil. 4 : 6.

Thanksgiving is the most neglected of all spiritual gifts. When the message of Jesus to the world began to be understood, the sheer joy of it affected the music in people's souls and gave the inspiration for all the triumphant harmonies of western music. Thanksgiving abounded. We in the twentieth century are so *blasé* about everything that it is as much effort to lift our hearts as it would be to climb a rope to the ceiling in a gymnasium. Only those can do it who have the habit.

Many people express thanksgiving only in return for material things. They measure their blessings by the number of *things* they possess, and gratitude then is synonymous with self-satisfaction. There is irony in that story of the old woman who summed up her blessings in the words,"I am thankful for two teeth that bite." When old age brings no higher satisfactions the soul has missed the whole meaning of life. What a contrast we have in the spirit of Habakkuk, the prophet, who soars above us all in his spirit. "For though the fig tree shall not blossom, neither shall the fruit be in the vines; the labor of the olive shall fail, and the fields shall yield no food; the flock shall be cut off from the fold, and there shall be no herd in the stalls: *yet I will rejoice* in Jehovah, I will joy in the God of my salvation." (*Hab. 3 : 17, 18*). If such a situation occurred in our agricultural districts we would appoint a day for mourning instead of thanksgiving.

When the Pharisee went up to the Temple to pray, our Lord says he prayed with himself and said, "God, I thank Thee that I am not as the rest of men —". Here gratitude is merely pride. How often we masquerade as thankful spirits when we are bursting with vainglory. This is one of the reasons why there is so little joy in our Christian life. We haven't yet learned the meaning of the word gratitude.

A group of students returned from Christmas holidays and were comparing notes. One was thankful for a large cheque; another rejoiced in a new car, and another in choice books. One boy was silent. When asked about his Christmas joy, he replied, "I was thankful to make ten little newsboys happy." He alone had the point of view of Christ. Thanksgiving is a spirit we call out in others; it is the spirit that gives rather than gets. How can we share the joy of God when we sit like the rich man in *Luke 16 : 19*, faring sumptuously, while the beggar lives on the crumbs that fall from our table. We cannot picture Christ sitting beside the rich man. He has nothing in common with the self-satisfied spirit. The true picture of the God we worship is found in the Shepherd who could not rest in the warm, protected fold while one sheep was out in the storm and darkness. Does His shout of thanksgiving wake any response in us, "Rejoice with me for I have found my sheep which was lost," (*Luke 15 : 6*).

Perhaps the reason why we find it hard to lift up our hearts is because we have not yet found the satisfaction of the Master.

> My heart is fixed, O God;
> I will sing, yea I will sing praises, even with my glory.
> I will give thanks unto Thee O Lord, among the peoples:
> And I will sing praises unto Thee among the nations.
> For Thy mercy is great above the heavens,
> And Thy truth reacheth unto the skies. *Psa. 108.*

THE SPIRIT OF MERCY

Our eyesight runs far ahead of our footsteps. Our living limps behind our knowledge of the truth. That which we know we should do, we do not always practice. Every day we have need to confess our shortcomings as we see ourselves in the light of Jesus Christ. We grow in wisdom and power from day to day reaching on and up to that moral perfection that God purposes for us. But we have not yet attained. Therefore our loving God meets the situation with the spirit of mercy and says, "Blessed are the merciful, for they shall obtain mercy."

It is significant that this beatitude comes immediately after the one which blesses those who "hunger and thirst after righteousness." Those of us who long to be right and realize our need so that we *hunger* for perfection, ought naturally to be filled with mercy toward others who are struggling on as we are. We know how it feels to fall short of our ideals. We know how hard it is to be true to our Lord, therefore we ought to appreciate the need of others. Strange as it may seem, it is one of the besetting sins of human nature that we apply the standard of perfection to others and fail to apply it to ourselves. Our judgment is more accurate than our practice. We find it hard to forgive in others that which we excuse in ourselves.

It is not easy to live up to two opposing standards at the same time. Righteousness and tenderness are blended to make mercy. We run from one extreme to the other. Our sense of righteousness makes us hard and unflinching and our tenderness too often is spineless. To achieve both at once, — that is the peculiar glory of the Christ whose whole life was spent in being just and merciful. His teaching is very clear and plain. We are to be merciful because we need mercy from God. Furthermore Jesus says very clearly that unless we show mercy to others we cannot expect mercy from God, and unless we forgive the shortcomings in others we cannot hope to be forgiven by Him. He taught us to pray that God would be as merciful to us as we are to others.

Herein lies the reason why some of us are yet slaves in sinning against our ideals. We cherish in our hearts bitterness and prejudice and malice until love is driven out and there is no inner atmosphere in which the Spirit of God can live and thrive. Love is the life energy going out to God and to others, and mercy is merely love in action. If love ceases to move toward others it ceases to move toward God and there can be no forgiveness, because without love we shall not desire to restore a relationship of love.

It is of the utmost importance to our peace of mind and health of body that we open our hearts to the spirit of mercy. Most of the influences that break down our health are the depressing and bitter experiences we have with other people. They are critical of us and we shrivel up. They oppose our progress and we spend wakeful hours in anxiety and fears. They are indifferent to us and we are lonely and depressed. If there rises within us a spirit of malice or anger we feel the effects of it at once in our minds and bodies. Sometimes sensitive souls are inhibited for years by some past experience with some one whom they cannot forgive. There is no remedy for soul or body until we begin to cultivate the inner spirit of mercy. It is used constantly by our Lord in reference to the undeserving and to enemies. Mercy loves its enemies, prays for them and pities them because of what they have to overcome before they can find peace. The spirit of mercy is the spirit of sympathy.

Jesus Christ pointed out a way in which we can rise to the height of assuring mercy for those who are undeserving. We are to turn away from the thought of their sins and to enter into our inner room, and there see ourselves in the light of God's presence, then we shall see how far short we have come in our own inner life and when we remember that, "his tender mercies are over all his works," while we struggle to have mercy toward a few, we realize our own shortcomings. From such a contemplation of fact we return with new tenderness and find it easier to let mercy have sway in our hearts.

There is also another method of releasing the spirit of mercy. When we begin to do others some real service, our attitude changes. We may not have any special emotion about it, but if our will is bent on right conduct, the sentiments will come in time. We are to do good whether we feel like it or not, and as we do it the feeling will come. There is nothing more sublime in all the life of Christ than the prayer he put into words at the very moment when He was being nailed to the Cross by His enemies, "Father, forgive them: they know not what they do." In the face of this supreme spirit of mercy we stand in silence, — His love never failed for one moment. The physical effort to concentrate on this act of mercy when he was suffering must have been beyond anything we know. Only a heart that was all love could have been able to do this.

A divine imagination can help us to be merciful sometimes when the enmity of others makes it especially difficult. We can look at facts as they are and then form a mental picture of what the unlovable soul would be like if the Spirit of Christ were released within him. Jesus looked at a fickle, impulsive, tempestuous man and said, "Thou art Simon, but thou *shalt* be Peter." And in the months that followed He helped the Simon to decrease and the Peter to increase. There is a Christ in chains in every life waiting to be released and to transform enmity into love, and malice into mercy. Perhaps we can help to hasten that day in the life of some one for whom we find it difficult to pray. Some day if we are faithful we may be one of those surprised souls who are to hear the word of their Lord. "I was in prison and ye came unto me . . . . inasmuch as ye did it unto one of these my brethren, even the least, ye did it unto me."

> "O God of mercy, God of might,
> In love and pity infinite,
> Teach us, as ever in Thy sight,
> To live our life to Thee.
>
> In sickness, sorrow, want, or care,
> Whate'er it be, 'tis ours to share;
> May we, where help is needed, there
> Give help as unto Thee."

FOR STUDY AND THOUGHT

And behold, a certain lawyer stood up and tempted him, saying, Master, what shall I do to inherit eternal life? And he said unto him, What is written in the law? how readest thou? And he answering said, Thou shall love the Lord thy God with all thy heart, and with all thy soul, and with all thy strength, and with all thy mind; and thy neighbour as thyself. And he said unto him, Thou hast answered right: this do, and thou shalt live. But he, desiring to justify himself, said unto Jesus, And who is my neighbour? Jesus made answer and said, A certain man was going down from Jerusalem to Jericho; and he fell among robbers, which both stripped him and beat him, and departed, leaving him half dead, and by chance a certain priest was going down that way: and when he saw him, he passed by on the other side. And in like manner a Levite also, when he came to the place, and saw him, passed by on the other side. But a certain Samaritan, as he journeyed, came where he was: and when he saw him, he was moved with compassion, and came to him, and bound up his wounds, pouring on them oil and wine; and he set him on his own beast, and brought him to an inn, and took care of him. And on the morrow he took out two pence, and gave them to the host, and said, Take care of him; and whatsoever thou spendest more, I, when I come back again, will repay thee. Which of these three, thinkest thou, proved neighbour unto him that fell among the robbers? And he said, he that shewed mercy upon him. And Jesus said unto him, Go, and do thou like-wise. *Luke 10 : 25-37.*

He hath showed thee, O man, what is good; and what doth the Lord require of thee, but to do justly, and to love mercy, and to walk humbly, with thy God.   *Micah 6 : 8.*

Mercy is a social spirit. It always involves a relationship with some one. It is the way we interpret the love of God to our fellows. In this matchless story of the Good Samaritan, Jesus binds together religion and ethics in practical living. Before His time religion and morality were not always inseparable. Obedience and justice were stern qualities and it was the teaching of Christ which united love for God and love for our neighbor in one indivisible bond. The ideal of mercy, which some of the prophets saw, became a great reality in the person of Jesus. Truth and mercy cannot be divided without destroying the Christian ideal.

The lawyer asked a pertinent question when he said, "Who is my neighbor?" or literally, "Who is near me?" If loving God and loving my neighbor are equally binding, how far am I to go in my human relation? Jesus describes both the neighbor and neighborliness in this story. A human being is robbed and left dying on the main highway. He cannot help himself. This man whose business is religion sees him and passes by without being merciful. Then the unexpected happens. Another human being of a country despised by the religious land comes along, and he stops and cares for the man and takes the time to bring him to an inn, and pays for his care. He must have been delayed in his business. It took time to show mercy. Perhaps the priest and the Levite had important religious engagements to keep so that they had no time for mercy. Some one has said that the godly are so unhuman and the human are so ungodly that the world cannot find a perfect revelation of the heart of God.

Jesus certainly meant us to be neighbor to anyone, anywhere, of any race, or faith. The whole world is our neighborhood. Our soul, our neighbor, and our God are so inextricably bound together that when we lose sight of one we lose sight of all. As Ernest Crosby puts it:

> "No one could tell me where my soul might be,
> I searched for God, but God eluded me,
> I sought my brother out, and found all three."

The world is getting smaller. Transportation outruns brother-hood. We can hear our brother whisper across the sea and the whole world knows when he is wounded. The spirit of mercy alone can insure our safety. Our animosities, our narrow prejudices must be put away or we shall have no peace. There are neighbors near to us who will never have a clearer vision of God than they get through us. Our lives are the only Bible they will read. Our own salvation depends upon the measure of mercy within us. "Forgive us our debts *as we forgive* our debtors," our Lord taught us to pray; which means that we are asking God to show us the same kind of mercy we show to others. Are we satisfied to have it so?

> Father of mercies, help us to remember what we owe Thee. May we give to others the care and love with which Thou hast surrounded us. Make us tender in heart, faithful in service, forgiving in spirit and understanding in sympathy. May the children of men find it easier to draw near to Thee because of us. Help us to hasten the time when all shall know Thee from the least unto the greatest; through Jesus Christ our Lord who came to seek and to find all those who have strayed from the true path. *Amen.*

THE SPIRIT OF TRUTH

When Pilate, the Roman governor, was conducting the trial of Jesus he asked curiously, "What is truth?" He received no answer. He was interested like many others in an academic discussion of an abstract idea. He was seeking a definition of words which would fit into his scheme of thinking, when at that moment the incarnate spirit of truth stood there before him.

That scene in the Judgment Hall has been reënacted countless times during the centuries since then. The One who said, "I am the Truth" has been ignored while men have questioned and argued, and tried to pare down the whole heaven to the dimensions of their little thoughts. But while they have been measuring infinite truth with their mental yardsticks, the great spirit of truth has escaped them and gone forth in power confounding their vision. Slowly people are beginning to realize that the whole of God's universe is included in the truth which we seek; that Jesus Christ is the personification of it; and that the Spirit of God unfolds it before our eyes as fast and as fully as we are able to understand it and to use it.

What wars and inquisitions, what strife and unhappy divisions, would the world and the Church have escaped had the plain teaching of Christ about the spirit of truth been followed! The experience of the world in seeking truth has been like the adventures of children on a mill pond. They have clambered into a flat-bottomed boat and skirted the shores which were in plain sight before them. They have seen the sandy bottom whose shallow depths were revealed by the sun and they have gone back to their evening meal with the comfortable sense of having conquered the laws of rowboat navigation. There was no mystery about the truth: it was fully understood and they rested their faith upon their understanding of it.

Others, however, have a different experience. They set sail on the sea of truth as men sail from New York for Liverpool. There is no shore line perceptible to the eye; only fog and mystery and waves, and unplumbed depths. They cannot see their destination, and all the laws of mill-pond navigation avail them nothing. They have to live by a new law, the law of faith. They go to sleep at night confident that somebody is on the bridge who knows what they do not know. They trust in him and at the appointed time they come to their destination, having learned the spacious dimensions of truth which include all they know and infinitely more.

Jesus said, "I am the truth," and when He went away He said, "the Spirit of truth will guide you into all the truth," thereby implying that it would be an unfolding revelation through all the days to come; it would also stretch to the limits of the universe of God, and comprehend all the laws of life. No one mind as yet can grasp it all. Each of us sees certain aspects of truth and others enrich our knowledge by the discoveries they have made. Two boys away at school were describing the same mountain which sheltered their home towns. One boy described it as long and low; the other spoke of its narrow peak. They disputed with one another and yet each was right, for they were looking at the mountain from opposite valleys. Most truths, as well as mountains, are too great to be grasped in their entirety from any one angle of vision. Pioneers, too, who climb to higher levels, get the first vision of the rising sun. As times go on, the light which they have discovered from the mountain top illumines the whole world.

Truth demands courage and that is why so many timid people are afraid of it or dare not utter it. There are thousands who live for years without being willing to face the truth which their own hearts know. They fool themselves with plausible excuses and live in a state of moral anarchy. They struggle against the pressure of that pervading spirit which cannot be resisted long because it is the law of the universe. Woe to him who pits his puny strength against the floodtides of God.

> "Truth crushed to earth will rise again,
>   The eternal years of God are hers."

All the blessing of human society would disappear if the spirit of truth were withdrawn. We build up every relationship and confidence in one another by the assurances of truth. No education is possible without a knowledge of things as they are. No friendship, no family life is possible unless the law of truth is the controlling law within it. So long as we can depend upon the truthfulness of others we can live in relationship with them. It is strange that we keep up so much sham and insincerity in our relationships: when we know that eventually the living truth will manifest itself. Nothing can resist it.

Modern psychology emphasizes the value of admitting to ourselves the truth concerning our thoughts and instincts in order to control them. If we repress them and refuse to recognize them they are likely to break forth in some abnormal way, often bringing on serious neurotic conditions. When, however, the disturbing thought of fear, or anxiety, or evil desire, comes into the mind and we recognize it clearly and acknowledge its character, we shall then be able to control it and redirect it to higher purposes. All the resources of the will come to our help when we are committed to truth in our inner life, and are ready to look facts in the face. We then can pray with a definite assurance that all the strength of God is with us to work out His purpose.

There is no one path of truth by which God manifests Himself to us. We see Him primarily in the Christ, and in the revelation of truth through His church, and in every good and perfect gift which comes from God. The parables of Jesus, the discoveries of astronomy, the Sermon on the Mount, and the laws of electricity are all part of the truth of God. The colors on the wing of an insect and the glories of the sunset are all one in the expression of the truth of God.

To be in harmony with the eternal spirit of truth is the most restful, and the most triumphant state to which any human being can attain. God then has right of way in our life and will do "exceeding abundantly beyond what we ask or think, according to the power that worketh in us." If only we have the courage to rank ourselves on the side of truth, to yearn for it as a hungry man yearns for bread and to follow it obediently, even the least of us may see the mighty works of God.

> Strong Son of God, immortal Love,
> Whom we, that have not seen Thy face,
> By faith, and faith alone, embrace,
> Believing where we cannot prove;
>
> Thou seemest human and divine;
> The highest, holiest manhood, Thou,
> Our wills are ours, we know not how,
> Our wills are ours, to make them Thine.
>
> *Tennyson 1850.*

FOR STUDY AND THOUGHT

Jesus saith unto him, I am the way, and the truth, and the life: no one cometh unto the Father, but by me. *John 14 : 6.*

I have yet many things to say unto you, but ye cannot bear them now. Howbeit when he, the Spirit of truth, is come, he shall guide you into all the truth: for he shall not speak from himself; he shall declare unto you the things that are to come. *John 16 : 12, 13.*

If ye abide in my word, then are ye truly my disciples; and ye shall know the truth, and the truth shall make you free. *John 8 : 31, 32.*

God is light, and in Him is no darkness at all. If we say that we have fellowship with Him, and walk in the darkness, we lie, and do not the truth: but if we walk in the light, as He is in the light, we have fellowship one with another, and the blood of Jesus His Son cleanseth us from all sin. If we say that we have no sin, we deceive ourselves, and the truth is not in us. *I John 1 : 5–8.*

For the fruit of the light is in all goodness and righteousness and truth. *Eph. 5 : 9.*

In his discussion of "The Religious Education of an American Citizen," Prof. Francis F. Peabody says in conclusion, "each step in this series of reflections on religious education brings one nearer to a single personality and influence. It is as though one's thought had revolved in the circumference of life, and was finally drawn as by some law of spiritual attraction toward a single centre. Each line of discussion or description, as it has been followed to its interior meaning, has led to some aspect of the teaching or example of Jesus Christ. . . . A modern life, as it interprets its own problems, is led inward to the teachings of Jesus; and the teaching of Jesus, followed outward, brings one to his immediate duty in the modern world. It is not so important to determine where to start as it is to find the Way. Jesus Christ may be either the beginning of a religious experience, or the end of it. . . . Whether light shall reach the eye directly or by reflection is not so important so long as one has light enough to see. Whether the Way leads from life to faith or from faith to life is not important so long as the Way is found and followed." The testimony of countless educators, and religious leaders of all faiths voices the same conclusion. Jesus *is* the way and the *truth*. No one can follow the truth without reckoning with Him any more than one can pilot himself across the seas without reckoning with the sun.

Most of us lose a lot of time in following one gleam of light after another. We are like children chasing a fire-fly in the darkness. When we think we have it in our hand, it is gleaming fitfully in the distance. Jesus gave us three guides to lead us into the light. The first is the indwelling Spirit of truth who is to guide us into all the truth.

> "And His that gentle voice we hear,
> Soft as the breath of even,
> That checks each thought and calms each fear,
> And speaks of heaven."

One cannot prove this statement by argument. We know it by personal experience. If the voice is faint, it is because we are not "tuning in" our heart.

The second guide is the life and teaching of Jesus. This has been said before, but it needs to be repeated again and again to us in order to induce us really to *begin to live with* the words of Jesus. We assent to this in our mind and then go on as before, letting every foolish book and any peddler of vagaries crowd out the truth for which our soul and body starves.

Why do we do this? Because we ignore the third guide; the light that is in the world for us as we walk from day to day. Do we find that the truth lived out in us means that we are closer one to another? Is it easier to overcome our sins and weaknesses? Does our truth separate us from holy living and holy loves, or does it lead to light? On all sides people are saying, "This is the truth; this is the way." How are we to know? Jesus' answer is the true test. "The truth shall make you *free*." It is possible to be free in thinking and enslaved in spirit. The freedom of Jesus brings no chaos to our being. Heart, soul, mind, and strength find their ordered completeness in Him.

> O God, we thank Thee that Thou hast revealed
> Thy truth to us through Jesus Christ our Lord.
> Grant unto us the Spirit of truth that we may
> be guided into right ways; lighten our darkness
> with Thy wisdom and grant that we fall into no
> error, for the sake of Thy Son, Jesus Christ.
> *Amen.*

AVAILABLE RESOURCES OF POWER

REWARDS FOR THE FRIENDLY HEART

Most of us agree with Ulysses, that hero of ancient Greek literature, when he says, "I am a part of all that I have met." Our personality becomes strangely intermingled with the personality of others, so that it is safe to say that no one is quite the same after meeting us and we too are influenced and charged by the impact of others on us. We are a blend of our own sentiments plus those which have been called out by our friends, and they in turn carry away with them a part of us. The truest portrait of anyone is that which has been etched on the hearts of those who have know him. That is the reason why we are often surprised at the true dimensions of a man after he has died. We thought him obscure and uninfluential and lo! a score or more of friends bear witness to his greatness, because of what he wrought out in them through friendship.

The spirit within is so much greater than the body which confines it that its only rest comes from the joys of friendship through which its power finds adequate satisfaction. "It is not good for man to be alone," we were told in the early record, and from that time down to the present we have needed friendship as a resource for our peace and health and power. When we shut ourselves away from others we are doing ourselves the greatest harm, in that we are limiting our possibility of greatness. The physical strain of loneliness testifies to this truth.

Friends are a source of power to us because through them we sense the reality of spiritual values. For example, we may have a theoretical idea of the value of honesty, but when we see it exemplified or wanting in the daily life of our friends it becomes a precious reality. Every virtue and every God-like characteristic is vivid only as we see it through some human relationship. One who has fifty friends has an understanding of the character of God fifty times greater than he would have if he lived only to himself.

Nothing gives such a peculiar buoyancy to one's spirit as the love of others. We know that God is love theoretically until we experience what it means through others. The leader of a mission which has reclaimed many a life from the scrap heap, once said that he had never been able to convince any man of the love of God who had not somewhere in his life had the love of a mother. No matter how far afield a man may go in his later years, the love of God is vivid to him if out of the memory of the past someone, like unto a mother, has personified love for him.

We need friends to hold us true to our best selves. The confidence which others place in us is the most effective stimulus for fine living. It nerves us for valiant achievement. My power for success is largely dependent upon the resources of confidence which are made available for me through my friends. Most of us would attempt the impossible if our friends expected it of us, after the manner of a small boy who will not refuse a dare. Most of our real courage also comes only when we are brave for the sake of others. The actual helplessness and expectation of those who depend upon us for help inspires a power beyond our own. Some of us are suffering from feeble health because we have succeeded in shutting ourselves away so completely from the need of others that we never get away from ourselves. An investment in friendship would yield large returns in physical buoyancy.

The achievement of others whom we love and long to be near is in itself a great influence which pulls us along in spite of ourselves. We do not like to be at the tail end of the procession. An invalid mother began to realize that her only son was beginning to outdistance her in his school studies. She resolved to keep up with him in order to hold his respect. Before a year had passed she was deep in special educational courses, and a well woman. Thus does the friendly heart inherit the ambitions of its friends. The tastes, careers, and standards of others become our own. We acquire them almost without effort. Few of us realize how we are influenced or inhibited by our social group.

Much is being written to-day about the power of the innumerable company, of those who have gone ahead of us, to reinforce us with their wisdom and protection. This is true in so far as it coincides with the law of friendship. The influence of a spirit does not depend on bodily presence. We may be sitting next to someone, and yet be thousands of miles apart; or we may be separated from our friends halfway around the globe and yet find them intimately near. Real absence is merely a retirement within oneself. When the mutual give and take of love is cut off between two human spirits, they are as remote as the east is from the west. Therefore the reality of a presence may be great or small as we will it to be. Jesus said to those who were to continue his work, "Lo, I am with you alway, even unto the end of the world." (*Matt. 28 : 20*). He took it for granted that their oneness with Him in love and purpose would bring His presence and help intimately nigh. Presence knows no limits of space or time. If God is present everywhere, surely those spirits who are one with Him, and with whom we are one in love, must be helping us with their love and strength every day. Thus our power is greater for personal victory and service. Our sense of values becomes more accurate, also, as we see them in the distance. The sublimation of our friendship enables us to judge its true value in contrast with our daily career.

It is a marvellous resource of power; — this connection through love with all the strength and kindred purpose of the ages. No matter how weak we may be in physical powers, our friendly heart may avail itself of all power. The kind of energy we draw upon is conditioned by the character of that with which we are at one. If we are one with evil, evil powers reinforce us; they cannot touch us unless they find a kindred spirit in us. Even so the powers of good are ours if the love of goodness is within us; if it is not there, they cannot help us.

> O may Thy soldiers, faithful, true and bold,
> Fight as the saints who nobly fought of old,
> And win with them, the victor's crown of gold
> > Alleluia!
>
> O blest communion, fellowship divine!
> We feebly struggle, they in glory shine;
> Yet all are one in Thee, for all are Thine
> > Alleluia!
> > > *W. Walsham How 1864.*

FOR STUDY AND THOUGHT

Paul, a prisoner of Christ Jesus, and Timothy our brother, to Philemon our beloved and fellow-worker, I beseech thee for my child, whom I have begotten in my bonds, Onesimus, who was aforetime unprofitable to thee, but now is profitable to thee and to me: whom I have sent back to thee in his own person, that is, my very heart: whom I would fain have kept with me, that in thy behalf he might minister unto me in the bonds of the gospel: but without thy mind I would do nothing; that thy goodness should not be as of necessity, but of free will. For perhaps he was therefore parted from thee for a season, that thou shouldest have him for ever; no longer as a servant, but more than a servant, a brother beloved, specially to me, but how much rather to thee, both in the flesh and in the Lord. If then thou countest me a partner, receive him as myself. But if he hath wronged thee at all, or oweth thee aught, put that to mine account
Philemon 1: 1, 10–18.

The true spirit of love transcends all social distinctions. What could be more perfect than this extract from the letter of St. Paul, that greatest apostle of Jesus, to the influential Philemon in the interests of a poor runaway slave Onesimus? In it are all the implications of friendship. If we could live according to this teaching, we should be able to solve every social and international problem.

Let us note that to St. Paul, the soul of a slave was of equal importance with the souls of Cæsar's household. Position is merely accidental. An emperor and a slave have the same capacity for immortality. Even though the days of opportunity for service were short, a slave, and a bad one at that, had a claim on the friendship of the representative of Jesus Christ. Jesus died for all; therefore all must be of vital concern to those of us who love Him. Think of what this belief would do in destroying our prejudices!

What an exquisite description of perfect friendship: *"His own person, that is, my very heart"*! Is this our ideal of love? How does it fulfill the command, "Thou shalt love thy neighbor as thyself?" We apply this description perhaps to one or two people whom we love: but how far would we have to change our ideals before we could say this truthfully about someone at the other end of the social ladder? St. Paul, the intellectual giant, finding his own heart in the person of an ignorant slave! We know that this is a God-like quality because it is so far from the ordinary human ideal.

Our civilization is torn by bitterness over class distinctions. Many social prophets trust to economic readjustments to remove the antagonism. If we looked at our personal relationships as not transient but eternal we would find it easier to transmute service into brotherhood. Friendship is our eternal bond. How our domestic life would be changed if everyone who serves the necessities of our life were not only a servant but *more* than a servant, a brother beloved. How far would our social order have to be reconstructed to put it on this basis? Are we ready to inherit the lasting rewards of the friendly spirit?

The friendly heart places its resources at the disposal of the friend who is in need. An ungenerous friend is a misnomer, for love is ever giving and using its resources to help establish brotherhood. Resources are merely opportunities for service; they were never meant to be opportunities for the display of power. How would our life be changed if we really received every one as the Master Himself? That will be the real test in that day when we shall have to give an account of our human relationships. "I was a stranger, and ye took me not in."

When? "Inasmuch as ye did it not unto one of these least, ye did it not unto me." (*Matt. 25 : 43–45*).

> Our Lord and Master, Thou hast given Thyself for the life of the world. Thou hast said that it is not the will of God that one of these little ones should perish. Forgive us that so many of Thy children perish and die while we care not for them. Take from us that spirit which indulges itself and withholds the means of life from others. How can we escape Thy wrath when we call Thee Lord, and yet refuse to minister unto Thee? Turn Thou our hearts we beseech Thee; through Jesus Christ our Lord. *Amen.*

SUBLIMATING OUR INSTINCTS

Every normal human being is born with certain instincts which are the inheritance of the ages. They are the stuff from which character is made. They cannot be acquired, or eliminated, therefore we are not responsible for having them.

Psychologists classify them differently, but the most important instincts are flight (with its emotion of fear), sex, parenthood, curiosity, the herd or social instinct, self-abasement, repulsion, ambition, self-assertion, acquisition and pugnacity. Every one of us has all of these, though they may not all be active at the same time. Sometimes an instinct may lie dormant in us for years until an occasion calls it forth. No one of us can glory over another, for all alike, good and bad, have the same instincts. They are like dynamos, full of emotional energy, supplying power alike to the passions and the will.

Our instincts are not good or bad in themselves, but they become so according to the purposes for which they are used. For example the instinct of ambition may be rightly directed toward the supply of the necessities of life, or it may be perverted and used for avaricious hoarding and robbery. We are discovering that many nervous diseases come from the repression of natural instincts which emerge into our conscious life in abnormal ways. We have already seen how fear when it is repressed shows itself in paralyzing effects and in moral diseases.

The dominance of certain instincts in us is largely due to early training and to circumstances; and our life careers are the natural result of this "bent" as we call it. A child in whom curiosity has been developed would be happy in scientific work, and unhappy in the rôle of business in which his acquisitive companion rejoices. It is also true that certain instincts succeed one another in power at different times. We see these desires asserting themselves in children at different ages. Each instinct in turn has its phase of activity. The training and education of the child determines which will be the strongest in adult life.

There are three things we need to know about our instincts: the original nature and end toward which they are directed; the precise danger of perverting them; and the possibility of redirecting their energy to higher ends. If we understand ourselves and our dangers we shall be able to work with the great purposes of God rather than to become the victims of our own ungoverned powers. We *can* sublimate every instinct if we will, and make it work out our salvation. We do not need to repress any of them; they can serve our highest purpose, and become the means of unfolding glories in life which we have scarcely suspected.

When we sublimate an instinct we direct it from its original end to some other end which is more satisfying and of real value. Even that common foe, fear, may become a virtue. We usually direct it toward anxiety or pervert it by attaching it to imaginary objects or those which ought not to inspire fear. We can sublimate it into alertness and caution. It should lead to a carefulness which is the opposite of carelessness. When we are told to work out our salvation "with *fear* and trembling" it is this sublimated fear which the writer has in mind. Much of the modern attitude toward the evil of all fear has resulted in a Christianity which is sickly and sentimental. A fear lest we come short of the highest ideals is necessary if there is to be any earnestness. One reason why we have so many perverted fears that are imaginary and nerve-racking is that we have removed all wholesome fear from life so that there is an *excess* of instinctive anxiety which takes its vengeance on our health and on our morals. The Psalmist was right when he sang, "The fear of the Lord is the beginning of wisdom." (*Psa. 111: 10*). We cannot eradicate fear from our hearts: therefore let us not pervert it, but direct it toward God and our destiny.

The instinct of sex is the most repressed and least understood of all our natural impulses. It is concerned with reproduction as a natural end. Most people have an excess of this repressed instinct because often there is no opportunity for its natural use, and also because of past training we try to ignore it as much as possible, as something of which to be ashamed. As a result comes sex perversion.

No instinct can be sublimated for such divine ends as the sex instinct. All the arts, like music, painting, poetry; all the creative work, the outreach of love, are the higher forms of this life force. We need all we have and more for this kind of sublimation. If people could realize what this costly power could do for them they would be less likely to throw it away on mere sex feeling. The creation of the race and all the creative work of the soul lie at the heart of this instinct. It is fair to suppose that most of us could find deliverance from many of our ills if we recognized this sex instinct as a precious possession and determined to use it to develop the latent genius within, instead of fighting it as an enemy. Herein lies spiritual victory. As Carlyle says, "Produce! Produce! Were it but the pitifulest infinitesimal fraction of a product, produce it, in God's name!"

No sublimation can be really satisfying unless it is of value to the community. We are all so interwoven with the social fabric that we dare not forget it. Our social instincts are so strong that they cannot be repressed without throwing the whole life out of balance. Each one of us reaches the highest self-expression when we find it in some work for the common good.

Christianity is the only power which enables us to take all of our instincts and use all their energy for our highest development. Even pugnacity can be sublimated by turning that force to account in overcoming evil with good. The Church satisfies the herd, or social instinct, and the acquisitive desire can be turned to laying up treasures of eternal value. Our love for the Christ brings in one central life of the soul. We cannot deal with ourselves in fragments. We reach our ideal only when we sublimate the whole.

> My soul, be on thy guard;
> Ten thousand foes arise;
> A host of sins are pressing hard
> To draw thee from the skies.
> Ne'er think the victory won,
> Nor lay thine armour down;
> Thy arduous work will not be done
> Till thou obtain thy crown. *George Heath 1781.*

FOR STUDY AND THOUGHT

But there was a certain man, Simon by name, which beforetime in the city used sorcery, and amazed the people of Samaria, giving out that himself was some great one.

Then laid they their hands on them, and they received the Holy Ghost. Now when Simon saw that through the laying on of the apostles' hands the Holy Ghost was given, he offered them money, saying, Give me also this power, that on whomsoever I lay my hands, he may receive the Holy Ghost. But Peter said unto him, "Thy silver perish with thee, because thou hast thought to obtain the gift of God with money. Thou hast neither part nor lot in this matter: for thy heart is not right before God. Repent therefore of this thy wickedness, and pray the Lord, if perhaps the thought of thy heart shall be forgiven thee. For I see that thou art in the gall of bitterness and in the bond of iniquity. And Simon answered, and said, Pray ye for me to the Lord, that none of the things which ye have spoken come upon me. *Acts. 8 : 9, 17–24.*

They were not able to enter in because of unbelief. Let us fear therefore, lest haply, a promise being left of entering into his rest, any one of you should seem to have come short of it. For indeed we have had good tidings preached unto us, even as also they: but the word of hearing did not profit them, because they were not united by faith with them that heard. *Heb. 3 : 19, 4 : 1, 2.*

The story of Simon illustrates the perversion of two primitive instincts: the desire for self-assertion and the instinct of acquisition. We could not do without the inborn impulse to self-assertion. All our individuality comes from it, and the advancement of the race and the growth of personality are dependent upon it. Simon perverted his desire for individuality by the use of sorcery which duped the mass of intelligent people around him. He asserted himself by illegitimate means. He was not really greater than those about him but advertised himself as great. Is he a unique character? In the light of this story it would be enlightening to read the modern publicity of those who claim to be able to do the works of God; to make people well, rich, successful by some infallible philosophy. One of the sure signs of this perverted instinct of self-display is that the instinct of acquisition is also perverted. Simon grew rich through the selling of his secrets of life. This was a perversion, because money cannot buy life and the power of God. Life is not a trick but an experience. The power of God is as free as the air we breathe and cannot be held, or given by anyone. Peter had the true insight to see that Simon's inner self was not right. Note that Simon is more afraid of personal hardship than of an insincere heart. We do well to ask ourselves whether we are being exploited by men or illumined by God. If the commercial spirit is evident, we are likely to find that we are being exploited by some modern Simon. There is no short cut to power. The teaching of Jesus will give us the open secret for ourselves.

In this warning to the Hebrews we have an illustration of the highest use of the instinct of fear. Its fruits are the virtues of diligence, prudence, caution, concentration, and humility. All these are sublimations of the fear element and without them we are likely to make grievous mistakes. Such a fear cleanses our hearts from ulterior motives and leads us into the highest wisdom. The thought that we may "come short" of our ideal keeps us from loitering along the path of life.

Note how faith is meant to work *with* fear when it is re-directed to higher ends. The tender mother is one who has the confidence to take her babe in her arms and yet fears lest she may hurt it. The greatest skill is a blend of confidence and carefulness. Where there is no fear there is no carefulness. Are there any phases of our national life to-day which are due to the lack of this blending faith and fear? How would our spiritual life be purified if we sublimated our fear and made it an intimate friend of faith?

Our Father, wilt Thou redeem all the instincts of our being so that they shall help us to attain to everlasting life. Deliver us from the heart of unbelief, from selfishness, and everything which exalteth itself above Thee. Purify every desire which burns within us. May we follow in the steps of Jesus who came to do Thy will. Thou hast made us as we are; help us to be reverent toward all our humanity because through Thy grace it may be transfigured with glory. Through Jesus Christ our Lord. *Amen.*

REINFORCING THE WILL

The human will has always been recognized as a fact of central importance for every individual, but it has not been clearly understood. Some people have assumed that the will has perfect freedom to do what it likes regardless of circumstances. Many teachers and religious leaders have regarded it as some extraneous instrument which the self could use or not as it chose. We speak of a man as inheriting a strong will or a weak will as if it were a matter of birth like the color of his eyes or the features of the face. St. Paul speaks as though we had two wills; the will to do the will of God, and a corrupt will which is antagonistic to the good will. Some psychologists regard the will as the activity of the *whole* self but that it is sometimes not strong enough to hold in firm control all the impulses of the mind. Tennyson in his immortal words is sure that whatever the will may be, it is only safe in the hands of God.

> "Our wills are ours, we know not how;
> Our wills are ours, to make them Thine.'

The British psychologist, Hadfield, throws much light on the subject. He writes, "When the organized self moves towards its own completeness we call it the *will*. The will is the organized self in function, the self in movement." In other words the will is not an entity, but a *function* of that part of the self which is made up of all the sentiments and dispositions which we have accepted for ourselves. Outside of this organized self, according to Dr. Hadfield, are the unexpressed instincts and the repressed sentiments, and those unacceptable experiences in life which were repugnant to us at the time and linger in our subconscious mind as repressed complexes. In this "Hinterland" as some one calls it, smouldering fires flame up into our consciousness from time to time and conflict with our will.

The *activity of the self*, *i e.*, the will, is ever moving toward its ideal. When it ceases to act, the self begins to disintegrate and we are again at the mercy of the conflicting instincts with which we were born. The great problem for us all lies in the task of uniting *all* our instincts and complexes into our common purpose so that there shall be peace because the will controls the whole situation. If only a few instincts are held together by a common purpose, we are likely to be swept away by some unsubdued instinct which is waiting its chance to come forth in power. Therefore the task of reinforcing our organized self is an important one both for health and morals, for the hidden fires devastate alike the mind and the body.

Our will is stimulated to action by an ideal and that ideal must be one which will produce completeness and happiness for the self. A complete self is a harmonious and free self; free to act with all its powers toward the goal of its desire. It is at this point that we see the scientific value and necessity for Christianity, because the Christ embodies the complete ideal for our whole nature.

At this point we ought to give thanks for parents and forebears who have inclined us to certain ideals and worthy ends so that the battle with our primitive instincts has been made easier for us. Some of us have not had this advantage, but we can take ourselves in hand now that we know what is at stake in our character. We may begin now, if complete inner harmony is so desirable to us that we make it our purpose and our will moves to that end.

One of the best methods of strengthening the will is to acquire the habit of mental reflection. The strong mind acts slowly; the weak mind acts quickly. In his "Education of the Will," Payot uses the illustration of a crystal plunged into a solution of saturated substances which in some mysterious way draws other molecules like unto itself until a large crystal of beauty is formed, *provided it is kept perfectly quiet*. If the solution is jarred, the deposit is irregular and imperfect. He then points out that, "If one keeps any psychological state whatever in the foreground of consciousness, it will insensibly, by an affinity no less mysterious than the other, gradually attract to itself other intellectual states of the same nature. If this 'crystallization' goes on slowly without disturbance or interruption it will acquire a remarkably strong character." All of this has been said before in the discussion of the habit of prayer, and Bible study, and meditation on what is true and good and beautiful, but it is well to see that these acts promote not only religion but mental self-control. Those who discount the value of Christianity will also have to discount modern psychology, for both emphasize the same principles.

Thinking intently is powerless without action. It gathers the forces of the mind together for united action, but of what use is force unless it moves something? It must turn the wheels of service or it will have to return to its original elements like steam that is blown off into the air. We strengthen the will by concentrated action in some one cause rather than by spasmodic efforts in many directions. It is good for all of us to reorganize our daily life on a systematic basis, making regular provision for certain tasks so that they become habitual. The power of good habits will overturn bad habits. A word needs to be said concerning system in *important* things, for some of us are enslaved by a system of trifles which are of no consequence to our character and prevent us from having any horizon for our soul.

At this point the Christian ideal is the way to victory. Loyalty to the Person of Jesus is more liberating than loyalty to a thing, however important it may be. It takes His Personality to satisfy our personality. Anything less than this does not offer completeness to the organized self. I, who choose what sentiments shall be acceptable, am by nature discontented with any goal save one which brings understanding fellowship with a Lord, the great Ideal for all humanity.

> My will is not my own
> Till Thou hast made it Thine;
> If it would reach a monarch's throne
> It must its crown resign:
> It only stands unbent
> Amid the clashing strife
> When on Thy bosom it has leant
> And found in Thee its life.   *George Matheson.*

FOR STUDY AND THOUGHT

Jesus therefore answered them, and said, My teaching is not mine, but his that sent me. If any man willeth to do his will, he shall know of the teaching, whether it be of God, or whether I speak from myself.
John 7 : 16, 17.

And why call ye me, Lord, Lord, and do not the things which I say?
Luke 6 : 46.

O Jerusalem, Jerusalem, which killeth the prophets, and stoneth them that are sent unto her! how often would I have gathered thy children together, even as a hen gathereth her chickens under her wings, and ye would not. *Matt. 23 : 37.*

Ye search the scriptures, because ye think that in them ye have eternal life; and these are they which bear witness of me; and ye will not come to me, that ye may have life. *John 5: 39, 40.*

Jesus always used the inductive method with His followers. He challenged them to test truth by the practical laboratory work of experience. Christianity is a way of life. It is based on laws which can be tested philosophically, but it has to be experienced in order to be understood. The teaching of Jesus is recognized as divine by those whose purpose and desire it is to be in harmony with God. The truth which comes out of life is the only kind which does not have to be proved. The thirsty man is the one who appreciates what water means. All the theories in the world amount to little unless there is some way of testing them in actual experience.

If the will is the function of the self, then there can be no sincerity in heart unless the self moves through the action of the will to the end which is in harmony with its desire. If we call on God in prayer and yet do not will those things which are pleasing to Him, it proves that our heart has not accepted His desires as our desires. We always will to do what we have accepted as our desire. It is like the act of Judas who said one thing with his lips and mocked that with the deed of betrayal. What we will to do is the thing we *desire* to do. It is a solemn fact that in religion as well as in other realms of experience, we use certain things without being inwardly committed to them. People have used the influence of the Church as a means of gaining certain ends without accepting that for which the Church stands. Every person in a prominent position knows well how many there are who desire to do mighty works by means of his influence without any real connection with him.

What a bitter disappointment it must have been to Jesus to find that after three years of patience and love and persuasion, the will of the people was still set against their own highest destiny. Even God with all His love cannot gather us under His protection if we will *not* let Him. All things do not come out right in the end without our willing coöperation. The heart of God is steadfast: if we are not enjoying His protection and care it is probably because we have run away from it.

Jesus in His person is the incarnation of all the truth and revelation of the scriptures. They pointed the way: He *is* the way. They described the life that is pleasing to God: He lived it. Even devils can quote scripture, but we cannot reconstruct the teaching of God from their lives. It is an easy thing to say, "I am a son of God because I search the scriptures." There is no escape from living what we believe. In truth, even now, our conduct is expressing what we have accepted as our standard. The will is performing its functions: the test of what we are is our resemblance to Jesus, the perfect embodiment of the truth.

O Lord God, Thou art an eternal will to all goodness. Grant that we may be as one in our beliefs and life as the sun and its rays are one. We thank Thee for the perfection of the character of Jesus. We thank Thee that in looking at Him we see what Thou wouldst have us be. May we have one desire only, — that Christ may be formed within our hearts that we may be One with Him as He is One with Thee. Help us to test our daily life by the standards of our Master. Through His name we come. *Amen.*

RESTORED YEARS

Wasted years are bitter enemies; — As we look back into the past most of us would give anything for the power to evade them. Lost opportunities cling to our minds with depressing effect the older we grow. Sometimes they were due to the foolish mistakes of youth, and oftener to the inadequate training for which we were not wholly responsible. The results however are the same. We have missed something which will never be ours again.

If the good news which Jesus brought into the world has anything to say about this, one of our heaviest burdens would be lifted. Is there any way of salvaging the past? Is there any part of the old building which can be used with which to build the new? The answer of the Bible is emphatically "yes."

Mistakes can be sublimated into wisdom after one sees their logical end. The natural law of cause and effect proves to us our folly, and we do not need further argument. The important moment comes when we decide what to do about the future. That is the point where our religion makes the great difference. If we have none, we will lean in the direction of our temperament, and those instincts which have usually ruled our conduct, and we shall be led again into difficulties. This is one reason why so few criminals are reformed by prison life. They have the habit of being led by evil instincts and restraint does not weaken their desires. What they need and all of us sinners need, is to discover the law of life which Jesus taught us by which the past can be transmuted into the wisdom of God. "He restoreth my soul," sang King David from a full heart after he had had to face his grievous mistakes. Religion, which reached its highest expression in the life and death of Jesus, is the only hope for those of us who regret a past. We may forget it, or ignore it, but we can never restore it apart from the principles of life which Jesus taught. The whole problem of sin is involved together with the necessity for forgiveness, for we are morally responsible.

We need also to salvage our outworn experiences. Some of us are still living in the past, crowding our souls down into the narrow confines of a child's intelligence. We may have minds that can grasp the most complicated problems of business and yet pray the little prayers of a five-year-old and live on some past experience which once was real, but has long ago been outgrown. Our crude and immature conceptions of God have never been replaced by an adult ideal of an adequate, understanding Father; — something stopped our spiritual growth in childhood, and since then we have been pitiful cases of arrested development. A fresh experience with the teaching of Jesus to-day might restore years of dwarfed life. To the simple child's faith might be added an understanding of God which would turn defeat into victory. A fresh study of Jesus' way of life never fails to restore withered and stunted ideals. The "down-and-outers" are not all in the bread line, or on the front seats in city missions, so far as spiritual powers are concerned; many of them are outwardly the most successful men and women in a community. It will take considerable restoration before they grow into full citizenship in the kingdom of God. It may take a physical breakdown, or some great shock or some insuperable obstacle before some of us come to ourselves and let God restore our blighted spiritual capacities.

After a year of happy life together a friend's husband died. To one of her sympathetic relatives she said proudly, "I would rather have had only twelve months of joy with my husband than fifty years with any other man I have ever known!" Love gave her a new sense of relative values. It is not length of life, but quality of life that satisfies. Who would not rather have lived for three years as Jesus lived in the power of God than to have been for fifty years a Napoleon! How much better, too, that the remaining ten years of our human incarnation should be lived in spiritual victory. If the mistakes of the past drive us to God *now*, we may yet overcome them all by this renewing of our mind.

There is another way also in which the past may be restored. Back in the hidden corners of our life, latent powers have been dormant for years because they were not called forth by a conscious relationship to God. They have been within us like seeds within the frozen earth. Chill winds and snows have kept them from growing. Months later, when the spring showers and sun reach down to them, they grow up to blossom and bear fruit. Had winter continued there would have been no harvest. In like manner our hidden powers come to fruition under the influence of Jesus and what we were unable to produce for years, now comes forth from us to bless the world.

Many of us are at the critical moment in life when we shall either sink back in disillusioned obscurity, or rise up in fresh spiritual vigor. We need restoration for soul, and body. Between us and the new life is a narrow door and we hear the voice of the Christ saying, "I am the door: by me if any man enter in, he shall be saved (*restored*) and shall go in and go out and shall find pasture." We bring our wasted years, our outworn ideas, our sins, and our needs: and giving them into the keeping of the Good Shepherd, we go into the new, open country of opportunity.

We shall really never know ourselves until we have this experience. What a surprise is in store for some of us who dare to venture. If by reading this, anyone sees how to sublimate a past and find a new life, he must not be disobedient to the heavenly vision or his last state will be worse than his first. If the seed does not respond to the sun and shower there is no future for it.

> "Perverse and foolish oft I strayed
> But yet in love He sought me
> And on His shoulder gently laid
> And home, rejoicing, brought me.
>
> And so through all the length of days,
> Thy goodness faileth never;
> Good Shepherd, may I sing Thy praise
> Within Thy house, forever."

FOR STUDY AND THOUGHT

Be glad then, ye children of Zion, and rejoice in the Lord your God: for he giveth you the former rain in just measure, and he causeth to come down for you the rain, the former rain and the latter rain, in the first month. And the floors shall be full of wheat, and the vats shall overflow with wine and oil. And I will restore to you the years that the locust hath eaten, the cankerworm, and the caterpillar, and the palmerworm, my great army which I sent among you. And ye shall eat in plenty and be satisfied, and shall praise the name of the Lord your God, that hath dealt wondrously with you: and my people shall never be ashamed. And ye shall know that I am in the midst of Israel, and that I am the Lord your God, and there is none else: and my people shall never be ashamed.
Joel 2 : 23–27.

For we know that the whole creation groaneth and travaileth in pain together until now. And not only so, but ourselves also, which have the first fruits of the Spirit, even we ourselves groan within ourselves, waiting for our adoption to wit, the redemption of our body. And we know that to them that love God all things work together for good, even to them that are called according to his purpose. *Rom. 8 : 22, 23, 28.*

Are ye so foolish? having begun in the Spirit, are ye now perfected in the flesh? *Galatians 3 : 3.*

Many a man has made a fortune from the waste products of manufacture. Good business requires that everything be utilized and be made to yield its share of profit. Why, then, should not God the Creator of all things be able to utilize the neglected "capacities" of

fasted and prayed for his sick son; but the child died. Jesus prayed three times for a way of escape from the cross and none came.

The reality of this experience of David's is one which our Lord shared when He hung on the cross. It was this Psalm which expressed His deepest emotion when He too felt God remote from Him. It was David's high honor to frame the words which described the most tragic moment of Jesus' life. David found in prayer something more than the answer to a petition; for his confidence in God is not shaken even though he feels deserted. There are greater issues involved on our prayer than can be met by an immediate answer. If our desire were satisfied at once, we would fail to press on into the larger victories of faith which take time to bring to pass. We win the goal by faith long before we arrive there just as we see the mountain top before we begin the climb. All the development of character would count for nothing if we arrived at the end without effort. All the prayer and yearning in the world will not give a college student his diploma before long weeks of study are completed. Unless, in the beginning, he really craves an education his prayer will never be answered.

To the thoughtful soul, prayer would be a hazardous business if we always obtained precisely what we ask. When St. Paul exclaimed, "Now I know *in part,*" he expressed the conviction of all the humble-minded. Even in the incidental happenings there is more wrapped up than we can at once see. Far-reaching consequences come from small things like the touch on a button which started the blast which blew up the Hellgate rocks. How can we be sure that what we wish to-day is really desirable in the light of tomorrow? If we were competent to decide what is best for us, then we would have little need for God. If a child is as wise as its father what is the need of family life? If we grant that we are ever likely to make mistakes in our prayers we can easily see that some of our petitions could not be answered if God really loves us. We get frightened at some of the circumstances of our life and forget that not even a sparrow falls to the ground without our Father knowing it and that to Him we are of more value than many sparrows.

As we study the lives of those people in the Bible who prayed, we see that their experiences in prayer corresponded with their spiritual development. God answered or denied their petitions according to the inner development which, in His judgment, they most needed. God's purpose and not their wish was the important thing. Whenever their desires and God's wisdom were one, all the powers on earth could not hold back the answer.

O God, the Father of us all, we trust Thy faithful heart.
Help us to believe in Thy love even when we cannot
see our way. Thou hast promised to lead the blind by a
way they know not. Wilt Thou make darkness light
before us and the crooked places straight, through
Jesus Christ the true way. *Amen.*

THE CHARACTER OF THE PRAYER

The character of our prayers often prevents their answer. We defeat ourselves by a wrong understanding of what our call upon God can accomplish. There is a certain region wherein we ourselves answer our own prayers, and there is another unlimited region where God must coöperate with us or our desires cannot be realized.

Prayer which expects God to be a substitute for our thinking will not find a response. God cannot rearrange the universe, to satisfy our muddled brains. Many Christians, looking upon prayer as an escape from all difficulties, are like the small child who prayed one night, "Dear God, please make Boston the Capital of Vermont, 'cause I said it was so in my examination paper and I want it to be right." Obviously God cannot answer such prayers. They place self-protection and vanity above truth. They ignore the laws of an orderly, growing, unfolding cosmos into which we must fit ourselves if we would inherit all things. There is the unescapable region of fact and law, of cause and effect, in which we are to work out our salvation. God has equipped our spirit with mind and judgment. He gives us the comradeship of other spirits wiser than ourselves, the knowledge of all generations in books ready for our use, and the world of nature, — His great laboratory in which we are free agents on discovery bent. All of this is ours that we may grow in grace and in the knowledge of God's power. And in it all we are not necessarily alone, but may have the inspiration of the Holy Spirit to guide us into the whole truth, for God is still working in His world as rapidly as He can secure coöperating spirits like ourselves through whom to work.

Sometimes our prayers are too dictatorial to deserve an answer. When importunity means the setting up of our own will, insisting that the blessings of heaven shall come in the precise form in which we decide we want them, we shut off our connection with divine power. Faith becomes presumption when demand outgrows petition. Egotism may replace coöperation and leave us, in the end, still groping for the secret power.

Many prayers go unanswered because they seek too little. They crave a small and immediate manifestation of God's love when delay would prepare our faith to rise to greater heights and rejoice in larger gifts. When we have to wait, let us examine the character of our prayer and take this time to make it effectual.

187

The opposite of this is also true. Many desires which we voice to God are so far-reaching that the answers can come only through long processes of working and waiting which may involve more than we dreamed. Is it not true with most of us that it is our childish insistence on having what we want now, without delay, that colors much of our doubt regarding prayer. Some day we may be in a realm where achievement follows instantly on the heels of desire, but on this material plane we may indeed be devoutly grateful if our dominant desires set in motion influences which ultimately will work out good for us.

Again, our prayer may be too insular, too unrelated to others about us, and so individual that our good might be another's harm. Perhaps we imagine that we ourselves, and God, are the only factors in the situation. Here again delay will help us to realize our narrow horizon. How often during the World War we found ourselves unable to pray definitely because we sensed in some feeble way that our good would be another's ill, and our social consciousness was too well developed to allow us to be selfish in our intercession.

Many people also do not know the difference between negative and positive prayer. Some of us, under the spell of an alluring temptation, go to God in all earnestness and ask for deliverance. Then we go out and speedily give way to the very temptation against which we prayed. The reasons are not far to seek. In all probability the desire for deliverance was nullified by weak purpose which did not fulfill the human side of the answer. Late hours of social dissipation often prevent any reply to a prayer for patience the next morning. The spirit may be willing, but the flesh has been rendered abnormally weak by our own volition.

The other reason is a psychological one. We tend toward that upon which we fix our attention. If our prayer is merely a recital of all the fears and inclinations from which we long to be delivered, we naturally strengthen the tendency to do that which we have re-impressed on our minds. In this case it is the negative prayer. Availing prayer for deliverance forgets its temptation in the presence of God, and is absorbed with contemplation, and praise, and worship of all the love and beauty and purity which is always shed within our hearts by the thought of God. From such prayer we go out with minds overcharged with an atmosphere of holiness which is a shield against all evil.

> Thou art where'er the proud
> In humbleness melts down;
> Where self itself yields up;
> Where martyrs win their crown;
> Where faithful souls possess
> Themselves in perfect peace.   *F. T. Palgrave 1867.*

FOR STUDY AND THOUGHT

Simon, Simon, behold, Satan asked to have you, that he might sift you as wheat: but I made supplication for thee, that thy faith fail not: and do thou, when once thou hast turned again, stablish thy brethren.

Luke 22 : 31, 32.

And by reason of the exceeding greatness of the revelations — wherefore, that I should not be exalted overmuch, there was given to me a thorn in the flesh, a messenger of Satan to buffet me, that I should not be exalted overmuch. Concerning this thing I besought the Lord thrice, that it might depart from me. And he hath said unto me, My grace is sufficient for thee: for my power is made perfect in weakness. Most gladly therefore will I rather glory in my weaknesses, that the power of Christ may rest upon me. Wherefore I take pleasure in weaknesses, in injuries, in necessities, in persecutions, in distresses, for Christ's sake: for when I am weak, then am I strong. *II Cor. 12 : 7-10.*

The making of character is responsible for many unanswered prayers. Latent greatness is locked up within every one of us as gold is confined within the rock. The refining process of life, watched over by God's love, brings out the eternal qualities. We are concerned about that which is confronting us; — an alluring prospect or something to shun. We pray according to our desire. We neither get what we want nor love what we do not want; we are given a chance to triumph over the things of sense and to develop certain powers which will bring us gifts far richer than those we desired.

How the thought of Jesus' prayer for him must have called out all the finest spirit in Simon Peter! Testings of strength, from which there was no escape, were coming to him. Jesus did not pray that he might escape the experience, but that his faith might be so victorious that multitudes would be inspired by his strength. Jesus was always reminding us of the others with whom we are connected. Every bit of heroism that is minted out of our life is of supreme value to society. God's power working *through* us is far more sublime than God's power for us. A child who loves music may desire merely to hear his master play for him, but if the great musician, by patient teaching, reproduces his genius in the child, he has answered the desire in the perfect way. Sometimes it takes us a long time to see this larger answer to our prayer but when we do, we are thankful that the immediate satisfaction was denied us.

We are all sensitive to our own weakness. Like Paul we long to be rid of the thorn in our flesh. We pray to be delivered from it. If it does not disappear by some special providence, we succumb to it and thereafter use it as an apology for inglorious living. It then becomes our pet weakness, and our pet excuse. We speak resignedly of the "nerves" or "liver trouble" or "headaches" which we inherited from our forebears, or the "temper," "melancholia," or "sensitiveness" etc., which has handicapped us. We say we have prayed for some escape from it, but God does not answer our prayer. Read once again this experience of Paul. How does he meet his limitations? He *"besought the Lord thrice;"* an expression of intense earnestness of desire that would not close until some relief came. He was so eager to be rid of this "thorn" that any deliverance by *any* means was welcome. This spirit of downright determination opened his eyes to see the supreme way out; to reduce the power of the enemy by bringing up huge reinforcements of spiritual power. The infinite strength of God must garrison his heart. No answer could be more perfect, because it gave him immunity not only from this thorn, but from all thorns.

The safety of a bank does not consist in locking the door against depositors who may organize "a run" on it, but in having such resources in its vaults that it can be indifferent to *any* "run." Toward which point is our prayer directed; against the "thorn" or toward the resources? Not in passive resignation, but active resolve, is our way of escape. Paul's paradox may be true for us, "When I am weak, then am I strong."

> I give Thee thanks, O Lord God, with my whole heart, because, though I walk in the midst of perplexities Thou dost guard me; Thou art acquainted with all my ways; Thy right hand upholdeth me; Thou wilt perfect that which concerneth me. My trust is in Thee. Through Jesus Christ, Our Lord. *Amen.*

THE NECESSITIES OF GOD'S PLANS

Many of our prayers are so wide in their scope that we, together with God, must wait in patience. Many other people may be involved with us in the expected blessings. The plan of God is the law of growth, "first the blade, then the ear, then the full corn in the ear!" It takes time to grow, time to educate our spirit, time to open our eyes to see new truth; to get rid of prejudices. Most of our petitions assume that God will turn people's hearts quickly and mould their wills in perfect obedience to His suggestion at a word. If we will look into our own spiritual experience and recall how slow we have been to respond to the suggestions of God's spirit, we shall understand how patiently God has to work in the hearts of others in order that they may do His will.

In the great plan of God for our life, there may be many gifts which He longs to give us, but as yet we are not full-grown in our spiritual strength to bear the responsibility of the blessing. Every parent knows this truth well. There are many things which we long to give our children but cannot until they grow up to an appreciation of what such provision means. Even then there must be intelligent coöperation between parent and child. A college education is a great boon; but many parents cannot give it to their sons because the sons do not appreciate it enough to ask for it and to work for it. Many other things in life require time for their fulfillment. We adjust ourselves to the situation; can we not believe that the same principle holds true in our relation to our Heavenly Father?

Oftentimes we ask for the shell when God intends us to have the kernel. Some of the great possessions of life come in the disguise of something seemingly irrelevant or insignificant, oftentimes mighty treasures are wrapped in insignificant parcels which we ignore. The great plans of God are usually seen just behind something that is near and accessible. While we are looking to heaven, behold there is the key at our hand. We sigh for a career in some unfamiliar life and mourn because it is withheld. Within reach of our hand the beginning of a career may be; but in our vanity we despise the day of small things! Our prayer has been answered, but we fail to recognize it. There is a divine providence in the environment, and "peculiar situation" in which we are placed. If we could bring to life some dominant desire out of the heart of our present situation we would find, as

191

Jacob found, a ladder reaching to heaven and say, "Surely God is in this place, and I knew it not."

Out of our limitations God will burst in triumphant power, if we accept them as the starting point for His miracle working. A blind man may have his dominant desire for sight answered through the prayer of faith, and live as a witness to the touch of God. Or he may be like the blind Milton, enduring physical darkness in order that the eyes of his mind might see the spiritual land of Paradise Lost and Paradise Regained. The same power of God may deliver a man from jail and give him a new chance for growth, or he may find in jail the quiet retreat in which to write "Pilgrim's Progress," as did Bunyan. With God nothing is impossible; but the closer we come in our relationship with divine love the more we shall pray the prayer of Jesus: "If it be possible, let this cup pass from me, nevertheless not my will but Thine be done." It is the purpose of our incarnation which we must discover and live out in our years on earth. The divine power will be seen not only in uncounted replies to our cries of need, but in a life-long process wherein, as the years go by, we shall discern a mysterious but personal guidance and one which will humble our hearts.

Of one thing we may be sure. The events of life are not accidental, nor the mere coincidences of endless permutations and combinations.

> "There's a divinity that shapes our ends
> Rough-hew them how we will."

There are countless gifts which come into the life of every child who possesses loving parents. Some of them come in answer to desires voiced by a child; but the greater number represent the foresight, and care, and tenderness of the parents. "If ye then," says Jesus, "know how to give good things to your children how much more will your heavenly Father give good things to them that ask Him." And the prophet of olden times discerned this truth when he caught this glimpse of God's heart in the word: "Can a mother forget her child? . . Yes, she may, yet will I not forget thee."

> "Thy ways are love; though they transcend
> Our feeble range of sight
> They wind, through darkness, to their end
> In everlasting light."

FOR STUDY AND THOUGHT

But as the time of the promise drew nigh, which God vouchsafed unto Abraham, the people grew and multiplied in Egypt, till there arose another

king over Egypt, which knew not Joseph. The same dealt subtly with
our race, and evil entreated our fathers, that they should cast out their
babes to the end they might not live. At which season Moses was born,
and was exceeding fair; and he was nourished three months in his father's
house: and when he was cast out, Pharaoh's daughter took him up, and
nourished him for her own son. And Moses was instructed in all the
wisdom of the Egyptians; and he was mighty in his words and works. . .
There came a voice of the Lord: I am the God of thy fathers, the God of
Abraham, and of Isaac, and of Jacob. And Moses trembled, and durst not
behold. And the Lord said unto him, Loose the shoes from thy feet: for
the place whereon thou standest is holy ground. I have surely seen the
affliction of my people which is in Egypt, and have heard their groaning,
and I am come down to deliver them: and now, come, I will send thee into
Egypt. This man led them forth, having wrought wonders and signs in
Egypt, and in the Red Sea, and in the wilderness forty years.

Acts. 7 : 17–22, 31, 32, 33, 34, 36.

The victory of the individual and the victory of the race are
intimately related. This is why many prayers cannot be answered at
once. It takes time for God's purposes to unfold. If human beings
were puppets, God could move us about at will without hindrance;
but because we are destined for likeness to God, the carrying out of
the divine plan is *immediately* affected by our decisions. *Ultimately*
no one of us can hinder God; but we have the chance now to work with
Him and inherit all things.

The history of Moses illustrates this. The countless prayers of the
enslaved Hebrews for deliverance from the cruelty of the Egyptians
apparently were in vain. The mother and father of the baby Moses
could not avert the fearful necessity of casting out their beloved child
to the forces of destruction. Then their prayers were partly answered.
The mother could nurse the baby, but he was to be the son of the
hated Pharaoh. This could not have been much comfort to the Levite
parents who, in the priestly line, must have desired their son to be
guardian of the faith and not to be trained as a pagan. They must
have wondered at the inscrutable purpose of God.

But God had a greater gift in store than they had asked in their
prayers. The training as the son of Pharaoh equipped Moses with the
education, the wisdom, and the intimate knowledge of court life
which was to make him the fearless deliverer of *all* his people. His
parents asked for his life and God answered by giving them the lives
of all their people. But it took years to accomplish it. The people
suffered for more than a generation while their leader was growing
up and being fitted to work with God for their deliverance.

There is no haste with God, because there is *no time* with Him.

Moses knew this. He prayed, in that immortal Psalm, "A thousand years in Thy sight are but as yesterday when it is passed, and as a watch in the night." (*Psa. 90 : 4*). Centuries after, in the midst of suffering, another friend of God, had to find his comfort, even after the triumph of the Christ, by writing, "Forget not this one thing, beloved, that one day is with the Lord as a thousand years, and a thousand years as one day. The Lord is *not* slack concerning His promise as some count slackness." (*II Peter 3 : 8-9*).

In the vividness of the moment, we lose our sense of eternity. We say, "I want this now! Why pray, if we have to wait for one thousand years?" Because the destiny of the future is hidden within our present desire. This moment is part of eternity — the *only* part we have *now*. Bring your desires to God. Many of them will be answered at once; some of them will be changed; others will start the unrolling of some mighty destiny. If we do *not* pray, we shall miss our chance for greatness and learn the bitter wisdom of uninspiring existence.

> Our Father, Who seest the end from the beginning and hast prepared for us who love Thee blessings beyond our understanding, grant us the patience to wait for Thee. Deliver us from fretfulness of spirit and anxiety of heart and may Thy peace which passes understanding keep our heart and thoughts in Christ Jesus. *Amen.*

THE REAL GIFTS OF UNANSWERED PRAYER

We may ask for material gifts and gain spiritual gifts: We may ask for certain spiritual gifts and gain others more needed for our growth. There are many spiritual gifts which come largely through delayed answers.

Chief among these blessings is the consciousness of a growing acquaintance with God. A delayed answer brings us to Him again and again until we grow in our capacity for a life of spiritual insight and meditation. We form a habit of prayer which is the beginning of all blessing, for it brings God intimately near.

There is also an added power and intensity which we would never have except for the discipline of delay. If the river of our desire flowed on without interruption we would soon become shallow and sluggish. Delay and hindrance build a dam in the river and the higher the wall the greater power we gather in flowing over it. The power thus stored up for future release can be harnessed to vast projects and bless multitudes of people. Thus the delay that comes to the waters is in itself the answer of power. The life of nearly every great man or woman speaks eloquently of such experiences.

Another spiritual gift is a steady purpose. Our desires become so much a part of our daily life that they become more vivid and pointed through the delay in realizing them. Purpose girds up the mind and makes it alert for action. We wait so long for the promise of the future that we are ready for it without delay when it comes, and we shall find that we shall accomplish in a short time what we never could have done without the time of waiting. Jesus waited thirty years before His career of three years began.

One of the necessary qualities of heart for any great life is a sacrificial love; a love which has been purified of self-interest and vanity, and self-importance and has lost itself in the purpose of God. The purifying fire burns more quickly when the blessing is withheld for a time. We search our hearts for hindrances, and reasons for the delay, and we fast in our spirits in the intensity of our prayer. Many people have been transformed in their character by unanswered prayer. A mother waits long years for the return of her boy and in the waiting becomes the very personification of forgiving, expectant love. We need not go about hunting for discipline in life. Fortunate indeed are we who know a heavenly Father who will "lead the blind by a way they know not." Nothing helps us to understand the heart of Jesus as this training in sacrificial love, waiting and yearning for the goal of desire.

We learn, too, to see the perfect blend of the material and spiritual in this world. If prayer were always answered at once, our desires would grow to be more material and we would merely seek great things for ourselves because of their easy possibility. In waiting for our prayers to be answered we learn that "the gift without the giver is bare," that we are all in the world, but not of it. It is the triumph of life to live in the spiritual plane while as yet we are still touching the material. Realizing this, we walk through life with a more than human power.

The gift of faith also becomes ours. We get the habit of visualizing the things we hope for and seeing more clearly the unseen and eternal world. We find too that our faith stands the strain, and steadies us through days of waiting. We have faith in what we ask because it has become a sixth sense, and has been strengthened by long use.

There is also a gift which we are slow to covet, but which helps us to enter into the secret wisdom of God. It is the gift of humility — Only the baffling experiences of life call it out. It is the pure gold minted out of life through the furnace of disappointment, perplexity, and waiting. — It is so subtle in its nature that as soon as we discover we have it we lose it: as soon as we can conquer our limitations we are likely to kill it. — If then for no other purpose than to teach us humility, God should delay the blessing we seek, we should be thrice grateful. It is the heart of the little child which finds rest for its soul and enters into the kingdom of heaven.

> Teach me to feel that Thou art always nigh;
> Teach me the struggles of the soul to bear,
> To check the rising doubt, the rebel sigh;
> Teach me the patience of unanswered prayer.
>
> *George Croly 1854.*

FOR STUDY AND THOUGHT

Now the Lord is the Spirit: and where the Spirit of the Lord is, there is liberty. But we all, with unveiled face reflecting as a mirror the glory of the Lord, are transformed into the same image from glory to glory, even as from the Lord the Spirit.   *II Cor. 3 : 17, 18.*

It is God, that said, Light shall shine out of darkness, who shined in our hearts, to give the light of the knowledge of the glory of God in the face of Jesus Christ. But we have this treasure in earthen vessels, that the exceeding greatness of the power may be of God, and not from ourselves; we are pressed on every side, yet not straitened; perplexed, yet not unto despair; pursued, yet not forsaken; smitten down, yet not destroyed; always bearing about in the body the dying of Jesus, that the life also of Jesus may be manifested in our body. For our light affliction, which is for the moment, worketh for us more and more exceedingly an eternal weight of glory: while we look not at the things which are seen, but at the things which are not seen: for the things which are seen are temporal; but the things which are not seen are eternal.

II Cor. 4 : 6, 7, 8, 9, 10, 17, 18.

In a Florentine picture gallery an art student sat before one of Raphael's masterpieces trying to copy it. When his work was nearly done, he stood back and compared the two. Then with his brush, he daubed over the face of his picture and exclaimed tragically! "How can I do what Raphael has done without the mind of Raphael!" Thank God our case is different when we start out to follow the Christ. "We have the mind of Christ" (*I Cor. 1 : 16*) as St. Paul says, because the Spirit of God dwells within us. Note what happens as we turn our attention toward Him. We are gradually transformed into the same image from character to character. This is not an obscure truth, — it is a law of life. We grow to be like that which we love; that to which we give our devotion. Our face and character become the personification of what has absorbed our attention. Consider what this means in the realm of prayer. Even our special petitions may be unanswered, there are rewards of spirit which in themselves enrich us. No one can come to God without being better for it in some way. His transforming Spirit works in us.

One would suppose that a man so devoted to the cause of Christ as St. Paul would have been free from afflictions and distresses of mind. If the prayers of anyone were answered, his should have been. Why then did he keep on in the face of all these experiences recorded in our lesson? It was because he looked at everything in the light of the endless life. He knew that every trial could be made to yield a more valuable gift just as the grapes put in the press come forth as wine. If one asks *why* wine cannot be made without pressure on the grapes, we can only say we do not know. It is a law of life. We do not know why we have to be baffled in order to grow any more than the lily understands why it had to push its way against the pressure of the dark earth up into light. All we know is that if the lily cease to push up, it dies. Therefore we, too, stretch up toward God, and pray continually, knowing that the reward is sure.

More and more each day we are becoming aware of mighty forces which we cannot see, and scarcely understand, but which we can use. Every scientific man knows now that the things which are seen are transitory and that the unseen forces are eternal as God Himself. The marvel is that St. Paul saw this long before modern science was imagined. How did he get it? By the illumination of the Spirit of God in his heart. He knew the laws as they were taught by Jesus, and we with our slow moving minds know that those laws are the same throughout the universe. Therefore when Jesus said, "Ask and ye shall receive," He will be proved right in the light of human experience.

O God, many are they that say, who will show us any good? Lord, lift Thou up the light of Thy countenance upon us. Thou hast put gladness in my heart, more than they have when their corn and their new wine are increased. In peace will I both lay me down and sleep: for Thou Lord, alone makest me to dwell in safety. *Amen.*

Psa. 4 : 6–8.

THE REALITY OF SEEMING UNREALITY

DISCOVERING A WORLD

A wise man once said, "at birth man enters the realm of dreams only to awaken to reality at death." Unreality is the common experience of us all. We look into the years behind us and everything is a hazy dream, — we look forward and the future is full of mystery.

It is a gigantic task — this struggle for reality. The life of every child proves this. It enters the world with a cry, and a mind unconscious of its surroundings. It has the whole world to discover and to make real, and this demands a lifetime. Slowly one discovery after another is made. Years pass between the time when a child discovers its fists, toes, and its mother's face until the day when a printed page becomes real in its meaning. Many more years pass before history, science, language, and philosophy open new worlds of thought to the mind. The world is limitless in possibilities for reality; and yet each one of us possesses only as much of it as engages our attention. As Anatole France once said:

> "The world though vast on every side,
> Is no wider than our thought is wide."

We spend years searching for reality in the world of things only to find that human spirits and their creative thinking are the only true reality. Even a child knows this. Each day a small boy returns from school. He opens the door and calls, "Mother, mother!" "Here I am, what is it?" "O nothing, I just wanted you to be here." Then he runs out to play with things, contented with the reality of his mother's presence.

We are all like that child. The world is real and satisfying in proportion to the presence of the living spirits who have touched us and blended their friendship with ours. It is the spirit which makes all things live and is immortal. Things have no value save as they express the spirit. Nevertheless we spend our short years trying to satisfy ourselves with things and measure human success by the size and the number of things we possess. Oue would do well to heed the lessons of the past. About five thousand years ago two men lived: One had

199

vast possessions, the other a mighty spirit. Both died. One was forgotten until the other day, when by chance his body was dug up, buried among all his things: the glory of King Tut. The other man has an unknown grave, but, since the day he died, he has been a living reality in every land where light and truth have been found and where law has safeguarded life. And still to-day Moses lives, and sways us with his ten commandments because he was a living spirit, to whom the spiritual life was the only reality.

It is the life of the spirit which gives reality to the world. It uses material things to express itself. Piano music might be described materially as the vibration of steel wires strung over a wooden board, but these alone would make noise and not music. It is only when a human spirit, filled with creative emotion, controls the sounds, that music comes into being.

The world has never yet yielded its full measure of reality and power because it has been an end in itself for most of us. We have not used it for the creation of eternal values, and therefore, as the years go by, our memories are a meaningless blur.

The disciples of Jesus overheard Him praying about our relation to the world. "As Thou hast sent me into the world *even so* have I sent them into the world. I pray not that Thou shouldst take them out of the world but that Thou wouldst keep them from the evil that is in the world." Christians have never measured the *"even so"* of this prayer. It includes the emphasis on the triumph of the spirit and the use of the world as an instrument for the expression of the soul. It has been difficult, however, for the followers of Jesus to see the possibilities of the world from a religious point of view. In the early centuries they were indifferent to it because of persecutions. When they lived in caves and dungeons it was not strange that they should have been more concerned with the future life than with the task of living on the earth. Even now many religious folk create a small world for themselves and deliberately stress an unsocial emphasis in that part of the prayer, "They are not of this world." There are others, too, who have not yet discovered the possibilities of this present age because their spirits are living either in the past or in the future. They are the influences and the ideals who are either behind or ahead of the present reality. They are our traditionalists and radicals who try to find reality in a world which they do not possess.

The real power is in the hands of those who identify themselves with the day in which they live and who accept the commission of their Lord when he said, "I have sent them into the world."

"To serve the present age,
My calling to fulfil;
O may it all my powers engage
To do my Master's will."

All about us are other human spirits. Some of them live so close to us that we lose our mental alertness and pass them by like wooden soldiers, and forget them. Our attention is absorbed by other things and our world shrinks to the range of our concentration. Sometimes it is no larger than our aches and pains and personal opinions. It is high time to awake and look around and see the vast possibilities for growth and service which are all about us in the world we do not know. Opportunities pass unheeded. We are like children filling our hands full of sand and letting it escape through our fingers.

How large is your world? Is it a mere heap of things or is it a living organism throbbing with the life of human spirits ready to help us to find reality? Perchance we are missing the whole meaning of life. If so, we do well to pray the prayer of Richard Watson Gilder:

"Oh, deeper lead
My soul into the living world of souls
Where Thou dost move."

Yea, we know thy love rejoices
O'er each work of thine;
Thou didst ears and hands and voices
For thy praise combine;
Craftsmen's art and music's measure,
For thy pleasure,
Didst design. *Francis Pott 1861.*

FOR STUDY AND THOUGHT

Be ye therefore imitators of God, as beloved children; and walk in love, even as Christ also loved you, and gave himself up for us, an offering and a sacrifice to God for an odour of a sweet smell. But fornication and all uncleanness, or covetousness, let it not even be named among you, as becometh saints; nor filthiness, nor foolish talking, or jesting which are not befitting: but rather giving of thanks. Wherefore he saith, Awake, thou that sleepest, and arise from the dead, and Christ shall shine upon thee. Look therefore carefully how ye walk, not as unwise, but as wise; redeeming the time, because the days are evil. Wherefore be ye not foolish, but understand what the will of the Lord is, and be not drunken with wine, wherein is riot, but be filled with the Spirit; speaking one to another in psalms and hymns and spiritual songs, singing and making melody with your heart to the Lord; giving thanks always for all things in the name of our Lord Jesus Christ to God, even the Father; subjecting yourselves one to another in the fear of Christ.

Eph. 5 : 1-4, 14-21.

A student once defended her rebellious attitude toward God by saying that her very religious father had read long portions from the Bible before breakfast until the food was cold and she went shivering to school. To be an imitator of God, and to walk in love at the same time is not always a simple matter, but it is the only way to make spiritual truths real. . . . . That was the triumph of Jesus. He fed the hungry multitude while he taught them. His disciples plucked the corn in the fields on the Sabbath day to the scandal of the religious leaders. Some one has said that the ideal Christian should be a *practical* mystic: he must have his head in the clouds and his feet on the earth.

Everything we touch in the world may be the means of making some spiritual discovery. The outer world must be the counterpart of the world within the man. We see what is within him by noticing what part of the world claims his attention. A vulgar mind notices the vulgar facts in the world. The man with an inner love of beauty discovers first the beautiful aspects of life. Filthiness, foolish talking and jesting are the realities of an earthly mind. Beauty, reverence, and exultant rejoicing are the realities of the spiritual mind. We might make significant discoveries about ourselves if we honestly listed those things in the world which have been most real to us in that we have regarded them and found them pleasurable.

The short years on earth are none too long for the discovery of our real selves. There is some reality in the world to appeal to every natural instinct. The difference between the wise and the unwise people lies in the kind of opportunities they buy as they walk through the days. What are the characteristics of the world which you have discovered? What has made the greatest appeal to you? The answer to these questions is a description of yourself.

The practical mystic is well described by St. Paul in his two counsels, "Be filled with the Spirit" and at the same time, "Subject yourselves one to another." The two are not incompatible. A commonplace life, lived in an uncommon spirit is an ideal which is possible for all, but is sought by few. There was nothing unusual or adventurous about the simple country life Jesus lived. Birds and flowers and His fellow-beings along the road were His world. But the spirit in which He tramped the dusty hillsides and talked with beggars and fishermen is an endless rebuke to our selfish pinings for thrills and adventures in the hope of discovering a different and larger world. It is not where we are, but what we are which makes real life. Just around the corner from where we are now lies a world waiting for our discovery. The flower on our window-sill enfolds an eternity of meaning if we will study it. The heart of our neighbor will require the strategy of a general if we enter it. Our community has within it, in miniature, the characteristics of a world. If we go through this "giving thanks always for all things" we shall be amazed at the joyous reality in our world.

> Our Father God, we thank Thee for the beauty of Thy world. We thank Thee for the love which has ministered to our joy. Help us to see Thee through the works of Thy hands and to worship in Thy holy temple. May we set our heart not on the things that are seen but on those which are unseen and eternal; through Jesus Christ our Lord. *Amen.*

THE TRANSFIGURATION OF LIFE

In a "Lost and Found" column of a newspaper a woman sought to recover an old-fashioned brooch. She offered a large reward and added, "Its intrinsic worth is small: I value it for sentimental reasons." There was the simple story of a great truth. A few stones and a bit of gold are worth many times their price because some loving human spirit has worn them and handed them down, radiant with the memory of her presence. In this way love transfigures the commonest possessions and adds to them deep meaning and joy and the consciousness of a spiritual presence.

In some such way the presence of Christ lingers over all nature and the homely duties of life because he used them to reveal the deepest truths about God. To those who love Him the most humdrum life may be transfigured: but to those who are indifferent to Him life is dull and uninspiring.

When the disciples of Jesus asked him why he spoke to the multitudes in parables, he replied: "Because seeing they see not, and hearing they hear not, neither do they understand." We who read those matchless stories of nature know how much the crowds missed because they were blind and deaf to the teaching of Jesus.

It is a fearful loss to any life to remain spiritually blind to God's world and to the hidden meanings beneath the surface of things. There is always something to be seen that cannot be seen save with the discerning eye of the spirit. These hidden values, these "sentimental reasons" are what make life worth living and full of meaning. Barren indeed is the experience which has never sensed the presence of God in His world. It is like separating the violet from its perfume, and robbing nature of all its golden sunlight.

> "Earth's crammed with heaven,
> And every common bush aflame with God:
> But only he who sees it takes off his shoes,
> The rest sit round it and pluck blackberries
> And daub their natural faces
> Unaware, more and more."

There it is, — the difference between people. One gets the divine vision through the visible expression; the others say, "It's only a blackberry bush. Let us eat."

If Moses had not had the eye of his spirit open, in the silences of the plains of Midian, he would have missed the glory of God burning in the bush, and never led his people out of captivity into the promised land. Literal-minded folk, who see only what can be seen on the surface of things, look at the material thing as an end in itself and satisfy themselves with things instead of their meaning.

The great majority of those who followed Jesus walked and talked with Him for three years, and at the end misunderstood Him. There were only three of His intimate friends who saw His transfiguration because their hearts were ready for the vision. The others did not know the nature of God even when He was with them.

We are even more dull in our comprehension to-day. Nature has unfolded her secrets and become ethereal in her substance and yet the majority of us are blind to all but the material wonder. We try to compress the majesty of God into a prescription, or a definition or a program when His presence is intimately near in the perfect harmony of natural and spiritual laws. If we could realize the truth that, "in Him we live and move and have our being" we would find new contentment and joy even in the simple things of life. So much of our ill health comes because we yearn for abundance of things rather than width of horizon.

Many of us will say, however, "That is not my difficulty. I want horizon and freedom of soul, but I am entangled by 'things' which demand attention and choke the life of my spirit. If I were only free from these vexing necessities, I, too, could have spiritual visions and exalted contacts." This is the common problem of all who work at tasks in order to live. There would be little hope for the spiritual life of most human beings if there were no divine principle to meet their pressing facts of daily experience. It shines out luminous in the experience of Jesus, and we may learn it from Him.

One evening, after a long walk with His disciples over dusty roads, He came with them to the upper room where they were to have their last conversation. Then they were tired and dusty, needing the refreshment of cooling water on their travel-stained feet. Perhaps they were too poor to hire a servant for this purpose or possibly he was detained by the passover crowds; but the menial task was not performed. The disciples were perhaps grumbling in their discomfort, at the very moment when they knew their Lord had important words to say. And Jesus, more than all of them, was burdened by the importance of these last hours with His disciples. A strange thing happens. Jesus knowing that He came from God and was going to God and that God had given *all things* into His hands, a consciousness of power that no

Roman Emperor could have had, "riseth from supper, and layeth aside His garments," and like a slave, "He took a towel and girded Himself. Then He poureth water into the basin and began to wash the disciples' feet, and to wipe them with the towel wherewith He was girded." Such an anti-climax! The Ruler of all washes dusty feet! Afterward He said, "If I then the Lord and the Master have washed your feet, ye also ought to wash one another's feet." From that time to this every towel has been transfigured, and every simple homely duty is radiant with the glow of a divine service.

> "The trivial round, the common task
> Will furnish all we ought to ask;
> Room to deny ourselves, a road
> To bring us daily nearer God."

If we follow the example of Jesus, every insignificant thing becomes the means of expressing the divine life. The preparation of a meal becomes the expression of love, and a sacrament. The washing of a child's hands becomes a holy art. The loaf of bread is the blend of God's creative work in the growing wheat and our creative part in the grinding and baking. If we have eyes to see, we may find everything in life a parable of God. Anything is endurable if it is transfigured. If things cease to be weights and become wings, we may be lifted up by them even to-day, into that realm where we shall find power for peace and health.

> "When he walked the fields, he drew
> From the flowers and birds, and dew
> Parables of God.
> For within his heart of love,
> All the soul of man did move:
> God had His abode.   *Stopford A. Brooke 1881.*

FOR STUDY AND THOUGHT

And he said unto them, Take heed, and keep yourselves from all covetousness: for a man's life consisteth not in the abundance of the things which he possesseth. And he spake a parable unto them, saying, The ground of a certain rich man brought forth plentifully: and he reasoned within himself, saying, What shall I do, because I have not where to bestow my fruits? And he said, This will I do: I will pull down my barns, and build greater; and there will I bestow all my corn and my goods. And I will say to my soul, Soul, thou hast much goods laid up for many years; take thine ease, eat, drink, be merry. But God said unto him, Thou foolish one, this night is thy soul required of thee; and the things which thou hast prepared, whose shall they be? So is he that layeth up treasure for himself, and is not rich toward God. *Luke 12 : 15-21.*

How this parable of Jesus goes against what we call sound wisdom! The instinct of self-protection is so strong in the average man and woman that the wisdom of Jesus does not appeal to us. We all want comfortable homes, bank accounts, provision against any rainy day that may come. We want to safeguard our children against hardships — in short we consider it good business to reduce life to a comfortable certainty. We consider anyone foolish who lives from hand to mouth. A stable society we say depends largely upon vested interests. Has the Master then only a few idealists in mind or is He speaking to humanity as a whole?

Our worldly wisdom is somewhat disturbed when Jesus puts His finger on the inner motive which lies at the heart of those who seek possessions. It is covetousness. The man who covets is devoted to things as his superior pleasure. His love goes out to what he wants. The synonym for covetousness is given us by St. Paul when he warns the church to beware of "covetousness which is idolatry." An idol takes the place of God. Therein is the danger. It is almost impossible for one to amass possessions and not be absorbed in them. Acquiring them takes all one's attention and caring for them afterward requires more attention. Worship of God becomes a luxurious exercise rather than the chief interest. A man has higher work to do than to be a mere caretaker of things, Jesus taught, particularly when those things do not represent his creative work any more than the harvest of a field is the work of the farmer. He merely fences off God's free gifts.

Sooner or later comes the distracted question. "What shall I do: because I have not where to bestow my fruits?" Then comes the acid test which shows the real motive of the heart. Shall we hoard these things and make the small idol into a big idol, or shall we transmute them into spiritual values? It is not possible to do both. We may collect a pile of wood, but when we begin to transmute it into the flaming fire to keep people warm, the wood begins to disappear; yet it is of no value to us or others until it begins to burn. Not long ago a man was found frozen to death covered only by newspapers. Under his pillow lay thousands of dollars. "The man was crazy," we say. No, he was merely chained to his idol. There are thousands of others like him. People with frozen hearts, without friends, lonely, suspicious, blind devotees of things. There is no light in their eyes because they see no heavenly glow of transfiguration shining in the common things of life.

In the picture of the heavenly city the apocalyptic writer sees the honor and glory of the nations brought into it. What is it that can be taken there? Dollar bills, or palaces, or the abundance of things which are only *things?* They are left behind. Only the spiritual values of those things can enter. How much glory can we bring with us?

O God, Thou hast made everything in life sacred because of Thy touch. May we, too, transfigure everything we touch by a self-forgetful love. *Amen.*

THE LAW OF THE HARVEST

When Jesus taught us to pray, "Give us this day our daily bread," He brought us into a close partnership with God for the realization of all our desires. The law of the harvest requires us to be co-workers with God for the satisfaction of our hunger. When we pray for bread we know that long before our petition, God began to set the forces of creation at work to produce the answer to our prayer. The food is there in reality because long before we called, God provided it.

Nothing makes God more real as a loving Father than the processes of nature which work continuously to meet our daily needs. "Your Father knoweth that ye have need of all these things" is the assurance of Jesus. All we need to do is to link our faith and labor to God's unfolding purposes and the harvest will be ours. "Look at that wonderful melon!" said a proud western farmer. "That shows what can be done when God and man are in partnership in the gardening business. It is infinitely better than the original product because I've done my full part, too"

That kind of pride is what God longs to see in us. The silent processes of life go on without season, waiting to reveal their strength whenever we join our strength to them. The growth will go on whether we help or not, but the richness of the harvest depends as much upon us as upon God. When we plant a few seeds in the ground the reality of the harvest is not tangible. We see it in faith and hope and patience. Days and weeks of change and growth pass by. We help it by the preparation of the ground, the cultivation and the reaping. At last the grain we planted comes back one hundredfold, and fills our barns, and our prayer for our daily bread is answered.

It is significant, too, how large a number of the social group enter into the answer of our prayer. The loaf of bread involves the baker, the coal workers, the millers, and the farmers, and the workers in transportation; also the labor for the means to buy the food. A large group unites its efforts for the blessing of each individual. And God back of it all brings life to the seed and increase to the harvest and moves upon the hearts of men to work together with him. Stolid indeed must be the heart that eats without giving thanks for the food which is life to the blood.

"Back of the loaf is the snowy flour,
Back of the flour is the mill,
Back of the mill is the earth and the shower
And the sun and the Father's will."   *Maltbie D. Babcock.*

There are spiritual laws which are illustrated in the laws of the harvest. We may rest upon them in full confidence. One of them shows the rational application of faith. No one can raise a crop without it. We plant in a faith which is "a conviction of things not seen." We know it is reasonable because God has always been faithful in the past and we know He has never failed. The real question is whether we have enough faith to back up our expectations with our coöperation.

The earth brings forth fruit after its kind. Figs do not grow from thistles, nor can one pluck violets from burdocks. As we sow, we reap. The increase of to-morrow is more of what grows to-day. There is a persistent growth which goes on whether we wake or sleep. Weeds and wheat both show vitality. They increase or decrease in response to our desires and efforts. The counsel of the old writing books is as true as the harvest.

> "Sow a thought and we reap an act,
> Sow an act and we reap a habit,
> Sow a habit and we reap a character,
> Sow a character and we reap a destiny."

It is equally true that we cannot hasten the processes of life. The corn does not come before the blade and the ear have developed. Every step in the heavenly growth is necessary. Many times we long to reap the harvest before God's time has come. It is useless to resent the slow process of growth. All the faith in the world will not do away with the necessity for patience. There is a precise moment when faith, effort, and growth arrive at full realization. When that time comes we shall find, as every farmer does, that a harvest is a responsibility and the long months of working and waiting have been a preparation for larger service.

When we grow tense with anxiety waiting for some cherished plan to come to fruition, we do well to remember the quiet persistence with which nature pushes on to full growth. Day and night, while we watch or sleep, the silent processes of life go steadily on to fulfilment. Our attention is caught by the noise and bustle of activity. Quietness in our world is mistaken for stupidity and inertia. We want to be reminded that things are moving and changing. Our gauge is publicity and efficiency which is apparent to the crowd. In our own life we measure our growth by our stirring experiences and emotions, and we are discouraged if there are few of them. All the while the law of God in nature rebukes us by surprising us with a harvest beyond all our hopes.

What peace would be ours, and what relaxation of nervous tension, if
we learned from nature, as did Matthew Arnold, the lesson:

> "Of toil unswerved from tranquillity!
> Of labour, that in lasting fruit outgrows
> Far noisier schemes, accomplished in repose,
> Too great for haste, too high for rivalry!"

It is no wonder that Jesus told us to enter our inner room and shut the
door and in the perfect silence of eternity to let the love and power of
God play upon our spirit until it begins to grow and expand with a
power that can bring to pass all of God's purpose for us.

> Joyful, joyful, we adore Thee,
> God of glory, Lord of love.
> Hearts unfold like flowers before Thee,
> Hail Thee as the sun above.
> Melt the clouds of sin, and sadness;
> Drive the dark of doubt away;
> Giver of immortal gladness,
> Fill us with the light of day!   *Henry Van Dyke 1908.*

FOR STUDY AND THOUGHT

And he said, So is the kingdom of God, as if a man should cast seed
upon the earth: and should sleep and rise night and day, and the seed
should spring up and grow, he knoweth not how. The earth beareth
fruit of herself; first the blade, then the ear, then the full corn in the ear.
But when the fruit is ripe, straightway he putteth forth the sickle, because
the harvest is come.   *Mark 4 : 26–29.*

I am the true vine, and my Father is the husbandman. Every branch
in me that beareth not fruit, he taketh it away: and every branch that
beareth fruit, he cleanseth it, that it may bear more fruit. Already ye
are clean because of the word which I have spoken unto you. Abide
in me, and I in you. As the branch cannot bear fruit of itself, except it
abide in the vine; so neither can ye, except ye abide in me. I am the vine,
ye are the branches: He that abideth in me, and I in him, the same
beareth much fruit: for apart from me ye can do nothing. *John 15 : 1–5.*

The most helpless man in the world is the farmer. He plants the
seed in prepared ground, and then waits for God to send sun and
showers and *growth* to the seed. The farmer cannot *make* the seed
grow. He can give it room and keep the weeds from choking it, but he
cannot add one cell to the life of the grain. "The earth beareth fruit
of herself." Jesus used this parable to show people how growth comes.
If growth is a spontaneous and inexplicable process entirely beyond
our control, why be anxious? The Heavenly Father has planted us
here. It is His responsibility to see that we grow. It is useless to tell

our children to grow; they cannot do it. The law of the harvest is a law of divine mystery. The grain must *wait* for God to work. The farmer can no more *make* anything grow than he can make the stars to shine or the wind to stop blowing.

We can encourage or hinder growth by the way we fit in with the process of nature in keeping the ground soft and bringing other natural elements near, through fertilization, which the plant can utilize for its silent creative work. When the fruit comes, we can gather it and use it, but the glory of it is not ours. The harvest is the work of God. The same principle is true in our spiritual life. All we can do is to surround ourselves with the light of God's truth and faith in His power to complete our transformation. Paul, from the depths of a Roman prison, is quietly confident, "that He who began a good work in you will perfect it," (*Phil. 1 : 6*). This is why it is short-sighted to seek to evade any of the experiences which come to us unsought. Who knows but that the very elements which we need most for our growth come to us in some unattractive disguise.

The illustration which Jesus used for the growth of the Christian was the ancient symbol of the grape vine which the prophets of old had used to describe the mission of the Hebrews. Nothing could be more perfect as an example of the life which finds itself by losing itself. The vine lives only for the fruit. Each year the branches are cut back in order to give strength to the grapes. It has no commanding presence; its power is in its service to man.

> "I am the True Vine"; saith our Lord, "and Ye
> My Brethren are the Branches," and that Vine,
> Then first uplifted in its place, and hung
> With its first purple grapes, since then has grown,
> Until its green leaves gladden half the world,
> And from its countless clusters, rivers flow
> For healing of the nations, and its boughs
> Innumerable stretch through all the earth,
> Ever increasing, ever each entwined
> With each, all living from the Central Heart.
> And you and I, my brethren, live and grow,
> Branches of that immortal human Stem. '
>
> *Eleanor Hamilton King.*

Our Father, may our life be centered in Thee as the branch is centered in the vine. Forgive us that we have ever thought we could come to fruition apart from Thee. Take from us all that saps our strength. May no faculty of mind or heart wither and die from inanition; may Thy word dwell in our heart to enrich all our service. Through Jesus Christ our Lord. *Amen.*

THE PERSONAL ELEMENT IN EVERYDAY LIFE

An American boy returned home from the Great War after seventeen months in France. In talking with a friend he said, "Do you know what kept me going straight over there? It was Dad. When we parted he was too deeply moved to speak, but he put his hand on my shoulder. It was strange, but during all those fearful months I could feel the pressure of his hand and it held me true."

A thousand times people have touched our shoulders, or shaken our hand and we never remembered anything but the fatigue of the crowd. Then again, someone — in a moment of need, grasps our hand and we go many days in the strength of that human touch. It was the human spirit reaching to us in that touch, just as the heart of the father enfolded his boy that day. It is the only thing in life that really holds us, — contact with someone's loving spirit.

Life is full of human pressure. We spend most of our time in the crowded walks of school, business, and social life. We are weary with the clamor of the crowds and the conflict of human opinion, and we wonder how much of what we do is really worth while. Our peace and health and power are affected by the pressure of living and most of us follow the crowd and do what the others do merely because it is the line of least resistance. Is there any rule by which life will put strength into us, instead of taking it out of us?

The answer is a simple one. Let the outreach of our spirit be the measure of our service. Our capacity for vital relationship with others varies. Some have more capacity for this than others. It varies also with our experience and strength. There are days when we can enter easily into the joys and sorrows and perplexities of others. Those are days when we have breathed in a larger measure of the life-giving power of God and have been lifted above our own fears and anxieties. We have a margin of strength for the service of others. At other times when we are weary from our own moral fight, we need to shun the crowd and to be touched ourselves by the victorious spirit of some friend, or better still take an hour off for prayer and the renewal of our strength.

Jesus was never too hungry or too weary to touch the spirit of those who were with Him. He was always ready with strength and help. One day in the midst of a crowd a sick woman drew near and touched His garment in expectant faith, and she was healed. Jesus

213

knew at once that a wistful spirit had touched Him, and He asked, "Who touched me?" and the answer came. "The multitudes press thee and crush thee." But Jesus said, "someone did touch me for I perceived that power had gone forth from me." (*Luke 8 : 46*).

It is always so. The contact of spirit with spirit draws on our power. It is life given to life. It costs something. There is nothing mechanical or professional in such service. We cannot deal with human spirits in the right way unless our life energy goes into our effort. This is one reason why, with all our highly-organized science, we accomplish so little with people. We cannot treat people impersonally and get personal response. People wait for the touch of the human spirit. No organization, however efficient, can take the place of the vital human contact which brings life to the spirit.

Some of us who are enamored of world issues and mighty movements which concern the destiny of thousands would do well to ask whether our supply of spirit warrants our desire to minister to multitudes. How much power is there available for the last man in the crowd? Service for large social groups will either widen the reach of our love or take away from us all that we have and leave us lifeless automatons. Mrs. Browning discerned this long ago when she wrote:

> "A red-haired child
> Sick in a fever, if you touch him once,
> Though but so little as with a finger-tip,
> Will set you weeping; but a million sick. . . .
> You could as soon weep for the rule of three
> Or compound fractions. Therefore, this same world
> Uncomprehended by you, must remain
> Uninfluenced by you."

God never redeems people's lives in the mass. He is adequate for the feeblest of His children and He enters into our individual needs as though we were the only recipients of His love. But the human spirit grows impatient with the slow process of one by one. We long to be omnipotent also, and we attempt it with the multitude only to find that we have failed in the one thing needful.

The other day a student went to a great library for help. The librarian took him out among the thousands of books and led him to the two or three of that number which could answer his questions. His omniscience extended to each volume and each had a special value for him. His success as a Librarian was conditioned by his appreciation of the books and their individual value. There is a limit to our influence and power. It is the length of the radius of our human interest in those about us. It is our loss if we restrict it by selfish

interests and self-centeredness, or by deliberately shutting ourselves
away from the world and its needs.

> "No one could tell me where my soul might be,
> I sought for God, but God eluded me —
> I sought my brother out, and found all three."

In the light of all that is expected of us in this day and generation,
the daily habit of prayer and intimate relationship with God is our
most immediate responsibility, and personal service to humanity is
our special privilege. We dare not neglect this, lest we lose our soul
and shut God out of our life. The need of our brother is the divine
call to us. Who of us can hope for peace, health or power if we fail
to respond to the call of God?

> " How silently, how silently,
> The wondrous gift is given;
> So God imparts to human hearts,
> The blessings of His heaven.
> No ear may hear His coming,
> But in this world of sin,
> When meek souls will receive Him still,
> The dear Christ enters in."   *Phillips Brooks 1868.*

FOR STUDY AND THOUGHT

And Jesus called unto him his disciples, and said, I have compassion
on the multitude, because they continue with me now three days and
have nothing to eat: and I would not send them away fasting, lest haply
they faint in the way. And the disciples say unto him, Whence should
we have so many loaves in a desert place, as to fill so great a multitude?
And Jesus saith unto them, How many loaves have ye? And they said,
Seven, and a few small fishes. And he commanded the multitude to sit
down on the ground; and he took the seven loaves and the fishes; and he
gave thanks and brake, and gave to the disciples, and the disciples to the
multitudes. And they did all eat, and were filled: and they took up that
which remained over of the broken pieces, seven baskets full. And they
that did eat were four thousand men, beside women and children. And
he sent away the multitudes, and entered into the boat, and came into
the borders of Magdala. *Matt. 15 : 32–39.*

This story is so characteristic of the Spirit of Jesus. The more
one studies His life the more one is amazed at the way in which details
of daily life and the consciousness of a stupendous task alike merit
the personal attention of the Master. A hungry soul and a hungry
body are both important to Him. What a contrast to our sense of
values! If we have a great work to do we seek to free ourselves from
what we call personal annoyances lest our meditation be disturbed.
This is probably the reason why so much of the truth we teach has no

meaning for common folk and is counted vague and theoretical by them because they perceive that we have little knowledge of the usual run of daily experiences.

Mere theory could not have held a multitude for three days in the desert. The questions of a lifetime were being answered. We are not told that they clamored for food; they were absorbed in the teaching of One who made them aware of their souls as never before. Notice the contrast between the attitude of Jesus and his friends. They feel no responsibility for two reasons: they had not asked the crowds to come, — they came on their own initiative; and furthermore, there was no adequate supply of bread, nor money with which to buy it. Jesus takes the attitude that facts are always to be reckoned with, and that the need of people is a legitimate claim on anything that we possess.

Situations like this bring us to the realm of the impossible, — the point where the power of God meets the extreme limit of man's ability. Most of us never get one peep into this realm because we hide away some of our resources. No one is ready to risk *everything* for a cause which is near to the heart of God. Therefore nothing wonderful happens, and we do our little bit sadly regretful that we couldn't do more — with safety to ourselves.

God is not moved by quantity, but by spirit. Many who read this may discount the miracle because they have never helped to create an atmosphere in which their little life could minister to thousands. It had to be experienced to be believed. A little child, sitting in a meeting where people were piously wishing they could find the means to help the destitute in their city, ran up to the chairman with a precious nickel saying ,"Here's all my money for them." The ringing sincerity of the childish voice pierced the selfishness of the grown-ups until there was enough and to spare, and the seemingly impossible came to pass.

> Yield thy poor best and nurse not how or why,
> Lest one day, seeing all about thee spread
> A mighty crowd, and marvellously fed,
> Thy heart break out into a bitter cry,
> "I might have furnished, I, yea, even I
> The two small fishes and the barley bread."
>> *F. Langbridge, Restful Thoughts for Dusty Days.*

O God, Thou dost care for the hungry sparrow, and the hungry man. Feed us with the bread of life. Help us to be tender toward all Thy children who faint by the way. Help us to share our abundance with them. Make us to be great in humble tasks and humble in great tasks; through Jesus Christ our Lord. *Amen.*

THE SIGNIFICANCE OF OUR OPPORTUNITIES

OUR SECRETS OF VICTORY

In his "Principles of Biology," Herbert Spencer calls attention to this truth: "Whatever amount of power an organism expends in any shape is the correlate or equivalent of a power that was *taken into it from without.*" In other words, our energy must first come from *without* before we can see it as personal power.

We know this is true in the physical life; food, oxygen, our environment in nature sustains the life of the body. The life of the mind too is sustained by association with other minds. Solitary confinement has often caused men to lose their minds. They were shut off from mental oxygen. What is the source of spiritual power? God. "The Lord is the strength of my life; of whom shall I be afraid?" (*Psa. 27 : 1*). We cannot generate spiritual power within ourselves. God is as necessary to our soul as the air is to our body. Before we can begin to give power we must take it in from without, from the environing presence of God.

The chief reason why we are weak in the life of our spirit is because we separate it from its natural environment. *To demonstrate power we must take in power.* This is such a simple fact that one would think it need not be emphasized; but somehow our failures do not seem to teach us because we forget that the faculty of faith and the resources of power are not identical.

Spiritual power can be used to influence the lives of other people through prayer for them. We are only beginning to see the scientific reasons why this is so. We know that mind influences mind, and even at a distance can make suggestions to other minds. Just how this is done we do not know. The power of friendship consists, to a great degree, in mutual and constant interchange of mental influence. We are influenced by love which is directed toward us by our friends if we are tuned to receive it. We feel also the positive enmity of an unfriendly spirit, but it cannot really touch us unless it finds a like spirit in us. There are natural human powers which we have known by instinct and occasionally experience without understanding the

217

laws by which they are determined. If this power of influence is true when we exert it consciously, how much more powerful must this same influence be when it is reinforced by the strength of God and directed unselfishly toward our friends. There are countless people whom we could help to sustain if we used our power of prayer for them. Many are unresponsive to God, but are responsive to us. If He is to win them He must use us as a distributing centre of power. Such unselfish service is the highest mark of friendship.

This is the reason why we call unselfish friendship eternal. It does not depend upon physical presence. Time and space are already being eliminated by wireless communication. Perhaps in its light we may understand better its spiritual counterpart between soul and soul. When that time comes, we shall see what we have missed in not taking the counsel of Jesus about the power of prayer.

There are no limits to the power of unselfishness. The little spring which bubbles up in the remote wood gives its waters freely to the brook, thence to the river and the ocean. When we give in unselfishness we may find ourselves encircling the world. All the social service, all the international friendships have come from the giving spirit. This old world needs nothing more than it needs the power of friendship given freely, without stint, as the spring empties itself continually into the brook. It is only when friendship becomes a *habit*, that we begin to sense its power. How much of this power have we? It is the supreme way of being God-like.

Ideals are also resources which our day and generation need. We do not need to wait for a common consent before we stand for them. If they are what people need we should take our courage in hand and be willing if necessary to die for them. Somebody's life-blood has to go into every advance. At present much of our vitality is used up in maintaining our own equilibrium. Our personal interests, our health, and our happiness absorb us and we have little to give to the world. If we should forget ourselves in the need of others, we might find new power for our own weakness.

Jesus seems to be teaching us once more the first lessons he taught. He touched people's bodies that they might find it easy to have faith in God. The closer the physicist, the chemist, and psychologist get to that realm of the unseen, the nearer ought the follower of Jesus to draw to them. A motor car in the hand of a child is a menace to himself and to the community, and the power to handle the unseen forces of nature without a corresponding growth in spirit is a menace to the human family. The scientific mind is recording new discoveries each day. How many discoveries of God do we make? We must keep pace in our experience lest humanity becomes drunk with power instead of being filled with God's Spirit.

Science and religion are looking at the same things from opposite points of view. Religion, in faith gives "substance to things *hoped for*," while science is finding "evidence of things *not seen*." Our day and generation need both science and religion to walk hand in hand. We need both for accurate thinking; and we need both for the health of our body. Faith in God's power and trust in the scientific knowledge of physical laws will bring in a new era of power for our day. We have been like birds flying only with one wing. It is not strange that we have fluttered in helplessness. What may we not do for the world when man and God are united in creative work?

> We would be one in hatred of all wrong,
> One in our love of all things sweet and fair,
> One with the joy that breaketh into song,
> One with the grief that trembleth into prayer, -
> One in the power that makes the children free,
> To follow truth, and thus to follow Thee.
>   *J. W. Chadwick 1864.*

FOR STUDY AND THOUGHT

Then came to him the mother of the sons of Zebedee with her sons, worshipping him, and asking a certain thing of him. And he said unto her, What wouldest thou? She saith unto him, Command that these my two sons may sit, one on thy right hand, and one on thy left hand, in thy kingdom. But Jesus answered and said, Ye know not what ye ask. Are ye able to drink the cup that I am about to drink? They say unto him, We are able. He saith unto them, My cup indeed ye shall drink: but to sit on my right hand, and on my left hand, is not mine to give, but it is for them for whom it hath been prepared of my father. And when the ten heard it, they were moved with indignation concerning the two brethren. But Jesus called them unto him, and said, Ye know that the rulers of the Gentiles lord it over them, and their great ones exercise authority over them. Not so shall it be among you: but whosoever would become great among you shall be your minister; and whosoever would be first among you shall be your servant: even as the Son of man came not to be ministered unto, but to minister, and to give his life a ransom for many.

Matt. 20 : 20-28.

There is special significance in the first word of this story. Jesus had been telling His disciples privately about the way His enemies would shortly condemn Him and put Him to death; all this was to happen at the end of their journey. *"Then,"* at such a tragic moment, two of the three men who were closest to Him came with their mother to ask that a selfish ambition should be granted. One of these men was John, the one on whom Jesus depended for intimate understanding.

It seems incredible that this could have been the same man to whom the fourth Gospel is attributed. They were thinking of themselves so much that they easily forgot the suffering heart of their Master, or perhaps, as has been suggested, they did not listen because they were busy plotting their future.

In the account by Mark, there is a significant sentence, "Master, we would that Thou shouldst do for us whatsoever we shall ask of Thee." In other words they looked upon Jesus as a means of getting anything they wanted. How familiar that suggestion sounds! Somewhere in the back of our minds we too have pet schemes, and some cherished ambition which we want God to further. We come to Him as these men came, so full of our own plans that we are blind to the great purposes and interests which concern the heart of God.

The answer of Jesus searches the hidden motive. Are you willing to pay the price for this great gift that you ask? Even God Himself cannot give the highest gifts to those who are not fitted to receive them. Everything that is worth-while costs a proportionate sacrifice. Are we able to meet the extreme test, and to *qualify* for power? There is a cup which must be drunk. It seems as though this needed to be shouted aloud to-day when we scramble in such keen competition for personal ambitions. We see this trait in others, but fail to see it in ourselves. The very disciples who were angry at the attempt of James and John to take the highest seats in the Kingdom had themselves been quarreling along the way about who was to be the greatest.

There is only one way to power; and that is through service. "He who loses his life shall find it," said Jesus. The greatest one is the servant of all. It is a fair test. *Everyone* can serve from the least to the greatest. Even he who gives a cup of cold water to a thirsty soul shall not lose his reward. After the death of our late President, one editorial said, "the honor of being President is merely a four-year opportunity to work harder than any other man in the land." That is true of every one who has come out first in any walk of life. Let us look at the dominant desires of our heart. Why do we want health, or privilege, or position? What is the motive as God sees it. Is it service or selfishness? Do we know what we ask?

> O God, help us to forget ourselves. May we learn the lesson of service and follow in the steps of our Master. As He gave Himself for others, let us also serve them in lowliness of mind, each esteeming others better than himself. Grant us a love that seeketh not its own, that we may grow up into likeness unto Thee; through Jesus Christ our Lord. *Amen.*

OUR DAY AND GENERATION

It is difficult for us to look ahead one hundred years and realize that the world will be as different then, from what it is now, as our day is different from that of one hundred years ago. Our special generation seems to us to be the only one that has ever really lived. When we think of those days with their despotic beings, slavery, and snail-pace transportation, we find it easy to believe in a progressive development. We are the last now in the long upward struggle of the centuries; the spire on the top of the building. It has taken endless work, endless aspiration to bring us to our present height.

Each generation has its glory and ours had a special glory; one which comes from certain common achievements. Let us look at our special environment and the opportunity each one of us had because of it.

First, let us consider the access every human being has to *all* the thoughts and deeds of the world, thousands of books, newspapers, schools, and last but not least, the education by pictures and radio so that even the most remote people in Greenland or the Sahara may be brought near to the heart of things. Time has ceased to delay. The miracle of this world panorama, in all its changing moods, is wrought for us day by day. We are *omniscient* as no other generation has been.

The world has become incredibly small so that human strain is at its greatest. We have to live, one with another in a different way. Only a few years ago if people came too close, we organized enemies and drove them away. Now we cannot. If we set fire to our neighbor's house we endanger our own. Cleverness has replaced force. We have to *rely on mind rather than brawn*, to hold our own.

The individual is far more important to-day. He is not tied down. His personality has a chance for self-expression. Even womanhood has become free to think and act as she chooses. The opinions of the people overturn governments and defy laws. The *individual more and more controls the state,* therefore his moral responsibility is greatly increased.

Our day is the day of leadership. This quality develops only where conditions are plastic and not crystallized. The whole *world is plastic,* and *sensitive to the power of an idea.* Even one mind may sweep it with the strength of his conviction. There was never before such a restless

221

seeking for new ideas and new power for leadership. The soul of man is beginning to assert itself.

The veil between the material and immaterial world was never so tenuous. *We are becoming omnipotent.* Powers of the air are doing our bidding. This little, feeble body of ours with its pains and aches contains a spirit which has already endless possibilities of power. It can project its influence around the globe at will and is only turning the first pages of the book of omnipotence.

We are proving the unity of the whole universe as no other generation has proved it. We know that the powers of that marvellous personality, Jesus Christ, are powers we are destined to have if we fulfil the conditions. We are learning how to make the physical obey the spiritual. In other days that power seemed miraculous; now we have glimmerings of a principle which is God's continuous purpose for humanity.

These are only a few of the stupendous possibilities of our day, — this day in which every reader of this page lives. There is one point on which the whole situation rests. It is contained in that fearful power of choice which each of us has. The great question is whether we are awake to the consequences of our decisions. The forces of life and the forces of death struggle in us all for the mastery. If the insight of the soul is denied by the desires of selfish greed, all that we have inherited from the centuries will be lost. No other generation has been able to snuff out its future as we are able to do, because no other day has had such universal powers. This is well illustrated by the words of Winston Churchill, whose authority is unquestioned in the light of his services as Minister of Munitions and as Secretary of State for War in Great Britain during the World War. He draws a vivid picture. He asks, "shall we commit suicide? Reciprocal extermination was impossible in the Stone Age. With the best will in the world to destroy his species, each man was restricted to a very limited area of activity. Meanwhile one had to live and hunt and sleep. So on the balance, the life forces kept a steady lead over the forces of death, and gradually tribes, villages, and governments were evolved." From this he turns to our powers now when we choose to take into our hands the forces of death. "It is probable — nay, *certain* — that among the means which will next time be at their (the nations') disposal will be agencies and processes of destruction wholesale, unlimited, and perhaps, once launched, uncontrollable. *Mankind has never been in this position before. Without having improved appreciably in virtue or enjoying wiser guidance, it has got into its hands for the first time the tools by which it can unfailingly accomplish its own extermination.* That is the

point in human destinies to which all the glories and toils of men have
at last led them. They would do well to pause and ponder upon their
new responsibilities." We feel like crying out as Byron did about
man:

> "He will perish
> And yet he must not."

We may not sit down in helplessness and say, "who can resist the
trend toward destruction?" There is One who gave His life on the
Cross in order that we might overcome the forces of death and push
through into immortal life. The decision is ours. Perhaps the final
chance to choose may pass within our lifetime. There are wise men
who think so. The responsibility is an individual one. May God give
us the strength to enter the gate that leads to life.

> To Thee our full humanity,
> Its joys and pains belong;
> The wrong of man to man on Thee
> Inflicts a deeper wrong.
> Who hates hates Thee; who loves, becomes
> Therein to Thee allied;
> All sweet accords of hearts and homes
> In Thee are multiplied. *J. G. Whittier 1856.*

FOR STUDY AND THOUGHT

Hear another parable: There was a man that was a householder, who
planted a vineyard, and set a hedge about it and digged a winepress in
it, and built a tower, and let it out to husbandmen, and went into another
country. And when the season of the fruits drew near, he sent his servants
to the husbandmen, to receive his fruits. And the husbandmen took his
servants, and beat one and killed another, and stoned another. Again,
he sent other servants more than the first: and they did unto them in like
manner. But afterward he sent unto them his son, saying, They will
reverence my son. But the husbandmen when they saw the son, said
among themselves, This is the heir; come, let us kill him, and take his
inheritance. And they took him, and cast him forth out of the vineyard
and killed him. When therefore the Lord of the vineyard shall come,
what will he do unto those husbandmen? They say unto him, He will
miserably destroy those miserable men, and will let out the vineyard
unto other husbandmen, who shall render him the fruits in their seasons.
Jesus saith unto them, Did ye never read in the scriptures, The stone
which the builders rejected, the same was made the head of the corner:
This was from the Lord, and it is marvellous in our eyes? Therefore say
I unto you, the kingdom of God shall be taken away from you, and shall
be given to a nation bringing forth the fruits thereof. *Matt. 21 : 33–43.*

In this story of the rebellious vine dressers Jesus describes the
spirit which put Him to death. It was embodied in the chief priests

and religious leaders of that time, but is as true to-day of all those who revolt against God's authority. There is a close parallel between then and now which will repay study.

The owner had a complete vineyard. Everything that would insure fruitfulness and success was done; a hedge to keep out wandering animals, a wine press to preserve the juice of the fruit and a tower to keep off the enemy. It was to be held in trust by the men who worked it and the owner went away, giving them perfect freedom, and depending on their faithfulness. Such a well protected bit of land undoubtedly yielded a large vintage. The men who worked it became prosperous. The love of riches grew in their hearts, so that they determined to have all the fruits for themselves even though they had to kill the servants of the owner, and even his son, the heir of the property.

This is a picture in miniature of the world to-day. — God has entrusted us with His world in which there is every possibility for success, for growth, and for coöperation with Him. It is not our world, but for some marvellous purpose we have been allowed to come here, to live in it and work in it and to carry out the divine purpose. A day is coming in which each of us must give an account of our privileges. At the present time, our generation has its day. We are responsible for the world. Soon our chance will be gone and others will be put in trust.

Some of us live as if we had a permanent right to everything. We even try to fix things so that our control in the world will outlast our lifetime. God has sent His messengers as He sent the prophets of old to turn the hearts of the people toward righteousness. Some listened; others rebelled. Then came the highest revelation of God to men and they killed Him. What shall our generation do with the Prince of Peace? Shall we acknowledge His right to reign in God's world or shall we kill Him again by our lust for power and wealth? Do we insist that we shall have preëminence even though we have to exterminate all other living spirits in order to get our way? What are the great national concerns to-day? Are they for service and education and the appreciation of the gifts of others? Or are we bent on greed and hatred? The individual has more power of initiative to-day than ever before. How are we using it? Are we some of those who throw stones at the Prince of Peace? There are two ways open before us: we may stand with all our strength for Him, even though it hurts, or we may yield to the spirit of rebellion against the kingdom of God and be utterly destroyed.

O God, save us from ourselves! Save us from the spirit of disobedience. We have sinned, and forgotten Thee days without number. We have been slothful in Thy service and selfish in our desires. O God make clean our hearts within us: and take not Thy Holy Spirit from us. Put within us the daily remembrance of Thee, that we may be faithful unto death — for Thy Name's sake. *Amen.*

OUR ONE WAY OF ESCAPE

All the progress that has ever been made has been bought by struggle and work. Muscles have been made strong by the discipline of exercise, learning has meant burning the midnight oil, and manners and morals have come through continuous restraints and conflict with the desires of the lower nature. In order to hold the fort, no furlough from fighting has been possible. Browning's experience is true of all of us.

> "And so I live, you see,
> Go through the world, try, prove, reject,
> Prefer, still struggling to effect
> Thy warfare; happy that I can
> Be crossed and thwarted as a man,
> Not left in God's contempt apart,
> With ghastly smooth life, dead at heart,
> Fame in Earth's paddock as her prize.
>
> .   .   .   .   .   .
>
> Thank God, no paradise stands barred
> To entry, and I find it hard
> To be a Christian, as I said."

Is life worth the struggle? What is it that keeps anyone climbing? Why do we have to go against the law of moral gravitation? There are two reasons for this; one is found in the unconscious urge of life which compels us to grow as it compels the lily to grow from the bulb. That accounts for some of the upward struggle. But there is a greater urge which we find it difficult to resist; the urge of the Christ. We may not admit it, or we may not be loyal to Him, but one thing is certain; since He came into the world, a new dazzling standard has been set up and the influence of His life has permeated all the thinking and judgments of the world. Millions of people have united their efforts, to all the longings of the past, in attaining this hope set before us. Henry Drummond, years ago, had this vision when he said, "The work of the ages had no apex. But the work begun by Nature is finished by the supernatural — as we are wont to call the higher natural. And as the veil is lifted by Christianity it strikes men dumb with wonder. For the goal of evolution is Jesus Christ. *The Christian life is the only life that will ever be completed.* Apart from Christ the life of man is a broken pillar, the race of Men an unfinished pyramid. One by one in the sight of Eternity all human ideals fall short, one by one before the grave all human hopes dissolve." Shall all hopes go? No, as St. Paul says, "When Christ who is our life shall appear, then shall ye also appear with Him in glory."

Suppose we do not take this one way of escape! What is the penalty? The penalty of being thirsty with rivers of waters *just beyond* our reach! The penalty of the tread mill, ever climbing and never reaching the top! The mockery of all desire. There is no remorse like this; and it is the future of every one of us who has seen the perfect satisfaction of life and yet decides to look back and down into darkness.

Why prolong the usefulness of a poor old body if the spirit within it is sick? The only hope for physical health, the only way to health is through a spirit which is throbbing with the life of Christ, and passes on its vitality to the body. It is as in the business world. A house in which some one lives is a better insurance risk than a house which is empty. The life of those within actually preserves the outer shell.

Some who are reading this book are disappointed because no infallible rule for the cure of the body has been given. It never can be given sincerely by anyone. The greatest possibilities for health, however, result from the health of the mind and spirit. If the mind of Christ be in us, and the spirit of Christ be in us there is hope for life now and forevermore. Without this we do ourselves the greatest injustice; we struggle up to the last and *fail* to enter in. It will be our failure and not God's. "It is not the will of your Father which is in heaven," said Jesus, "that one of these little ones should perish." (*Matt. 18 : 14*).

Like the people in the time of Jesus, we, too, would like some sign from heaven which would help us to gain the height of our desire at a single bound. The real miracle is the miracle of a heart that fixes its eye upon God, and centers every part of its life in *faithful* coöperation with His purpose. To be able to do this in the teeth of moral gravitation is as much a miracle as the flower which unfolds, pure and white, from the black mire of the swamp.

Some of us may assume an indifference to our own future and yet be unwilling to drag others down with us. There are always others to be considered. No one of us lives to himself. Our failure makes it harder for some one else. For their sakes if not for our own we dare not give up the struggle. Even the animals sacrifice themselves for their young. Surely we are not so absorbed in our egotism that we are deaf to the appeal of our friends who expect great things of us. We do not fight alone. Most of us are in communities where we are held in spite of ourselves. Society as a whole is interested in helping us work out our salvation. Schools, welfare organizations, hospitals, the spirit of reformers, the Church, most Governments are concerned for the victory of the individual. If any of us loses our chance it will be because we are *bent* on our own destruction. Is there any one of us so ungenerous that he is unwilling to do "his bit" to roll the world onward into light?

> Come, labour on.
> Away with gloomy doubts and faithless fear!
> No arm so weak but may do service here:
> By feeblest agents may our God fulfill
> His righteous will. *Jane Borthwick 1859.*

FOR STUDY AND THOUGHT

Thou therefore, my child, be strengthened in the grace that is in Christ Jesus. Suffer hardship with me, as a good soldier of Christ Jesus. No soldier on service entangleth himself in the affairs of this life; that he may please him who enrolled him as a soldier. And if also a man contend in the games, he is not crowned, except he have contended lawfully. The husbandman that laboureth must be the first to partake of the fruits. Consider what I say: for the Lord shall give thee understanding in all things. Of these things put them in remembrance, charging them in the sight of the Lord, that they strive not about words, to no profit, to the subverting of them that hear. Give diligence to present thyself approved unto God, a workman that needeth not to be ashamed, handling aright the word of truth.

II Tim. 2 : 1, 3, 4, 5, 6, 7, 14, 15.

The last counsels of a man facing death are likely to be the dominant ideal of his life. In a Roman prison St Paul, facing death, because of his faith, writes to his closest friend who is to take up his work. There is no flinching in his spirit. He is sure that Jesus Christ is worth all that it may cost. It is sure to be a struggle involving hardship and the courageous endurance of a soldier. There is something in us which thrives on difficulty. We prize that which has cost effort. The athletic trophy is worth winning merely because it is not easy to win. The distant view from the mountain peak is desirable because it is so difficult to attain. They who are unwilling to work soon lose the ability to win, — and they are not crowned!

What we need to-day is to blaze new trails into the larger life of the spirit. We get so "entangled in the affairs of this life" that we are not free to achieve spiritual power. As someone puts it, "It is better to say, 'This one thing I do', than to say 'These forty things I dabble in.'" If anyone suggests that this means a narrow, restricted experience, he is indeed mistaken. What the Christian needs is a purpose so simple and direct that all of life centers around it. Many of us have such purposes but they are not always large enough to include everything. St. Paul surely had such people in mind when he urged Timothy to charge his fellow workers, "that they strive not about words." The cause of Christian service has been hindered mightily because we have talked more than we have prayed, and have been intent on details rather than on the spirit.

The spirit which holds a straight course in spite of opposing forces, keeping its eye on Jesus, is bound to be crowned with immortality. Browning describes this victorious soul in his epilogue;

> "One who never turned his back but marched breast forward,
> Never doubted clouds would break,
> Never dreamed though right *were* worsted
> Wrong would triumph,
> Held we fall to rise, are baffled to fight better,
> Sleep to *wake*."

Such a man was St. Paul; and such must we be if we are to win heaven and eternal life. The conception of the Christian life as a glorified life insurance policy which will come due at death has no place in the thinking of the great apostle. He does not promise his successor anything less strenuous. If some of us were following in his footsteps we would not have time to think of ourselves. If St. Paul had thought of himself and not been willing to endure hardness, we should probably not be here in an enlightened age enjoying the fruits of Christian peace. There are limitless fields of thought to explore and new experiences into which we too must lead the way for others. The hope of the future is in our faithful following of the Christ to-day. Phillips Brooks sang of Him:

> "The hopes and fears of all the years
> Are met in Thee tonight."

The same might be said of us, — "And working together with Him, we intreat also that ye receive not the grace of God in vain." (*II Cor. 6 : 1*).

> Now unto Him that is able to guard you from stumbling, and to set you before the presence of His glory without blemish in exceeding joy, to the only God our Saviour, through Jesus Christ our Lord, be glory, majesty, dominion and power, before all time, and now, and forevermore. *Amen. Jude 24.*

OUR CONFIDENT HOPE

If a human being is the highest achievement of the organic kingdom, what of the future? To what goal does all this endless striving tend? This is the question which haunts us more and more the longer we live. We are born weak, and grow up to physical strength and then gradually lose those bodily powers which we attained. In the realm of the mind, the case is different. We begin as children with the whole world to discover. Gradually one experience after another makes us wiser until at the time when our body is weakening, our mind is at its highest point in knowledge and general equipment for life. Problems are easily solved; we see a thousand possible careers open to us, and are just ready for our best work. Our spirit, too, has been disciplined and trained for nobility of character, and our insight into the meaning of life is keener than ever. Can it be possible that death ends all?

Sir Oliver Lodge writes, "I will not believe that it is given to man to have thoughts, nobler or loftier than the real truth of things." In other words, he is sure that eternal life must be really true or we would not have such a persistent feeling for it and urge toward it in all our life. We have a sense of eternity about all our larger interests. Our educational systems cover far more than what is needed in order to supply our economic necessities. Whenever we build anything, we strive to give it lasting qualities. We yearn to write books that will live on for centuries. Even our business corporations assume financial indebtedness in bonds which mature long after all present directors will have finished their work on earth. Why would we have this persistent attitude toward the future if there were no future? Why work so hard if there is no future growth possible? If we take life seriously and aim for permanence, why should we think of God as interested only in what is temporal? Is not His plan for our lives infinitely greater and more far-reaching than our pitifully small desires can be? Where did we get this sense of eternity, anyway, if not from the Father of our spirit?

We have hope, too, because of the inherent greatness of our personality. What is the use of developing a self-conscious spirit, capable of mighty prowess if we are to be mocked, at the moment of our greatness, by a disintegration of all that we have grown to be through the costly processes of the ages? Things must be different from what they seem to be. The disappearance of a train along the far stretch of track does not mean that it is not somewhere else. The stars seem to disappear with the rising of the sun, but we know they are still in the heavens, out of sight. When a personality goes beyond our sight, why should it not be growing and working out its desires elsewhere? We have a strange way of inferring that in the realm of the future we can gain evidence only by some voice from the future. We do not reason this way about other things. We find a workable law here, and depend, in cold business sense, on its working in the future.

We *have* had a Voice from the future. In powers and achievement, Jesus belongs to a realm infinitely superior to ours. He had much to tell us about the working of the law of eternal life. He made no attempt to project the material into the immaterial. He stated the law of life explicitly in these words, "Except a man be born of water and the spirit, he cannot enter into the kingdom of God. That which is born of the flesh is flesh; and that which is born of the spirit is spirit." (*John 3 : 5–6*). While we may be the final word in the organic kingdom, we are babes in the spiritual kingdom, destined for a mighty future in the likeness of Christ. Henry Drummond, as a biologist, describes the process. "Man, or the spiritual man, is equipped with two sets of correspondences. One set possesses the quality of everlastingness, the other is temporal. But unless these are separated by some means, the temporal will continue to impair and hinder the eternal. The final preparation, therefore, for the inheriting of Eternal Life must consist in the abandonment of the non-eternal elements. And this is effected by death. Death is the necessary result of imperfection, and the necessary end of it. But it is the claim of Christianity that it can abolish death. And it is significant to notice that it does so by meeting this very demand of science — it abolishes imperfection."

Our hope and confidence, then, must be placed in the reality of the life of the spirit. It involves our working out our salvation according to the principles of the spiritual life which we have been studying. Our spiritual growth must be won by us just as truly as our physical growth has been won by an observance of physical laws. Human wisdom has been gained by concentrated effort, and heavenly wisdom will come in the same way through the Master Teacher, Jesus Christ. Just as the realm of humanity is higher than the animal, so the realm of the Christian life is higher than the human life. As Dean Bennett, of Chester Cathedral, writes, "Christianity just seems to me to be the last, the final stage, as far as this world is concerned, of the age-long process for the making of immortal out of immortable individuals — in other words, for the making of the sons of God. If any are to inherit eternal life, for it they must qualify themselves. God Himself cannot do for us what can only be done by us."

The birth of the Christ life within us is the work of God. As has been said many times in this book, it comes in reply to our prayer and our willingness to let "the law of the Spirit of life in Christ Jesus" make us "free from the law of sin and of death." This is the hope of the world; your hope and mine; our *only* hope, but an adequate hope, — as God Himself is adequate.

> For lo! the days are hastening on,
> By prophets seen of old,
> When with the ever-circling years,
> Shall come the time foretold,
> When the new heaven and earth shall own
> The Prince of Peace their King,
> And the whole world send back the song
> Which now the angels sing.   *E. H. Sears, 1846.*

FOR STUDY AND THOUGHT

It is written,

> Things which eye saw not, and ear heard not,
> And which entereth not into the heart of man,
> Whatsoever things God prepared for them that love him.

But unto us God revealed them through the Spirit: for the Spirit searcheth all things, yea, the deep things of God. For who among men knoweth the things of a man, save the spirit of the man, which is in him? even so the things of God none knoweth, save the Spirit of God. But we received not the spirit of the world, but the spirit which is God; that we might know the things that are freely given to us by God.   *I Cor. 2 : 9-12.*

Who shall separate us from the love of Christ? shall tribulation, or anguish, or persecution, or famine, or nakedness, or peril, or sword? Even as it is written,

> For thy sake we are killed all the day long;
> We were accounted as sheep for the slaughter.

Nay, in all these things we are more than conquerors through him that loved us. For I am persuaded, that neither death, nor life, nor angels, nor principalities, nor things present, nor things to come, nor powers, nor height, nor depth, nor any other creature, shall be able to separate us from the love of God, which is in Christ Jesus our Lord.   *Rom. 8 : 35-39.*

Even before Christ came what a quiet confidence has come down through the centuries concerning the wondrous purposes of God for those who love Him! It took a great faith in those days to be sure that God was far more loving than any heart had ever imagined Him to be. The conception is so beyond the usual thinking of humanity that it must have come to the prophet by inspired insight.

It takes a human being to understand a human being. I understand human things because I have a human spirit within me. I am human and not God; so that in order to understand Him I must have the Spirit of God within me. This receiving of the Spirit of God is what Jesus meant by saying, "Ye must be born anew" (*John 3 : 7*). This relation is surely a guarantee of eternal life. Here is a relation of spirit with spirit which will never cease. It is a new power which brings us into direct connection with God and triumphs over death. It has survival power over all physical change. Our spirit has become vitalized with power and we see through the mists of earth, and begin to know, within us, the things of God. The assurance comes again through St. Paul in those words, "If the Spirit of Him that raised up Jesus from the dead dwelleth in you, He that raised up Christ Jesus from the dead *shall quicken also your mortal bodies through His Spirit that dwelleth in you.*" (*Rom. 8 : 11*).

Note the list of all those things which threaten to separate us from our relation of love to Christ. They are all changes in *physical* environment, — famine, anguish, sword, perils; these are the enemies of the body which cause us to disappear from our human incarnation. They *seem* to be able to defeat all our work and make existence impossible. It is, though, only seeming defeat for *in all these things* the spirit is untouched and is released for larger life.

The victory of the spirit is even more complete. After being driven from the earth there are other forces with which it may have to reckon; death, powers, angels, height, depth, or some other condition. Even there the love of God will keep us in our union with Christ. Jesus said to His disciples, "All authority hath been given unto me in *heaven* and on earth," (*Matt. 28 : 18*) and the promise of His Presence was to extend to the end of the world. No loophole has been left for fear. The Christian faith is confident and serene before *all* facts of life and death.

> I know not what the future hath
> Of marvel or surprise,
> Assured alone that life and death
> His mercy underlies.
> I know not where His islands lift
> Their fronded palms in air,
> I only know I cannot drift
> Beyond His love and care. — *Whittier.*

150
CR 5/25